California Asset Forfeiture Law & Procedure

Including statutory
revisions effective January 1, 2018

By Brenda Grantland, Esq.
Mill Valley, California

First Edition
published May 1, 2018

ISBN # 13: 978-0-9847859-3-3

Published by
Brenda Grantland
20 Sunnyside Suite A-204
Mill Valley, CA
https://brendagrantland.com

Table of Contents

About this book

This book focuses on asset forfeiture under California state law. Although it briefly covers federal forfeiture law that a state forfeiture litigant may encounter, such as federal adoption of a state seizure, coverage of federal law and procedure is very limited. If a forfeiture case is brought in federal court, the law and procedures outlined here do not apply. Consult a treatise on federal forfeiture law.

Forfeiture law and procedure are very complicated, and there is a substantial learning curve – even for experienced lawyers. Forfeiture law incorporates laws and procedures from many areas of law and procedure, on top of a body of law peculiar to forfeiture.

Forfeiture is really too complicated for most claimants to represent themselves well, but sometimes they are forced to because they can't afford an attorney, or a lawyer would cost more than the property is worth. For their sake, this book endeavors to explain all of the steps and procedural requirements even if they may be common knowledge to seasoned civil and criminal litigators. This benefits lawyers as well, because it puts all the applicable rules at your fingertips.

Litigating forfeiture cases often requires researching a wide variety of legal areas – criminal law, search and seizure law, civil procedure, constitutional law, evidence, real property law, marital property law, and partnership and corporate law, among others. It was impossible to pack everything you may need to know from all of those subjects into one book. To get more detail, consult separate treatises on search and seizure law, property law, and other subjects.

Guide for pro se claimants

If you are representing yourself, it is very important that you thoroughly research your issues and the rules before filing anything, and that you comply with all of the rules of civil procedure. If you don't comply with the procedural rules, your filings will be rejected and you'll have to redo them. You also run the risk of annoying your judge, and some judges have little sympathy for *pro se* litigants.

The laws do not require judges to give *pro se* litigants a break just because they are not lawyers. The California Supreme Court said:

> mere self-representation is not a ground for exceptionally lenient treatment. Except when a particular rule provides otherwise, the rules of civil procedure must apply equally to parties represented by counsel and those who forgo attorney representation....

(*Rappleyea v. Campbell* (1994) 8 Cal.4th 975, 986).

Legal writing format

Case books and court pleadings look weird to non-lawyers, but this is the format you will have to use in your motions and other court documents.

When a block of text is indented on both sides that means it is an exact quote from the case or statute. The citation to the quoted matter appears immediately after the set-in block.

Inside quotes, square brackets are used to indicate the matter inside the brackets was modified by the author to make the tense agree, supply missing information, etc.

In this book I use the citation format generally used in state court, instead of the "blue book" format used in federal courts. In California courts, either citation format is proper as long as you are consistent, but most state court judges still prefer the California Style Manual format.

Download the California Style Manual from http://www.sdap.org/downloads/Style-Manual.pdf.

The Bluebook: A Uniform System of Citation is copyrighted and you have to buy it or find it in the library. You don't need it in state court. You can use the California Style Manual instead. If you decide to use blue book format, there is a free guide for commonly asked questions:
http://www.law.georgetown.edu/academics/academic-programs/legal-writing-scholarship/writing-center/upload/everything_bluebook.pdf.

Case citations

When reading a treatise, case, or court filing, the citations in parenthesis are the source of the immediately preceding quotation, or immediately preceding summarized matter.

A case citation looks like this: *Rappleyea v. Campbell* (1994) 8 Cal.4th 975, 986.

Citations to cases are comprised of (1) the case name, (2) parenthesis containing the year and sometimes the abbreviation for the court, and (3) the place where the case can be found in legal books called "reporters" (a large set of consecutively numbered volumes). The third section of the citation has three parts: (a) volume, (b) abbreviation for the reporter, and (c) page number.

Federal cases have the abbreviation for the court inside the parenthesis with the year, unless the case is from the U.S. Supreme Court.

Sometimes the page number is followed by another number or series of numbers (for example, 231 Cal.App.3d 167, *173-174*). That second number or series of numbers – called the "jump cite" - is the place where the matter quoted or cited can be found, within the case.

There are many different reporters. The California Appellate Reports (Cal.App.") series contains appellate court decisions. The California Reporter ("Cal. ") series contains California Supreme Court decisions. The Federal Reporters ("F.2d and F.3d") contain federal appeals court decisions. Federal Supplement ("F.Supp. or F.Supp.2d") contains federal district court opinions. The U.S. Supreme Court cases are reported in United States Reports ("U.S.") and Supreme Court Reports ("S.Ct."), and Lawyer's Edition, U.S. Supreme Court Reports ("L.Ed."). These three reporters report the same cases, but with different volumes and case numbers. You only need one cite to find the case.

Many of these reporters have gone beyond the first series and started a new series that starts over with volume one. The 2d, 3d, or 4th is the series number. When you get to the area where particular reporter is shelved, look for the series number ("2d," "3d," etc.) after the title before you select a volume, because the volume numbers start over at one when the reporter starts a new series.

You can look up a case in a law library by looking on the spines of the books for the name of the reporter and series in your citation, and selecting the book with that volume number, then turning to the page.

An easier way to look up a case is to type the citation (without the jump site) in the Google Scholar search engine. The case will appear on your screen, and you can print it out. On Google Scholar, the internal page numbers within the reported decision appear in the left margin.

Google provides free access to California and federal cases on Google Scholar at this link: https://scholar.google.com/. Select

“Case law” and then “California courts.” Put the citation into the blank and press the blue button with the magnifying glass to the right of the blank.

Statute citations

Citations to federal statutes are to C. The number before "U.S. Code" is the title of U.S. Code it is in. The title number will appear on the spine. After "U.S. Code" you'll see a section symbol or the abbreviation "Sec.", followed by the section number where the statute can be found.

Citations to state statutes are simpler. They start with the abbreviation for the state code it is in, followed by the section symbol or abbreviation and the section number. See the list of code abbreviations below.

For free online access to California statutes go to http://leginfo.legislature.ca.gov/faces/codes.xhtml.

For further explanation of how to read citations go to http://www.saclaw.org/citations-guide.

Statute citation abbreviations

Bus. & Prof. Code – Business and Professions Code

Code Civ. Proc. – Code of Civil Procedure

Evid. Code – Evidence Code

Fin. Code – Financial Code

Gov. Code – Government Code

Health & Saf. Code – Health and Safety Code (includes controlled substances laws)

Pen. Code – Penal Code (general criminal provisions)

Pub. Util. Code – Public Utilities Code

U.S. Code – United States Code (federal statutes)

Veh. Code – Vehicle Code

Legal terms

Note: The California Style Manual, which is still the preferred citation style book in many California state courts, recommends italicizing some Latin legal terms but not others. See pages 146-147 of that manual for list of legal terms that are italicized and those that are not.

Et seq. – Latin for "and the following." Following the citation for a statute it refers to the statutory sections that follow the section number listed. For example – Health & Saf. Code Sec. 11470 et seq. means section 11470 through 11474 (or the last of that division in the code).

Ex parte – a motion or judge's ruling made by one party, without hearing from the other party, usually because of the sensitive or privileged nature of matter that needs to be discussed without the opposing party present.

Ibid. – the same exact cite that was last cited in the paragraph.

Id. – the same case that was last cited, but with a jump cite to the specific page number where the matter was found.

In camera – means "in private," as a hearing held in the judge's chambers or in the courtroom with the public excluded.

In limine motions – (Latin for "on or at the threshold") are motions prior to trial seeking rulings to prevent the opposing party from introducing inadmissible or unfairly prejudicial evidence before the jury.

In rem – a type of legal proceedings in which the lawsuit is against property instead of against a person, organization or corporation. Civil forfeiture is an in rem proceeding against the property targeted for forfeiture.

In pro per (or pro se) means the party is representing himself/herself without a lawyer.

Lis pendens – a notice of pending litigation that would affect title to property, which is filed at the Recorder of Deeds, so that it will show up in a title search for the real estate.

Pendente lite – means "pending litigation." A pendente lite order means an order that is in effect only while the case is pending, such as an order restraining property pending trial.

Res – (pronounced "race") means "thing" – the seized property that is the subject matter of the forfeiture case.

Sua sponte – when a judge makes a ruling on his/her own accord, without either party moving for the ruling or requesting it, it is sua sponte.

Supra – Latin for "above." Used with a partial citation to indicate the full citation appears earlier in the same paragraph.

Introduction

In 1994, California passed a landmark civil forfeiture reform bill, based on the recommendations for forfeiture reform urged by Forfeiture Endangers American Rights ("FEAR") in its position paper, which I authored. Our position paper was introduced into the record of the U.S. House Government Operations Committee hearings on forfeiture abuse in November 1992. California Assemblyman John Burton got a copy of it and his aide called to tell me Burton wanted to introduce a California forfeiture reform bill based on FEAR's recommendations. I just happened to be moving to California, and was fortunate to be able to participate in making forfeiture reform happen here.

California FEAR built a large and dedicated grass roots movement that made lobbying trips to Sacramento, meeting with legislators on both sides of the aisle. We were able to recruit cosponsors of every political persuasion, in every part of the state. We enlisted the help of a wide variety of non-profit organizations and amassed public support across the state.

Many of our activists were forfeiture victims. Their powerful first-hand accounts taught legislators that average law-abiding citizens were losing their property even though they were innocent. Before then, the legislators had only heard the propaganda pushed by the California Correctional Peace Officers Association, which painted forfeiture as an "effective weapon" against "drug dealers," conveniently omitting the fact that forfeiture's broad sweep harmed innocent people too. It was difficult to overcome the force of the law enforcement propaganda. The CCPOA is the most powerful lobby in the state. Forfeiture was a huge source of off-budget funding for law enforcement agencies, without any significant oversight – and the CCPOA wanted to keep it that way. They told legislators that supporting forfeiture reform would send the wrong message to drug dealers and would make legislators look "soft on crime."

It took two years and many, many trips to Sacramento to meet legislators and testify at hearings. Quite often our activists would travel to Sacramento at their own expense and sit in the audience all day waiting to testify at the hearing, only to be told at the end of the day that the hearing would have to be postponed to another day.

Balanced against our volunteer activists, taking the day off work and paying travel expenses out of their own pockets, were hundreds of law enforcement spokespeople, chiefs of police, and state prosecutors – being paid for the day, and having their travel expenses paid by their departments.

Amazingly they did not wear us down. Some of the most active victims, including the late Byron Stamate, showed up at every scheduled hearing.

Eventually we got our bill passed, but it wasn't the normal way.

As the 1993 legislative session was drawing to a close, FEAR volunteers and other forfeiture reformers went to Sacramento to meet with John Burton. While we were waiting in the hall outside his office, we heard a lot of yelling in his office. It turned out to be prosecutors browbeating Burton into slipping their provisions and edits into his bill. Curse words were hurled, but then John Burton is famous for his colorful language.

When the prosecutors filed out an hour later we knew from the smirks on their faces that they had gutted our bill.

It didn't take much study to see that the Burton bill as revised by the prosecutors was worse than existing law. The existing forfeiture law was due to sunset (cease to exist) on January 1, 1994. We assumed that if the current law were allowed to sunset, state law would revert to the forfeiture statute that existed in December 1988, which had been replaced by the sunsetting statute.

The previous statute was not as bad as the revised Burton bill. We decided to ask legislators to vote against the Burton bill and let the law sunset instead.

How to communicate that to them was the question. This was before the internet, and with only a few days to spare before the end of the legislative session, we had only one alternative. We prepared a one-page flyer telling legislators that the Burton bill had been revised into something worse than current law, and asking them to let the law sunset instead. We put that flyer in a packet with a reprint of Gary Webb's "The Forfeiture Racket," and a few volunteers went to Sacramento and hand delivered the packet to every single legislator's office in Sacramento. I can remember who those volunteers were – Byron Stamate, Prof. Dick Korn, Georgetown Gazette publisher Tom Daly, and myself. We fanned out and hand-delivered the packets to every legislator's office.

It worked! The Burton bill was voted down and the law was allowed to sunset.

At the time it did not seem like a victory.

Later I started piecing together the previous statute to see what the law would revert to in January and discovered that the previous statute had a sunset provision in it too. It had sunset in 1988!

I called other California FEAR lawyers and we had a big laugh – what if the sunset scheduled for January 1, caused the law to revert to a previous law which had itself already sunset and there was no forfeiture law? We laughed about it for a while and then I called a friend I had made in one of our sponsor's offices. He had worked in the legislature for years. He said we could be right, and called his friend in the legislative counsel's office and asked him to look into it.

FEAR lawyers started filing motions to dismiss their pending forfeiture cases on the grounds that the forfeiture law had sunset completely. Courts began dismissing cases! I settled Byron Stamate's $450,000 case with the government keeping $1,000 and giving Byron the rest back. The prosecutor didn't want to chance losing and setting bad precedent for his other cases. If the court had adopted our reasoning, the prosecutor's entire forfeiture case load would have been dismissed.

Then Legislative Counsel issued an opinion agreeing with us!

Armed with that opinion, we had the upper hand. The law enforcement lobby was desperate to get a forfeiture statute in place before the old law's sunset. All of those pending cases would be dismissed if they didn't work quickly to restore some forfeiture law — any forfeiture law.

John Burton got them to agree to our ideal Burton bill, with no revisions, and it was quickly enacted. That bill was still in effect, unchanged after 22 years, until California passed forfeiture reform legislation which was signed into law by Governor Jerry Brown on September 29, 2016 — improving existing law, which had remained unchanged since the Burton bill!

Several reforms in the 1993-94 Burton bill set the California reform bill apart from the laws of other states and the federal government, setting an example for other states — and the federal government — to reform their forfeiture laws to help even the playing field for citizens, as we had done.

First and foremost of the reforms, California's 1994 forfeiture law required a criminal conviction of the property owner before certain property, such as a house, could be forfeited. It also set a higher burden of proof — clear and convincing evidence — for some categories of property.

Prosecutors did not like these provisions because it made it much harder for them to win.

As soon as the Burton bill was signed into law, police and prosecutors scrambled to find a way around it. They found the perfect end run – federal adoption.

Federal adoption is a process set out in 21 U.S.C. Sec. 881(e)(3)(A) that allows state and local police to seize property and hand it over to a federal agency for forfeiture under federal law. The feds then give the local and state agencies up to 80% of the proceeds of the forfeiture case depending on the relative degree of work each agency did on the investigation and prosecution of the forfeiture case.

Because the police began seizing property and turning it over to the feds under the federal adoption program, the state forfeiture statute was generally used only for lower value property seizures that the feds didn't want.

Forfeiture reformers began trying to pass legislation to curtail federal adoption but the powerful police lobby fought hard against it. Bills were frequently introduced, gathered support, and sometimes even passed in one branch of the legislature, then failed in the other.

For 8 years, FEAR and other activist groups continually pushed for federal forfeiture reform, culminating in the passage of the Civil Asset Forfeiture Reform Act of 2000 ("CAFRA"). Provisions to limit federal adoption did not make it into the final version of CAFRA, however. There was too much opposition from the police lobby, and our Congressional sponsors refused to include it, saying restricting federal adoption would be a bill killer because of law enforcement's opposition.

The movement to abolish federal adoption continued in Congress. In January 2015, outgoing Attorney General Eric Holder issued a policy order appearing to limit federal adoption, but it contained a loophole that allowed the police to get around the policy order by merely putting a federal agent on their task force. (This is the same policy order that current Attorney General Jefferson Beauregard Sessions made such a big deal about repealing.)

In November 2015 Congress cut $1.2 billion from the Justice Department's budget appropriation that had traditionally funded federal adoptions. This forced the DOJ to suspend equitable sharing payments temporarily, but the DOJ promised the program would resume as soon as they found the money. Intense blowback from the International Association of Chiefs of Police and other police lobbying groups sent DOJ scrambling for money, and in March 2016 the DOJ announced they had increased their federal forfeiture income enough to self-fund the Federal Adoption/Equitable Sharing program.

Efforts to curtail federal adoption through federal legislation will continue, and will probably be beaten back as long as the Republicans remain in control of Congress.

Now it is incumbent on state legislatures to limit federal adoption from their end, to make sure the state and local police don't use federal adoption to make an end-run around improvements in state forfeiture law.

California finally achieved the goal of reining in federal adoption when it passed SB443, which took effect January 1, 2017. It is still too early to see how it will effect federal adoptions in California, but most certainly it will cut them drastically since the cops won't be able to get equitable sharing payments from the feds without convictions in most types of property seizures.

1. Recent changes in California forfeiture law

As I was saying in the Introduction, John Burton's forfeiture reform bill passed in 1994 and California forfeiture law remained unchanged until January 1, 2017, when SB 443 took effect. Both the 1994 Burton bill and SB 443 only amended the Health and Safety Code (drug law) forfeiture provisions, but forfeiture statutes for other types of crime share the same features.

A. Federal adoption

SB 443 was introduced in 2015 by State Senator Holly Mitchell (Dem. 30th District, Los Angeles). Like many bills that were introduced but failed to pass, it contained a provision – Health & Saf. Code Sec. 11471.2 – which limits state and local police participation in the Federal Adoption program.

Under the federal adoption program, state and local police can ask a federal agency to adopt a seizure of property made by state or local police under state law, and if the feds adopt the case, the forfeiture is processed by federal prosecutors, in federal court, using federal law. This allowed police to get around the state law's conviction requirement and higher burden of proof. If successful, the feds share up to 80% of the proceeds of the forfeiture with the state or local police that seized the property. See Chapter 15.

First the new law forbids state agencies from seizing property under state law and seeking federal adoption.

> State or local law enforcement authorities shall not refer or otherwise transfer property seized under state law authorizing the seizure of property to a federal agency seeking the adoption of the seized property by the federal

> agency for proceeding with federal forfeiture under the federal Controlled Substances Act.

(Health & Saf. Code Sec. 11471.2(a)). Sec. 11471.2(a) does not prohibit federal agencies from seizing property under federal law and sharing forfeiture proceeds with state or local agencies who work in joint federal investigations or federal task forces.

Even when local and state agencies merely participate in joint investigations leading to federal forfeitures, the new law prohibits state or local agencies from sharing in the proceeds

> unless a defendant is convicted in an underlying or related criminal case for which Sec. 11470 or 11488 authorize forfeiture, or an offense under the federal CSA which includes all the elements of an offense under Sec. 11470 or 11488.

(Health & Saf. Code Sec. 11471.2(b)). Section 11471.2(b) does not apply to seizures of cash or negotiable instruments totaling more than $40,000. For those larger amounts there is no conviction requirement as a prerequisite to equitable sharing. Under Sec. 11471.2(c) a conviction is also not required if the defendant is charged but flees to evade prosecution.

B. Burden of proof

SB 443 increased the government's burden of proof. In contested Health & Safety Code (drug forfeiture) cases involving any property other than $40,000 or more in cash or negotiable instruments, the government has to prove grounds for forfeiture beyond a reasonable doubt. In these larger money seizure cases, grounds for forfeiture must be proven by clear and convincing evidence – a standard substantially higher standard than the normal preponderance of the evidence. In cases other than $40,000 or more in cash or negotiable instruments, the burden of proof in the forfeiture case is beyond a reasonable doubt.

C. Reports

A provision codified at Health & Saf. Code Sec. 11495(c), requires the Attorney General to publish a report each year stating:

(1) the number of forfeiture actions: initiated under state law, initiated by a joint task force, and adopted by the federal government;

(2) the number of cases, with the administrative number or court docket number for which forfeiture was declared;

(3) the number of suspects charged with drug violations;

(4) the number of cases charged under federal or state law;

(5) disposition of the criminal cases (plea, jury acquittal, etc.)

(6) value of assets forfeited;

(7) the recipients of the forfeited assets, amounts received and date of disbursement.

D. Disbursement and audit of federally shared funds

Under Health & Saf. Code Sec. 11495(a), all funds received by law enforcement agencies from forfeiture under state law must be deposited into an account maintained by the Controller, county auditor or city treasurer, who must maintain a record of all disbursements from the funds. The records are open for public inspection, unless privileged under Evid. Code Sec. 1040 (official information withheld in the public interest), 1041 or 1042 (pertaining to revealing an informant's identity). The governing body of the jurisdiction (e.g. the county board of supervisors) can order an audit of the funds. (Health & Saf. Code Sec. 11495(b)).

2. Basic principles of asset forfeiture

A. Forfeitures are disfavored

> "Statutes imposing forfeitures are not favored and are to be strictly construed in favor of the persons against whom they are sought to be imposed." (*People v. $ 28,500* (1996) 51 Cal.App.4th 447, 463-464....) This disfavor applies "notwithstanding the strong governmental interest in stemming illegal drug transactions...."

(*People v. $10,153.38* (2009) 179 Cal.App.4th 1520, 1526, quoting *People v. Ten $ 500 etc. Traveler's Checks* (1993) 16 Cal.App.4th 475, 479).

Critics have long complained that forfeiture has a corrupting influence on police. Allowing police to profit from asset forfeiture skews police priorities toward forfeiting property instead of investigating and prosecuting crimes – especially crimes that do not trigger forfeiture. It also encourages law enforcement to stretch the truth or even lie to make a forfeiture case.

The California legislature sought to curb those corrupting tendencies by including this provision in the drug forfeiture statute:

> (a) Law enforcement is the principal objective of forfeiture. Potential revenue must not be allowed to jeopardize the effective investigation and prosecution of criminal offenses, officer safety, the integrity of ongoing investigations, or the due process rights of citizens.

(b) No prosecutor's or sworn law enforcement officer's employment or salary shall be made to depend upon the level of seizures or forfeitures he or she achieves.

(Health & Saf. Code Sec. 11469(a)-(b)).

These are inspiring words to quote in your motions, but the reality is that the government and many courts are biased in favor of asset forfeiture because it brings in money for law enforcement agencies and the criminal justice system.

Under Health & Saf. Code Sec. 11489, proceeds of forfeited cash or the sale of forfeited property are distributed first to bona fide or innocent purchasers and lienholders, up to the amount of their lien, and the balance is distributed as follows:

65% to the state or local law enforcement agencies that participated in the case, in proportion to their contribution;

15% to a special local fund for drug abuse prevention and to divert gang activity;

10% to the prosecuting agency (the prosecutors get a cut!);

24% to the California general fund, with the first $10 million earmarked for school safety and security;

1% to a nonprofit organization composed of local prosecutors to provide statewide education and training for prosecutors and police in ethics and proper use of forfeiture laws. (Health & Saf. Code Sec. 11489(b)(2)(A)-(D)).

All funds allocated to the state department of justice and all payments to the state from federal forfeiture programs must be paid into the Department of Justice Special Deposit Fund's state asset forfeiture account, and used for law enforcement.

Funds distributed to state or local entity pursuant to Health & Saf. Code Sec. 11489(b)(2)(A) or (B) "shall not supplant any state and local funds" that would otherwise be budgeted for those agencies. (Health & Saf. Code Sec. 11489(d)).

B. Civil vs. criminal forfeitures

Forfeiture lawyers who generally practice in federal courts may find themselves confused by the differences between state and federal forfeiture law, and just assume that certain concepts they are accustomed to from federal courts also apply in state courts. Although state law was patterned after federal law to a great extent, they are not identical.

Federal law has both civil forfeiture and criminal forfeiture, with completely different sets of procedures. For most federal offenses the prosecutor has a choice of whether to prosecute a case as a civil forfeiture or criminal forfeiture, and sometimes they use both simultaneously. In federal cases, criminal forfeiture is done inside the criminal case, with a civil third party process tacked onto the end.

California forfeiture laws are basically civil forfeiture, with aspects of criminal forfeiture. The forfeiture case is filed as a separate case from the criminal case, except in computer crime forfeitures, which are more like federal criminal forfeiture procedure. See Chapter 3 Section D.

The Code of Civil Procedure applies to the early parts of the forfeiture process. However most California forfeiture provisions require a criminal conviction. If there is a conviction the forfeiture trial commences after the criminal trial, often before the same jury — even though they were separate cases.

Most California forfeiture provisions require a criminal conviction of the property owner for the forfeiture-triggering offense, and the burden of proof in the forfeiture case is often beyond a reasonable doubt. Some forfeitures only require clear and convincing evidence, but the only forfeiture statutes that have the civil "preponderance of the evidence" burden of proof are computer crime forfeitures and vehicle forfeitures for unlicensed driver and DUI offenses. See Chapter 3 Sec. D-3 and F-3.

State forfeiture statutes sometimes exempt third parties (owners of interests in the property other than the criminal defendant) from the reach of forfeiture. In those cases all the third party has to do is file a claim and, if the government challenges the claim, they must show standing to defend the property, that is, an ownership or possessory interest.

Property owners don't have to prove they were "innocent" under state law, as claimants do under the federal innocent owner defense – the government always has the burden of proof. Even when the statute requires the non-defendant to show lack of knowledge and consent to the illegal use, the government has the burden of proof on those issues.

C. Applicability of federal law to state forfeitures

Federal statutes do not apply in state forfeiture cases, but where there is no state court precedent interpreting a state statute, California courts will look for guidance to federal cases interpreting a similar federal forfeiture statute.

> Because the California drug asset forfeiture statutes are modeled on the federal forfeiture laws, federal case law, while not controlling, is highly persuasive in deciding drug forfeiture issues.

(*People v. $ 8,921* (1994) 28 Cal.App.4th 1226, 1232. See also *People v. Property Listed in Exhibit A* (1991) 227 Cal.App.3d 1).

State and federal law are identical on some issues – generally because the procedure or defense originated from Supreme Court rulings interpreting the U.S. Constitution. On such issues, state courts often rely heavily on federal appellate court decisions interpret the constitutional rulings of the U.S. Supreme Court.

1. The U.S. Constitution applies to state forfeitures

a. Fourth Amendment – search and seizure law

The Fourth Amendment exclusionary rule applies in civil forfeiture cases. (*One 1958 Plymouth Sedan v. Commonwealth of Pennsylvania* (1965) 380 U.S. 693, 701-702.) Forfeiture claimants can file motions to suppress illegally seized evidence by following the procedures used in state criminal cases. When there is a related criminal case, the suppression motion would be filed and litigated in the criminal case.

Many forfeiture cases are won when the illegally seized evidence is suppressed. However, the finding that the seizure was illegal does not automatically immunize the property from forfeiture. The government can still prove its case with other evidence that was not tainted by the illegal search and seizure. See Chapter 11 Section C, below.

b. Fifth Amendment – self-incrimination, due process, double jeopardy

The Fifth Amendment privilege against self-incrimination also applies in forfeiture cases. (*Boyd v. United States* (1886) 116 U.S. 116.)

In *Boyd*, the Supreme Court held that the privilege against self-incrimination applied because forfeiture was quasi-criminal, but that reasoning has since been repudiated. Now the justification for applying the privilege to civil forfeiture cases is the possibility of incriminating oneself in the parallel criminal case – or the mere possibility of a future criminal prosecution for any offense – state or federal – based on an incriminating statement elicited in the civil forfeiture case.

> The privilege against self-incrimination does not depend upon the likelihood, but upon the possibility of prosecution and also covers those circumstances where the disclosures would not be directly incriminating, but could provide an indirect link to incriminating evidence. The only way the privilege can be asserted is on a question-by-question basis, and thus as to each question asked, the party has to decide whether or not to raise his Fifth Amendment right.

(*Doe v. Glanzer* (9th Cir. 2000) 232 F.3d 1258, 1263). See Chapter 10 Section I-5, below.

The Fifth Amendment's Due Process clause has been the source of numerous judicial reforms of civil forfeiture procedure. The U.S. Supreme Court held in *United States v. James Daniel Good Real Property* (1993) 510 U.S. 43 that Due Process prohibits real estate from being seized prior to trial except in exceptional circumstances. The owner cannot be ousted from possession of real estate until after a verdict of forfeiture. The right even applies when the property is rented out to tenants. It does not apply to personal property such as money or vehicles. See Chapter 5 Section A.

The Fifth Amendment's Double Jeopardy clause does not apply to civil forfeiture, the Supreme Court held in *United States v. Ursery* (1996) 518 U.S. 267. The *Ursery* decision overturned precedents in a majority of federal circuits and many state courts that had ruled in favor of claimants and defendants on double jeopardy/forfeiture issues, so if you come across forfeiture cases from the 1990s that discuss double jeopardy as a defense, don't get excited — those cases are all overruled.

The Supreme Court explained the apparent conflict between *Ursery* and its earlier decision in *Austin v. United States* (1993) 509 U.S. 602 — that civil forfeiture is sufficiently punitive to trigger the Eighth Amendment Excessive Fines clause — by reasoning that some constitutional rights are broader than others. The Double Jeopardy clause does not apply to forfeiture.

c. Sixth Amendment – right to counsel, speedy trial, jury trial

The Sixth Amendment only applies to criminal cases, as it clearly indicates by its own language. It begins with "[i]n all criminal prosecutions the accused shall enjoy the right...." And then enumerates the rights.

The right to counsel – which originates from the Sixth Amendment – does not apply to civil forfeiture cases, either under federal or state law. (*People v. Madeyski* (2001) 94 Cal.App.4th 659 (forfeiture under Pen. Code Sec. 502.01 is civil, not criminal); *People v. $4,413* (1996) 47 Cal.App.4th 1631, 1638 (forfeiture under Health & Saf. Code Sec. 11488.4 is civil)). Federal statutes have provisions authorizing appointment of counsel for forfeiture victims in two narrow categories of cases, but there is no equivalent California statute authorizing appointment of counsel in a state forfeiture case.

Although the right to speedy trial originates from the Sixth Amendment, the U.S. Supreme Court has extended speedy trial principles to civil forfeiture cases, through the Due Process Clause. (*United States v. $8,850* (1983) 461 U.S. 555, incorporating the standards of *Barker v. Wingo* (1972) 407 U.S. 514.) Chapter 4 part D, below.

The Sixth Amendment's right to jury trial only applies to criminal cases, but the Seventh Amendment gives civil forfeiture litigants the right to trial by jury – because jury trials were required in forfeiture cases when the Constitution was written.

d. Eighth Amendment – excessive fines

The Eighth Amendment applies to forfeiture – not through the Cruel and Unusual Punishments clause, but through the Excessive Fines clause. Proportionality is determined in forfeiture cases under the standards of *United States v. Bajakajian* (1998) 524 U.S. 321. See Chapter 4 part E, below.

2. The California Constitution also applies

The California Constitution has many provisions that are similar to the provisions in the U.S. Constitution, but sometimes the California Constitution is interpreted more protectively of citizens' rights than the U.S. Constitution.

> The California Constitution is a document of independent force that may be interpreted in a manner more protective than the United States Constitution. (Cal. Const., art. I, § 24; *People v. Fields* (1996) 13 Cal.4th 289, 298 [52 Cal. Rptr.2d 282, 914 P.2d 832]; *Raven v. Deukmejian* (1990) 52 Cal.3d 336, 353-354 [276 Cal. Rptr. 326, 801 P.2d 1077] [invalidating constitutional amendment by initiative measure which would have altered this rule for wide spectrum of rights].) However, the general policy is that "cogent reasons must exist before a state court in construing a provision of the state Constitution will depart from the construction placed by the Supreme Court of the United States on a similar provision in the federal Constitution." (*Raven*, supra, 52 Cal.3d at p. 353.)

(*People v. $4,413* (1996) 47 Cal.App.4th 1631, 1639).

Check the state cases interpreting the state constitutional provision to determine whether the state constitution is more protective than the equivalent provision of the U.S. Constitution.

D. Legal concepts encountered in forfeiture cases

1. Contraband

Contraband is any item or substance that by its nature is illegal to possess or sell. Contraband is seized and "summarily forfeited" – that is, the owner is divested of ownership rights to it without a forfeiture hearing.

Under Health & Saf. Code Sec. 11475, "controlled substances listed in Schedule I that are possessed, transferred, sold, or offered for sale in violation of this division are contraband and shall be seized and summarily forfeited to the state." A list of the controlled substances that are listed in Schedule I are set out in Health & Saf. Code Sec. 11054. See Chapter 3 Section A-3-a, below.

> [S]pecies of plants from which controlled substances in Schedules I and II may be derived which have been planted or cultivated in violation of this division, or of which the owners or cultivators are unknown, or which are wild growths, may be seized and summarily forfeited to the state.

(Health & Saf. Code Sec. 11476). Schedules I and II are set out in Health & Saf. Code Sec. 11054 – 11055.

Cannabis (marijuana) is currently classified in Schedule I. (Health & Saf. Code Sec. 11054(d)(13)). Medical marijuana and recreational marijuana are legal now in California (though highly regulated, with criminal penalties still imposed for noncompliant cultivation and distribution). Federally, marijuana remains classified in DEA Schedule I. Under California law, possession of marijuana in California takes it out of the state definition of contraband if the person is possessing it in compliance with state laws. That does not apply to controlled substances seized by federal agents and prosecuted in federal court.

2. Furnished or intended to be furnished

In a typical drug enforcement reverse sting, undercover police or informants posing as drug dealers agree to sell drugs to a person. The person arrives with money to purchase the drugs and the undercover agents arrest him and seize the money. There may never have been any real drugs because the agents were only posing as drug dealers to set him up. Still, the money the defendant brought to the transaction is forfeitable as money "furnished or intended to be furnished" to purchase drugs. (Health & Saf. Code Sec. 11470(f)).

In the above hypothetical scenario, the intent to be furnished for drugs is clear from the undercover transaction.

Where a large amount of currency is seized but no drugs are found, and there are no incriminating statements, the government has to use circumstantial evidence to prove the money was "furnished or intended to be furnished." These factors are relevant:

> First, the large amount of currency found at this one location is strong circumstantial evidence the money is connected to narcotics trafficking. While some federal courts have suggested possession of "[f]ifteen to twenty thousand dollars is hardly enough cash, standing alone, to justify more than a suspicion of illegal activity," the courts have also recognized the converse. (See *U.S. v. $ 191,910.00 in U.S. Currency* (9th Cir. 1994) 16 F.3d 1051, 1072.) A large stash of cash supplies "strong evidence" the money was exchanged for illegal drugs. (*U.S. v. $ 39,873.00* (8th Cir. 1996) 80 F.3d 317, 319 ["possession of a large amount of cash [nearly $ 40,000] is strong evidence that the cash is connected with drug trafficking"]; *U.S. v. $ 67,220.00 in U. S. Currency* (6th Cir. 1992) 957 F.2d 280, 285 [carrying a large sum of cash is strong evidence of some relationship with illegal drugs]; *U.S. v. Currency, in the Amount of $ 150,660.00* (8th Cir. 1992) 980 F.2d 1200,

1206 [several courts have held the possession of a large amount of cash is strong evidence the cash is connected with drug activity]; *United States v. $ 93,685.61 in U.S. Currency* (9th Cir. 1984) 730 F.2d 571, 572 [the extremely large amount of money found in the household itself is strong evidence the money was furnished or intended to be furnished in return for drugs].) ....

A second circumstance the courts have found to support an inference the money is connected to drug trafficking is the way currency is wrapped or stored. (*People v. $ 30,000 U. S. Currency* (1995) 35 Cal.App.4th 936, 939 [41 Cal. Rptr. 2d 748] [$100 bills stapled together in stacks of $ 1,000 secreted in spare tire of abandoned vehicle in backyard]; *People v. $ 28,500 in U.S. Currency,* supra, 51 Cal.App.4th 447, 450 [currency was placed in brown paper bag inside brown plastic bag]; *U.S. v. $ 31,990 in U.S. Currency, supra,* 982 F.2d 851, 854 ["[w]hile we recognize that the method of bundling may be probative of drug activity, we emphasize that it is but one factor weighing in favor of a finding of probable cause"]; cf. *U.S. v. Jenkins* (8th Cir. 1996) 78 F.3d 1283, 1288 ["the defendant had over $ 100,000 in cash stored in a garbage bag in his home. A jury certainly could have concluded from this evidence that the defendant was aware that the money in question had resulted from drug activity"]; *U.S. v. $ 29,959.00 U.S. Currency* (9th Cir. 1991) 931 F.2d 549, 553 [currency found in men's clothing dresser and hidden in a man's sock]; *U.S. v. U.S. Currency, $ 83,310.78* (9th Cir. 1988) 851 F.2d 1231, 1235-1236 [currency found in a brown shopping bag].) ...

Moreover, the money was found in a house containing the tools of the money-laundering trade. (Cf., e.g., *People v. 25651 Minoa Dr., supra,* 2 Cal.App.4th 787, 793 [relevant circumstance was discovery of drug paraphernalia and cutting agent found in claimant's home office from which he sold drugs].) The officers found money-packaging materials and a laundry dryer with its insides removed. Law enforcement officers described how narcotics traffickers often use these modified dryers to conceal large bundles of cash and to transport it from one location to another or smuggle it out of the country.

Third, courts consider it significant the money is found at a location connected to a drug-trafficking and money-laundering organization. (*See People v. $ 30,000 U.S. Currency, supra,* 35 Cal.App.4th 936, 939 [currency found near greenhouse in backyard containing 95 marijuana plants and near garage housing methamphetamine lab]; *U.S. v. Saccoccia* (1st Cir. 1995) 58 F.3d 754, 782; *U.S. v. Ramirez* (5th Cir. 1992) 954 F.2d 1035, 1039-1040.) ...

A fourth circumstance present here, the dog's detection of cocaine on claimant's cash, provoked the most discussion in the briefs. Claimant argues the canine alert to illegal drug residue does not constitute sufficient evidence to support the forfeiture because of the large amount of contaminated money presently in circulation in the United States. Indeed several courts have questioned the value of a canine alert due to the same argument the claimant offers here. (*See U.S. v. $ 5,000 in U.S. Currency* (6th Cir. 1994) 40 F.3d 846, 849-850; *U.S. v. U.S. Currency, $ 30,060.00, supra,* 39 F.3d 1039, 1041-1044.) At the same time, however, many courts continue to consider canine alert as probative evidence the currency is related to narcotics trafficking. (*People v. $ 28,500 in U.S. Currency, supra,* 51 Cal.App.4th 447, 452-454; *U.S. v. Saccoccia, supra,* 58 F.3d 754, 777; *U.S. v. $ 215,300 U.S. Currency* (9th Cir. 1989) 882 F.2d 417, 419.) Moreover, even claimant's cited

> cases concede a dog alert is relevant and probative of drug activity when combined with other credible evidence clearly connecting the money to illicit drugs. (*U.S. v. U.S. Currency, $ 30,060.00, supra,* 39 F.3d at p. 1042.)"

(*People v. $497,590* (1997) 58 Cal.App.4th 145, 155 – 157).

People v. $497,590 was brought under an earlier statute, when the government's ultimate burden at trial was a mere preponderance of the evidence, and the government's burden on a claimant's motion for return of property was "probable cause to believe the property was subject to forfeiture." *Id.* 58 Cal.App.4th at 151. Now that the prosecution's burden of proof has been raised to "clear and convincing evidence" or "beyond a reasonable doubt" this type of circumstantial evidence may not be enough.

Cases based on circumstantial evidence can be refuted with defense evidence.

In another early case, $47,050 was seized during execution of a search warrant inside a home, along with one-third gram of cocaine, 84.5 grams of marijuana, guns, and a digital scale. Defendant's house was 3,600 sq. feet with an electric gate, guarded by two Rottweilers. Based on these factors the government's drug expert stated his opinion that the money was furnished or intended to be furnished for drugs. The court did not allow the expert to rely on allegations in the search warrant affidavit in forming his opinion. The amount of cocaine was so small that the expert admitted there was no evidence it was possessed for sale, and the amount of marijuana was so small that the defendant got diversion. The scale was not a type typically used by drug dealers. Claimant testified he owned a construction business and his tax returns showed substantial legitimate income. Applying a preponderance of the evidence standard, the court found insufficient evidence for forfeiture.

> [T]here is nothing in the record beyond speculation to support the conclusion that his security concerns related particularly to the protection of drug trafficking activities.
>
> Ultimately, in order to establish that the cash was either "furnished or intended to be furnished" in exchange for a controlled substance, we are left only with Bastida's expert opinion that, regardless of the source of the cash, he believed that the cash was to be used to purchase narcotics. Although an expert's opinion on an ultimate issue of fact is admissible, and may constitute substantial evidence (see *People v. Douglas* (1987) 193 Cal.App.3d 1691, 1695 [239 Cal.Rptr. 252]), the conclusion by itself does not constitute substantial evidence without an adequate factual foundation. (*See, e.g., United States v. $38,600.00 in U.S. Currency* (5th Cir. 1986) 784 F.2d 694 [court found no probable cause despite expert's testimony that money found in car was part of a narcotics transaction, because no evidence of nexus between cash and narcotics trafficking].)"

(*People v. $47,050* (1993) 17 Cal.App.4th 1319, 1324 – 1325).

When money is seized from a vehicle stopped for non-narcotic enforcement reasons, and "there [is] no evidence to connect the money, the vehicles, or the occupants of those vehicles with narcotics trafficking" and police have only "a mere suspicion the money was the proceeds of some sort of illegal activity," the government cannot make its burden of showing the money was furnished or intended to be furnished for drugs. (*People v. $497,590* (1997) 58 Cal.App.4th 145, 157, discussing the holdings in two federal cases: *United States v. $30,060* (9th Cir. 1994) 39 F.3d 1039 and *United States v. $31,990* (2nd Cir. 1993) 982 F.2d 851.)

a. "Furnished... in exchange" and "traceable proceeds"

In drug cases, the court may forfeit money, negotiable instruments and other things of value "furnished... by any person in exchange for a controlled substance, [and] all proceeds traceable to such an exchange." (Health & Saf. Code Sec. 11470(f)). "Furnished... in exchange" is synonymous with "proceeds."

"Traceable proceeds" allows the government to forfeit proceeds of crime after they have been invested in other property.

In forfeiture cases involving banking offenses "any property which constitutes or is derived from proceeds traceable to" the offense is forfeitable. (Fin. Code Sec. 5320). See Chapter 3 Section B, below.

In criminal profiteering forfeiture cases, all property acquired through the pattern of criminal profiteering, and all proceeds of the pattern of profiteering and all things received in exchange for proceeds immediately derived from the activity are forfeitable under Pen. Code Sec. 186.3(b) & (c), provided the factors of Pen. Code Sec. 186.5(d) are proven, beyond a reasonable doubt. See Chapter 3 Section C, below.

When a defendant is charged with human trafficking which involves a sex act involving a victim under 18 years of age, "the alleged proceeds or instruments" of the crime are subject to forfeiture. (PEN Sec. 236.8(a)). The procedures are the same as those used in criminal profiteering cases.

Defendants convicted of dogfighting or cockfighting forfeit "[a]ny property interest, whether tangible or intangible, that was acquired through the commission of" an offense under Pen. Code Sec. 597.5(a) or 597b(b). (Pen. Code Sec. 598.1).

A proceeds theory can be proven with circumstantial evidence, such as drug dog alerts and other factors mentioned in relation to the "furnished or intended to be furnished" theory. See Chapter 2 Section D-2, above.

1. Commingling with clean funds does not taint the clean funds

The fact that some proceeds of forfeiture-triggering crime were deposited into a bank account already containing funds does not make the entire bank account forfeitable.

In *People v. $9,632.50* (1998) 64 Cal.App.4th 163, the Fifth Appellate District rejected the government's argument that "once some drug money was commingled with other funds, the other funds became tainted and subject to forfeiture, even though the original drug money could be quantified." Noting the lack of state case law on point, the court looked to federal cases and ruled that "the only amounts traceable to drug transactions are the $700 that the court ruled was drug money and any interest actually earned on that sum. The remainder of the account, as legitimate funds not traceable to drug transactions, must be returned to claimant."

Apparently this is the only reported California forfeiture case tracing proceeds that have been commingled with clean money.

The federal forfeiture cases discussed in *People v. $9,632.50* provide guidance in other different scenarios.

The Fifth Appellate District found *United States v. Pole No. 3172, Hopkinton* (1st Cir. 1988) 852 F.2d 636, to be "most helpful." (*People v. $9,632.50* (1998) 64 Cal.App.4th 163, 169).

Pole No. 3172 did not involve proceeds deposited in a bank account with clean proceeds, but drug proceeds used to pay mortgage payments on a house on which the prior payments had been made with legitimate funds. Rejecting the government's argument that the entire property was forfeitable, the court stated:

> We agree that the interest acquired as a result of mortgage payments made with the proceeds of drug transactions should be forfeitable. We do not believe, however, that forfeitability spreads like a disease from one infected mortgage payment to the entire interest in the property acquired prior to the payment. After all, only the actual proceeds of drug transactions are forfeitable. Unless [§ 21 U.S.C.] section 881(a)(6) deprives persons accused of dealing drugs of the right to own any property, the existence of an undivided interest in a felon's property which constitutes proceeds cannot mean that his entire property is proceeds.

(*Pole No. 3172*, 852 F.2d at 639-640). That case is widely cited in federal forfeiture cases as well.

Criminal money laundering cases, such as *People v. Mays* (2007), 55 Cal.Rptr.3d 356, have similar rules regarding commingling of tainted funds with clean funds, but those are not the standards applicable to forfeiture. The crime of money laundering does not require tracing of a particular amount of proceeds into a particular account, it only requires a deposit of at least $5,000 in criminally derived proceeds into an account, or one of two other alternatives. This transfer of $5,000 in proceeds is enough to convict the defendant but does not render the whole account forfeitable because it is not a forfeiture statute.

2. Appreciation in value is forfeitable as traceable proceeds

The court in *People v. $9,632.50* (1998) 64 Cal.App.4th 163 also looked to cases where proceeds were used to purchase an asset that subsequently appreciated in value. In that scenario, courts routinely reject the argument that only the amount of the actual proceeds invested in the asset should be forfeited.

> [A]ny increase in property value was also forfeitable, since it resulted from the use of drug money. *Id.* at 645-46. We agree that any profits, appreciation, or income from drug money proceeds is forfeitable – profits from tainted proceeds are still tainted.

(*United States v. One 1980 Rolls Royce* (5th Cir. 1990) 905 F.2d 89, 91, citing *United States v. Real Estate Located at 116 Villa Rella Dr.* (S.D. Fla. 1987) 675 F. Supp. 645).

If the defendant spent the proceeds on something other than the property seized for forfeiture, the government can't substitute it as "substitute property" as federal courts allow.

The court in *People v. $9,632.50* (1998) 64 Cal.App.4th 163 rejected the government's argument that because the defendant spent his drug proceeds on routine living expenses and banked his legitimate paychecks, "any assets the claimant would not possess had he not been able to use drug money for routine financial needs" became forfeitable proceeds.

> Respondent's view of profits includes not only the interest the drug money itself might have earned, but also includes any asset obtained by a drug dealer which he might not have been able to afford if he had not been dealing drugs, regardless of whether it can be shown that the asset was actually purchased with tainted funds. This view is tantamount to saying that persons accused of dealing drugs should be deprived of the right to own any property (*cf. Pole No. 3172, supra,* 852 F.2d at p. 640). The statute authorizes forfeiture only of proceeds traceable to an exchange for a controlled substance. It does not authorize forfeiture of the increase in net worth that would not have occurred but for the person having

acquired drug money. Such an expansion of the forfeiture law should be left to the Legislature.

(*People v. $9,632.50* (1998) 64 Cal.App.4th 163, 174).

b. Intended to be furnished

Under the drug forfeiture statute, negotiable instruments and other things of value "...intended to be furnished by any person in exchange for a controlled substance" are subject to forfeiture. (Health & Saf. Code Sec. 11470(f)).

This differs from the proceeds theory because the transaction has not been consummated yet. If a person makes an offer to buy controlled substances and tenders an amount of cash, that cash becomes forfeitable even if the drug transaction never occurs. Proof of the intent to furnish the cash in exchange for a controlled substance is shown by the buyer's statements.

3. Facilitation

In drug cases, boats, planes, and vehicles used to facilitate manufacture, possession for sale, or sale of controlled substances are forfeitable. (Health & Saf. Code Sec. 11470(e)). Real property is also forfeitable under a facilitation theory if the property owner is convicted of violating Health & Saf. Code Sec. 11366, 11366.5 or 11366.6 with respect to that property, unless it is used as a family residence or co-owned with an innocent owner. (Health & Saf. Code Sec. 11470(g)).

Under Health & Saf. Code Sec. 11470(f), forfeitable property also includes money or other items of value "used or intended to be used to facilitate" a violation of Health & Saf. Code Sec. 11351, 11351.5, 11352, 11355, 11359, 11360, 11378, 11378.5, 11379, 11379.5, 11379.6, 11380, 11382, or 11383, a felony violation of Health & Saf. Code 11366.8, or a violation of Pen. Code Sec. 182 – if:

> the offense involves manufacture, sale, possession for sale, offer for sale, or offer to manufacture, or conspiracy to commit at least one of those offenses, if the exchange, violation, or other conduct which is the basis for the forfeiture occurred within five years of the seizure of the property, or the filing of a petition under this chapter, or the issuance of an order of forfeiture of the property, whichever comes first.

(Health & Saf. Code Sec. 11470(f)).

4. Abandonment

Under certain circumstances personal property that comes into the possession of the government, including law enforcement agencies, can be treated as abandoned and escheated to the state (declared legally the property of the state).

When personal property suspected of being used to cultivate or transport marijuana is seized and no prosecution results, the property is not being held for evidence, and the owner is not known or has not claimed the property, it can be treated as abandoned. The police must send notice to the owner or tenant of the real property where it was found, post notice at the location and also publish notice. If no owner comes forward after 90 days the property can be treated as abandoned and sold or transferred to a government agency or community service organization. (Health & Saf. Code Sec. 11485).

Money or personal property worth $1,000 or less can be declared escheated to the state under the process set out in Code Civ. Proc. Sec. 1415. The statute requires preparing a "return" (a the list of the property to be declared escheated), with the property's description or the amount of money, the name of the owner or claimant and his last known address if known, the name and address of the agency delivering the property to the State Treasury, and the facts and circumstances causing it to escheat or vest in the state. The notice is posted for public inspection in the Controller's Offices of the cities of Sacramento, San Francisco and Los Angeles, and published in newspapers of general circulation in those three cities at least once per week for two consecutive weeks. Once the return is published the owner has five years to come forward and claim it or will be forever barred. An owner who is an infant or incompetent person has a period of one year after the disability is removed to come forward and claim it.

Under Code Civ. Proc. Sec. 1519, all tangible personal property held for the owner by a government agency that has remained unclaimed for three years escheats to the state. Intangible personal property can also escheat to the state, provided the requirements of Code Civ. Proc. Sec. 1510 are met.

Unclaimed property that escheats to the state can be sold and distributed according to the provisions of Code Civ. Proc. Sec. 1564.

In the past, the abandoned property process has been abused by some police agencies to confiscate and keep property that was not really abandoned. Before agencies can treat property as abandoned they are supposed to make reasonable efforts to locate the property owner and give them notice.

Where property is seized by police and held a long time without an ongoing forfeiture case, it is important that the property owner periodically make inquiries (in writing, to create a paper record), giving his/her current address.

Owners who are in prison need to write the agency holding their property to let the agency know they are incarcerated, and update their prison address if moved to another prison. If the prison mail is not reliable, they should give an address of a responsible person on the outside (or their lawyer) where correspondence concerning their property should be sent.

Even after taking those precautions the property owner should have someone on the outside monitoring their mail at their residence and promptly advising them when registered or certified mail arrives.

When a person who is not charged with a crime has property detained as evidence in a criminal case, it is very important that they notify the prosecuting agency and the police that they want their property back when it is no longer needed. They too need to keep the agency apprised of changes of their address, because they will lose by default if notice is mailed to them at their old address and they miss the deadline for filing a claim.

5. Relation back

The relation back doctrine is a peculiar concept — a legal fiction that "all right title and interest" in forfeitable personal property vests in the government at the time of the illegal act, subject to it later being proven forfeitable. (Health & Saf. Code Sec. 11470(h)(1) or Veh. Code Sec. 14607.6(e)(6)).

If it were literally true that the government obtained ownership of forfeitable property at the time the property was tainted by a criminal act, the government would own everything in the country by now. So what does relation back mean?

The statutory relation back doctrine has exceptions — the doctrine does not affect the interests of third parties, and it cannot be used to defeat the claims of bona fide purchasers or encumbrancers who acquired their interests from the defendant after the act which divested the defendant of ownership under the relation back doctrine.

Although relation back is still embodied in the forfeiture statute, it may not have much meaning now, after the U.S. Supreme Court rolled back the government's overly expansive view of that doctrine in the 1993 case *United States v. 92 Buena Vista Ave.* (1993)

507 U.S. 511. In that case a woman had bought her house with money her ex-boyfriend had given her. Years later, long after they broke up, the ex-boyfriend was charged with dealing drugs and her house was seized as proceeds. She had argued that she was an innocent owner. In its Supreme Court brief the government argued that "no one other than the United States can acquire a valid ownership interest in property after it becomes subject to forfeiture" and that "the 'innocent owner' defense can only be asserted by a claimant who acquired an interest in the property before commission of the act triggering the forfeiture." (Brief for the United States in *United States v. 92 Buena Vista Ave.*, S.Ct. No. 91-781, p. 4).

> Under this doctrine the government's title to forfeitable property vests at the time the property was used unlawfully, and the government's title is superior to that of any subsequent purchaser, transferee, or owner of the property. Because of the relation back doctrine, property that is tainted by unlawful acts in, say, 1986 remains forfeitable today even against someone who purchased it in 1990....
>
> The impact of the relation back doctrine is easy to comprehend. Using it, the government can invalidate numerous asset transfers, however legitimate, by linking the history of an asset to some unlawful act that occurred while the asset was in the custody of an earlier owner or user. In short, the relation back doctrine affords the government a type of continuing hidden lien or title claim to property that is not discernible through normal commercial channels.

(Terrance G. Reed, "American Forfeiture Law: Property Owners Meet the Prosecutor," Cato Policy Analysis No. 179, Cato Institute, Washington D.C. Sept. 29, 1992)).

As you can imagine, this overly expansive doctrine would wreak havoc on real estate titles, among other things. The mortgage bankers association and title companies filed amicus briefs asking the Supreme Court to curtail the doctrine. And it did.

Noting that the government's expansive theory "would effectively eliminate the innocent owner defense in almost every imaginable case in which proceeds could be forfeited" the Court concluded that Congress could not have intended such an inequitable result. The Court held:

> If the Government wins a judgment of forfeiture under the common law rule – which applied to common law forfeitures and to forfeitures under statutes without specific relation-back provisions – the vesting of its title in the property relates back to the moment when the property became forfeitable. Until the Government does win such a judgment, however, someone else owns the property. That person may therefore invoke any defense available to the owner of the property before the forfeiture is decreed.

(*United States v. 92 Buena Vista Ave*. (1993) 507 U.S. 111, 127).

In response to *Buena Vista,* Congress amended the federal forfeiture statute to require subsequent purchasers who raised the innocent owner defense to prove they are bona fide purchasers for value without knowledge that the property was subject to forfeiture.

The California drug forfeiture statute now provides that relation back cannot be used to defeat the claim of a bona fide purchaser or encumbrancer, even if he/she acquired the property from a defendant whose property interest was divested by the relation back doctrine. (Health & Saf. Code Sec. 11470(h)(2)).

Given *Buena Vista*'s limitations on the doctrine, why is it still in the statute? What does relation back do today?

In a case decided a few years before *Buena Vista,* relation back was used to defeat a claim that property detained for forfeiture should be released so the defendant could retain counsel. (*People v. Superior Court* (*Clements*) (1988) 200 Cal.App.3d 491, 499 – 500). The court reasoned that stolen loot cannot be used to retain private counsel, and that jeopardy tax assessments (by which the IRS can freeze funds in a taxpayer's accounts if he/she owes the IRS money) have been upheld over claims that they caused the defendant to not be able to retain counsel. The court also relied on the availability of court appointed counsel for defendants who were rendered indigent by the pretrial seizure of property targeted for forfeiture. (*Id.* at 500 – 501).

People v. Superior Court (*Clements*) has been cited in more recent cases but not for the relation back doctrine. It is not clear what effect the special vesting rule of "relation back" still has, if any).

6. Standing

> Standing is a threshold legal issue in proceedings initiated under the California forfeiture statutes. (*People v. $28,500 United States Currency* (1996) 51 Cal.App.4th 447, 467, 59 Cal.Rptr.2d 239.) The claimant bears the burden of establishing a legally cognizable interest in the subject property sufficient to confer on him standing to challenge the government's forfeiture action. (Ibid.) "Under both the federal and state systems, a claimant must show he has a recognizable legal or equitable interest in the seized property in order to establish standing. Standing has been recognized where the potential claimant has a bona fide ownership, possessory, or security interest in the property seized." (Ibid.)

(*People v. $241,600* (1998) 67 Cal.App.4th 1100, 1107 (internal citation omitted)).

> The doctrine of standing seeks to insure that courts decide actual controversies and not abstract questions. Absent standing, the claimant in a forfeiture action cannot contest the government's decision to seek forfeiture; this is the rule in state and federal proceedings. (*People v. $28,500 United States Currency,* supra, 51 Cal.App.4th [447,] 467, 59 Cal.Rptr.2d 239 [involving a former version of section 11488.4].) If it were otherwise, "persons with no interest whatsoever in seized property could make a handsome living filing claims." (*U.S. v. Certain Real Prop. Located at 16510 Ashton* (6th Cir.1995) 47 F.3d 1465, 1473 (Boggs, J, dissenting).) Thus, "a claimant [in a civil forfeiture proceeding] must show he has a recognizable legal or equitable interest in the seized property" in order to establish standing; it is the claimant's burden to establish an "interest in the seized property" sufficient to satisfy the court of his standing to contest forfeiture. (*People v. $28,500 United States Currency,* supra, 51 Cal.App.4th [447,] 467, 59 Cal. Rptr.2d 239.) This is a threshold legal issue. (*Id.* at pp. 466-467, 59 Cal.Rptr.2d 239; *People v. $241,600 United States Currency* (1998) 67 Cal.App.4th 1100, 1107-1108, 79 Cal.Rptr.2d 588; § 11488.4, subd. (g).)"

(*Jauregi v. Superior Court* (1999) 72 Cal.App.4th 931, 938).

Hearsay is not admissible to prove standing. (*Id.*)

In *$241,600,* the claimant said he found the cash in a rest room at a rest stop, before the police seized it from him. When the police seized it from him he signed a disclaimer that the police presented to him, stating he did not want anything to do with the money. When the forfeiture petition was served on him he filed a claim. Later the government moved for summary judgment, arguing he lacked standing because he had disclaimed the money. Because he allegedly found the money the government also argued that under the relation back doctrine, all right, title and interest in the property vested in the state government "when the alleged drug trafficking offense occurred, before claimant found the money." (*People v. $241,600,* supra, 67 Cal.App.4th 1100, 1108).

The superior court judge granted summary judgment for the government, holding the claimant lacked standing to defend the money. He appealed, arguing he had a legal interest in the money as the finder of lost or abandoned property, and that he had not signed the waiver and disclaimer knowingly, intelligently and voluntarily.

On appeal the Fourth Appellate District reversed. On the government's relation back argument, the court noted that the Health & Saf. Code Sec. 11470 relation back doctrine's vesting rule

> shall be limited to circumstances where its application will not defeat the claim of any person, ... which interest arose prior to the seizure or the filing of the complaint for forfeiture pursuant to this chapter, whichever occurs first, notwithstanding that the interest in the property being claimed was acquired from a person whose property interest would otherwise have been subject to divestment pursuant to this subdivision.

(*People v. $241,600,* supra, 67 Cal.App.4th 1100, 1108).

With regard to the claimant's argument that the money was his because he found it, the court noted that CIV Sec. 2080.3 provides a process by which a person can acquire ownership of found property worth $250 or more. If the true owner is not known, and no one appears and claims ownership within 90 days the police department must publish notice in a newspaper, and if the owner does not come forward and claim it within 7 days, the person who found it is declared the owner, as long as he/she pays the publication costs. The police did not follow that procedure, and the time had expired for the department to do so.

The appellate court concluded the evidence was sufficient to raise triable issues of fact as to whether the claimant knowingly and voluntarily waived and disclaimed his interest, and whether the claimant had an interest in the money and standing to oppose its forfeiture. Id. at 594. The summary judgment was reversed and the case remanded for trial.

Aguilar, the claimant in *People v. $28,500,* did not fare as well on the standing issue. Aguilar claimed to have loaned the money to the person from whom it was seized. The court held he lacked standing to defend it.

> Once the loan was made, Aguilar no longer retained an ownership interest in the actual dollars loaned to Esqueda. (*United States v. $47,875.00 in U.S. Currency* (5th Cir.1984) 746 F.2d 291; 1 Smith, Prosecution and Defense of Forfeiture Cases, supra, ¶ 9.04, p. 9-68.17.) Instead, Aguilar had an unliquidated, unsecured, debt owed to him by Esqueda – a debt which would not become due until roughly six months after the money was seized. All right, title and interest in any property found to be subject to forfeiture under section 11470 vested in the state upon commission of the illegal act which gave rise to forfeiture...

(*People v. $28,500,* 51 Cal.App.4th 447, 469, collecting cases holding unsecured creditors lack standing to defend seized property).

7. Fugitive disentitlement

If the defendant willfully fails to appear in the related criminal case, or flees to evade prosecution, the government does not have to obtain a criminal conviction as a prerequisite for forfeiture. (Health & Saf. Code Sec. 11488.4(k)). Forfeiture will be ordered by default if the government's application for default shows it exercised due diligence trying to locate the defendant. However, the government must still establish a prima facie case, proving all of the elements of forfeiture. (Health & Saf. Code Sec. 11488.4(k)).

If the fugitive disentitlement doctrine applies or if the defendant dies before the forfeiture case is tried, there is no conviction requirement as a prerequisite to equitable sharing. (Health & Saf. Code Sec. 11471.2(c)).

8. Interpreting statutes

When there is a question of how to construe a statute, courts rely on the rules of statutory interpretation (also called "statutory construction.")

> As in any case involving statutory interpretation, our fundamental task here is to determine the Legislature's intent so as to effectuate the law's purpose." (*People v. Murphy* (2001) 25 Cal.4th 136, 142, 105 Cal.Rptr.2d 387, 19 P.3d 1129.) "[W]e look first to the language of the statute. In interpreting that language, we strive to give effect and significance to every word and phrase." (*Copley Press, Inc. v. Superior Court* (2006) 39 Cal.4th 1272, 1284, 48 Cal. Rptr.3d 183, 141 P.3d 288; *Szold v. Medical Bd. of California* (2005) 127 Cal. App.4th 591, 596, 25 Cal.Rptr.3d 665.) "We give the words of a statute their ordinary and usual meaning and construe them in the context of the statute as a whole." (*American Liberty Bail Bonds, Inc. v. Garamendi* (2006) 141 Cal.App.4th 1044, 1052, 46 Cal.Rptr.3d 541; *Hassan v. Mercy American River Hospital* (2003) 31 Cal.4th 709, 715, 3 Cal.Rptr.3d 623, 74 P.3d 726.) "We must presume that the Legislature intended 'every word, phrase and provision... in a statute ... to have meaning and to perform a useful function.'" (*Garcia v. McCutchen* (1997) 16 Cal.4th 469, 476, 66 Cal.Rptr.2d 319, 940 P.2d 906.)

> If there is no ambiguity in the language of the statute, then the Legislature is presumed to have meant what it said, and the plain meaning of the language governs. Where the statute is clear, courts will not "interpret away clear language in favor of an ambiguity that does not exist." (*Lennane v. Franchise Tax Bd.* (1994) 9 Cal.4th 263, 268, 36 Cal.Rptr.2d 563, 885 P.2d 976; *People v. Benson* (1998) 18 Cal.4th 24, 30, 74 Cal.Rptr.2d 294, 954 P.2d 557.) "[T]he 'plain meaning' rule does not prohibit a court from determining whether the literal meaning of a statute comports with its purpose.... Literal construction should not prevail if it is contrary to the legislative intent apparent in the statute. "Statutes should be construed so as to be given a reasonable result consistent with the legislative purpose.... 'The court should take into account matters such as context, the object in view, the evils to be remedied, the history of the times and of legislation upon the same subject, public policy, and contemporaneous construction.'" (*Rincon Del Diablo Municipal Water Dist. v. San Diego County Water Authority* (2004) 121 Cal.App.4th 813, 818-819, 17 Cal.Rptr.3d 666; *Thornburg v. Superior Court* (2006) 138 Cal.App.4th 43, 49, 41 Cal.Rptr.3d 156.)
>
> If the statute is ambiguous, we may consider a variety of extrinsic aids, including legislative history, the statute's purpose, and public policy." (*American Liberty Bail Bonds, Inc. v. Garamendi*, supra, 141 Cal.App.4th 1044, 1052, 46 Cal. Rptr.3d 541; *Coalition of Concerned Communities, Inc. v. City of Los Angeles* (2004) 34 Cal.4th 733, 737, 21 Cal.Rptr.3d 676, 101 P.3d 563.)

(*People v. Mays* (2007) 148 Cal.App.4th 13, 29-30 (some internal citations omitted.))

> The goal of statutory interpretation is determining legislative intent. To accomplish that goal, courts must

> look first to the language of the statute and give effect to its plain meaning. If the words are clear, courts may not add to or change them to accomplish a purpose not apparent on the face of the statute or from its legislative history. (*Burden v. Snowden* (1992) 2 Cal.4th 556, 562 [7 Cal. Rptr.2d 531, 828 P.2d 672].) Moreover, notwithstanding the strong governmental interest in stemming illegal drug transactions, forfeiture statutes are disfavored and must be construed strictly in favor of the owner of the property. (*People v. One 1937 Lincoln etc. Sedan* (1945) 26 Cal.2d 736, 738 [160 P.2d 769]; *Baca v. Minier* (1991) 229 Cal. App.3d 1253, 1265 [280 Cal. Rptr. 810].)

(*People v. Ten $500 travelers checks* (1993) 16 Cal.App.4th 475, 479).

One very important rule of statutory interpretation for forfeiture claimants is the

> well-settled proposition that "'[s]tatutes imposing forfeitures are not favored and are to be strictly construed in favor of the persons against whom they are sought to be imposed.'" (*People v. $ 28,500 United States Currency* (1996) 51 Cal.App.4th 447, 463–464 [59 Cal. Rptr. 2d 239].) This disfavor applies "notwithstanding the strong governmental interest in stemming illegal drug transactions ...." (*People v. Ten $ 500 etc. Traveler's Checks* (1993) 16 Cal.App.4th 475, 479.)

(*People v. $10,153.38* (1987) 179 Cal.App.4th 1520, 1525 – 1526).

3. Offenses that trigger forfeiture

A. Drug offense forfeitures

1. Triggering offenses

Note: the parenthetical information following the section numbers below was added by the author to give a basic idea of the activities prohibited in that section. The provisions of the statute are often much broader. Please consult the statute itself for accuracy. For free online access to California statutes see http://leginfo.legislature.ca.gov/faces/codes.xhtml.

Under Health & Saf. Code Sec. 11488(a), police officers making or attempting to make an arrest for violation of Health & Saf. Code Sec. 11351 (possession for sale of Schedule III, IV or V narcotic drug), Sec. 11351.5 5 (cocaine base); Sec. 11352 (transport, sell, import Schedule III, IV or V narcotic drug); Sec. 11355 (offer to furnish Schedule III, IV or V narcotic drug); Sec. 11359 (cannabis); Sec. 11360 (cannabis); Sec. 11378 (non-narcotic drug from Schedules III, IV and V); Sec. 11378.5 (phencyclidine or analog or precursor); Sec. 11379 (non-narcotic drug from Schedules III, IV and V); Sec. 11379.5 (transport or sale of phencyclidine or analog or precursor); Sec. 11379.6 (manufacturing substances in Schedules I through V); Sec. 11380 (use of a minor in drug crime); or Sec. 11382 (give or sell Schedule III, IV or V non-narcotic drug); or Penal Code Sec. 182 (conspiracy) involving the manufacture, sale, or purchase for sale of one of those offenses may seize any item subject to forfeiture under Sec. 11470(a) – (f).

See Chapter 3 Section A-2 for property that may be forfeited.

a. The DEA schedules

Schedule I controlled substances are those that the U.S. DEA claims have no currently accepted medical use in the United States, a lack of accepted safety standards for use, and a high potential for abuse. Of course medical experts sometime dispute the characterization of some substances in this list, especially with regard to cannabis. Schedule I includes: opiates, heroin, Ibogaine, LSD and other hallucinogens, marijuana and its cannabinoids, MDMA ("ecstacy"), mescaline and peyote, methaqualone, peyote, psilocybin, and analogs of those substances. The complete list is contained in Health & Saf. Code Sec. 11054.

Schedule II controlled substances, according to the DEA, have "a high potential for abuse, with use potentially leading to severe psychological or physical dependence." However, this class of drugs has accepted medical uses, and may be obtained or administered with a doctor's prescription. Without a prescription, possession is illegal. Schedule II includes: amphetamine, barbiturates, cocaine, codeine, diphenoxylate, fentanyl, hydrocodone, hydromorphone, methadone, methamphetamine, methylphenidate, dexmethylphenidate, morphine, nabilone, opium, oxycodone, oxymorphone, Nembutal, pethidine, phencyclidine (PCP) secobarbital, and tapentadol. The complete list is contained in Health & Saf. Code Sec. 11055.

Schedule III contains substances with a currently accepted medical use, less potential for abuse, and abuse may lead to moderate or low physical dependence or high psychological dependence. Without a prescription, possession is illegal. Schedule III includes anabolic steroids, some barbiturates, ketamine, Marinol, paregoric, secobarbital and pentobarbital. See the complete list in Health & Saf. Code Sec. 11056.

Schedule IV substances have a currently acceptable medical use, a low potential for abuse relative to Schedule III, and abuse may lead to limited physical or psychological dependence relative to Schedule III. Without a prescription, possession is illegal. Schedule IV substances include Xanax, Librium, Klonopin, Valium, and Ambien. The complete list is contained in Health & Saf. Code Sec. 11057.

Schedule V substances have a currently acceptable medical use, a low potential for abuse relative to Schedule IV, and abuse may lead to limited physical or psychological dependence relative to Schedule IV. Without a prescription, possession is illegal. Schedule V substances include cough suppressants containing codeine, Pyrovalerone, and Lyrica. The complete list is contained in Health & Saf. Code Sec. 11058.

b. Relevance of schedules to forfeiture

The schedule of a drug determines the criminal penalties, and the penalties factor into proportionality analysis for purposes of the Excessive Fines defense, which allows forfeitures to be reduced if forfeiting the entire property would be grossly disproportionate punishment for the offense.

2. Property that may be forfeited

California drug laws are set out in the California Uniform Controlled Substances Act, Health & Saf. Code Sec. 11000 – 11651. The forfeiture provisions are set out in Health & Saf. Code Sec. 11470 et seq.

The following are subject to forfeiture under Sec. 11470:

(a) controlled substances in violation of statute;

(b) raw materials and equipment used/intended for use;

(c) all property except real estate or boats, airplanes & vehicles used as a container for (a) or (b) property;

(d) books records & research materials;

(e) boats, planes, vehicles used to facilitate manufacture, possession for sale, or sale of controlled substances of a certain quantity or more (except where person other than defendant owns a community property interest and it is the only vehicle available to immediate family;

(f) money, negotiable instruments, securities & things of value furnished in exchange for illegal controlled substances; and

(g) real estate, if the owner is convicted of Health & Saf. Code Sec. 11366, 11366.5 or 11366.6 with respect to that property, but not if the property is used as a family residence or co-owned with an innocent owner.

The provisions for forfeiting vehicles, boats and airplanes do not apply to common carrier or an employee acting within the scope of his employment. (Health & Saf. Code Sec. 11490).

3. Procedures

The drug forfeiture statutes were amended by SB 443, effective January 1, 2017. The forfeiture case is a separate civil case, but the forfeiture and criminal cases are filed in the same court and closely coordinated. (Health & Saf. Code Sec. 11488.4(a)(1)).

a. Administrative forfeiture

The drug laws have a separate administrative forfeiture process that does not exist in other forfeiture schemes. It only applies in drug cases where the seized property is personal property worth less than $25,000.

The chief difference in administrative forfeitures is that the claimant has to file the first paper to commence the case in court.

The government serves a written notice of its intent to forfeit the property administratively, and then the claimant must file a claim in court, commencing a judicial action. See Chapter 7 for details of the administrative forfeiture process.

Claimants who fail to file a claim within 30 days after being served with the notice of administrative forfeiture lose by default. Defaults can be vacated under certain circumstances. See Chapter 14 Section C.

Unless he/she qualifies for a waiver the claimant has to pay a filing fee to file the claim in superior court. The claimant must serve a certified copy of the claim on the district attorney.

Once the claim is filed, the government has 30 days after service of the claim to file a petition for forfeiture. (Health & Saf. Code Sec. 11488.4(j)(5)(C)).

b. Judicial forfeiture

The judicial forfeiture provisions of the Health and Safety Code are similar to those used in most other California forfeiture statutes. It is applicable to all forfeiture cases involving property worth $25,000 or more. In those cases the forfeiture case is commenced in court with the government's filing of a petition of forfeiture. See Chapter 6 Section A.

If forfeiture is sought against property of a minor who has a pending juvenile proceeding growing out of the circumstances giving rise to the forfeiture case, the forfeiture will be continued until after the adjudication of the juvenile petition. In that circumstance the forfeiture hearing is not held in juvenile court. (Health & Saf. Code Sec. 11470.3(c)).

c. Summary forfeiture of contraband

Items that are "summarily forfeited" may be destroyed or otherwise disposed of without any formal forfeiture proceedings.

> Controlled substances listed in Schedule I that are possessed, transferred, sold, or offered for sale in violation of this division are contraband and shall be seized and summarily forfeited to the state.

(Health & Saf. Code Sec. 11475).

> Species of plants from which controlled substances in Schedules I and II may be derived which have been planted or cultivated in violation of this division, or of which the owners or cultivators are unknown, or which are wild growths, may be seized and summarily forfeited to the state.

(Health & Saf. Code Sec. 11476).

Note that cannabis (marijuana) is currently classified in Schedule I, which makes it disposable as contraband. However, medical marijuana and recreational marijuana are legal now in California so long as it is possessed and/or distributed in compliance with the state and local regulations. Legal possession under California law takes it out of the state definition of contraband, so a defendant or claimant who prevails in showing he/she possessed it legally may seek return of the seized marijuana in a motion for return of property. See Chapter 14 Section A-1-a-(i), below. That does not apply to marijuana prosecuted in federal court.

d. Disposal of abandoned property

When personal property suspected of being used to cultivate or transport marijuana is seized and no prosecution results, the property is no longer being held for evidence, and the owner is not known or has not claimed the property, it may be treated as abandoned. The police must send notice to the owner or tenant of the real property where it was found, post notice at the location and also publish notice in a newspaper. If no owner comes forward after 90 days the property can be treated as abandoned and disposed of by transfer to a government agency or community service organization or sale. (Health & Saf. Code Sec. 11485).

Any property – other than vehicles, boats, airplanes, money, or negotiable instruments – which has no value may be ordered destroyed. Uncontaminated science equipment which is found not to be legally possessed may be donated to a school at the request of a law enforcement agency. (Health & Saf. Code Sec. 11473).

4. Burden of proof and criminal conviction requirement

A criminal conviction is required for forfeiture, except when the property is cash or negotiable instruments totaling $40,000 or more. (Health & Saf. Code Sec. 11488.4(i)(4)).

If there is a related criminal case, the forfeiture case is tried in conjunction with the criminal case, but the trial is bifurcated. Trial is by jury unless waived by all parties. (Health & Saf. Code Sec. 11488.4(i)(5)).

The government has the burden of proving grounds for forfeiture beyond a reasonable doubt, except when the property is $40,000 or more in cash or negotiable instruments (Health & Saf. Code Sec. 11488.4(i)(2)). Where the seized property is $40,000 or more in cash or negotiable instruments, the government must prove grounds for forfeiture by clear and convincing evidence. (Health & Saf. Code Sec. 11488.4(i)(4)).

When the seized property is $40,000 or more in cash or negotiable instruments, there is no conviction requirement, and the forfeiture case can proceed without a parallel criminal case. (Health & Saf. Code Sec. 11488.4(i)(4)).

If the defendant willfully fails to appear in the related criminal case, a criminal conviction is not required as a prerequisite to forfeiture. Forfeiture will be ordered by default if the government's application for default shows it used due diligence in trying to locate the defendant.

Even though the defendant is a fugitive and loses by default, the government still must establish a prima facie case for forfeiture, that is, present evidence sufficient to establish all the elements required for forfeiture. (Health & Saf. Code Sec. 11488.4(k)).

B. Banking offenses

1. Triggering offenses

Fin. Code Sec. 5320 authorizes forfeiture for certain banking offenses. The triggering offenses are:

(a) Fin. Code Sec. 5303 – false entry or omission in books by banking employee or agent.

(b) Fin. Code Sec. 5304 – corrupt solicitation to influence transaction of savings association.

(c) Fin. Code Sec. 5305 – misapplication of funds or credit of savings association.

(d) Fin. Code Sec. 5306 – scheme to defraud savings association.

(e) Corp. Code Sec. 25540 – states the penalties for violations of Corp. Code Sec. 25400 – 25402 (fake trading in securities; false statement in sale of security; and illegal insider trading.)

(f) Corp. Code Sec. 25541 – scheme or artifice to defraud in connection with sale or purchase of securities.

(g) Pen. Code Sec. 487 – grand theft.

(h) Pen. Code Sec. 504 – embezzlement by public employee.

A conviction for one of the above offenses is required before property can be forfeited. (Fin. Code Sec. 5320).

2. Property that may be forfeited

A defendant convicted of one of those specified banking offenses forfeits "any property which constitutes or is derived from proceeds traceable to that violation." (Fin. Code Sec. 5320).

3. Procedures

The prosecutor commences the action by filing a forfeiture petition in the court where the offense is prosecuted.

> A notice regarding the petition shall be provided, by personal service or registered mail, to every person who may have an interest in the property specified in the petition.

(Fin. Code Sec. 5321(a)). However, if notice cannot be given that way notice may be published. The notice must inform claimants to file a verified claim by the deadline. (*Id.*)

To forfeit real property the prosecutor must file a lis pendens in each county in which the property is situated. (Fin. Code Sec. 5321(b)).

If a forfeiture petition is filed for a banking offense before criminal charges have been brought, the prosecutor must give notice to any parties that they are targets of the anticipated criminal action, (Fin. Code Sec. 5321(c)), and the government must indict or file a criminal complaint within 120 days after filing the forfeiture petition or the forfeiture petition must be dismissed. Once dismissed it cannot be refiled until after criminal charges are filed by complaint or indictment. (Fin. Code Sec. 5321(d)).

Only the convicted criminal defendant's interest is forfeitable. "The judgment of forfeiture shall not affect the interest in real property of any third party which was acquired prior to the recording of the lis pendens." (Fin. Code Sec. 5321(b)).

However, a third party can lose his/her interest by default. The claimant must file a verified claim within 30 days after receipt of actual notice – or the date notice is published if service is by publication. (Fin. Code Sec. 5322(a)). If a non-defendant fails to file a claim by the deadline, they are declared in default, but the prosecutor must submit proof of forfeitability. (Fin. Code Sec. 5322(b)(1)).

If the defendant fails to file a claim the court will enter a response of denial on the defendant's behalf. (Fin. Code Sec. 5322(b)(2)). If a defendant is convicted, the forfeiture trial may be before the same or a different jury. Jury trial is required unless waived by all parties. (Fin. Code Sec. 5322(c)(2)). The prosecution has the burden of proving beyond a reasonable doubt that the property is forfeitable. (Fin. Code Sec. 5322(d)).

"No property solely owned by a bona fide purchaser for value shall be subject to forfeiture." (Fin. Code Sec. 5324(a)).

Claimants other than the defendant do not have to prove anything except that they are owners of interests in the property, or lienholders. If the jury finds the person has a valid lien or interest, but does not find that the person obtained his/her interest with actual knowledge that the property was to be used" in a forfeiture-triggering offense, the person's interest is not forfeited. (Fin. Code Sec. 5324(b)).

If the property is found to be forfeitable as to the defendant, owners and lienholders can buy the property from the government by paying the difference between the appraised value of their interest and the appraised value of the property. If they don't want to buy the government out, the government will sell the property and pay them the appraised value of their interest or lien. (Fin. Code Sec. 5324(c)).

C. Criminal profiteering

1. Triggering offenses

The California Control of Profits of Organized Crime Act was enacted to punish and deter criminal activities of organized crime through forfeiture of profits acquired through criminal activities. The legislative intent of the legislation is "to punish and deter only such activities" (i.e. organized crime). (Pen. Code Sec. 186.1).

This is very similar to the federal RICO statute, 18 U.S. Code Sec. 1962 *et seq.*

Although the criminal statutes it incorporates are garden variety crimes, the forfeiture statute is triggered only when there is a pattern of criminal profiteering activity. See Chapter 3 Subsection C-1-b below.

a. Criminal profiteering activity defined

Pen. Code Sec. 186.2(a) defines "criminal profiteering activity" as "any act committed or attempted or any threat made for financial gain or advantage, in violation of any of the following sections:"

(1) Arson, (Pen. Code Sec. 451).

(2) Bribery, (Pen. Code Sec. 67, 67.5, and 68).

(3) Child pornography or exploitation, (felony violations of Pen. Code Sec. 311.2, 311.3 or 311.4).

(4) Felonious assault, (Pen. Code Sec. 245).

(5) Embezzlement, (Pen. Code Sec. 424 and 503).

(6) Extortion, (Pen. Code Sec. 518).

(7) Forgery, (Pen. Code Sec. 470).

(8) Gambling, (Pen. Code Sec. 337a through 337f, and Sec. 337i), except for activities solely as an individual bettor.

(9) Kidnapping, (Pen. Code Sec. 207).

(10) Mayhem, (Pen. Code Sec. 203).

(11) Murder, (Pen. Code Sec. 187).

(12) Pimping and pandering, (Pen. Code Sec. 266).

(13) Receiving stolen property, (Pen. Code Sec. 496).

(14) Robbery, (Pen. Code Sec. 211).

(15) Solicitation of crimes, (Pen. Code Sec. 653f).

(16) Grand theft, (Pen. Code Sec. 487a).

(17) Trafficking in controlled substances, (Health & Saf. Code Sec. 11351, 11352, and 11353).

(18) Corporate securities law violations, (Corp. Code Sec. 25541).

(19) Obscene matter offenses (Pen. Code Sec. 311 – 312.7) and offenses relating to harmful matter (Pen. Code Sec. 313 – 313.5) – if they may be prosecuted as a felony.

(20) False or fraudulent claim, (Pen. Code Sec. 550).

(21) False or fraudulent activities, schemes, or artifices (Welf. & Inst. Code Sec. 14107).

(22) Money laundering, (Pen. Code Sec. 186.10).

(23) Counterfeit registered mark offenses, (Pen. Code Sec. 350), or offenses relating to piracy, (Pen. Code Sec. 653w).

(24) Unauthorized access to computers, computer systems, and computer data, (Pen. Code Sec. 502).

(25) Conspiracy to commit any of the crimes listed above, (Pen. Code Sec. 182).

(26) Criminal street gang activity, (Pen. Code Sec. 186.22(a)), or a felony subject to enhancement under Pen. Code Sec. 186.22.

(27) Fraud or theft against the California beverage container recycling program, (Pub. Resources Code Sec. 14500 et seq.)

(28) Human trafficking – that is, depriving a person of personal liberty "with the intent to obtain forced labor or services," (Pen. Code Sec. 236.1(a)).

(29) Any crime in which the perpetrator induces, encourages, or persuades a person under 18 years of age to engage in a commercial sex act. For purposes of this paragraph, a commercial sex act means any sexual conduct on account of which anything of value is given or received by any person.

(30) Any crime in which the perpetrator, through force, fear, coercion, deceit, violence, duress, menace, or threat of unlawful injury to the victim or to another person, causes a person under 18 years of age to engage in a commercial sex act. For purposes of this paragraph, a commercial sex act means any sexual conduct on account of which anything of value is given or received by any person.

(31) Identity theft (Pen. Code Sec. 530.5).

(32) Theft of a motor vehicle (Veh. Code Sec. 10851).

(33) Abduction or procurement by fraudulent inducement for prostitution (Pen. Code Sec. 266a).

(34) Insurance fraud, (Unemp. Ins. Code Sec. 2106, 2108, 2109, 2110, 2110.3, 2110.5, 2110.7, and 2117).

b. Pattern of criminal profiteering activity defined

In order to forfeit property under this provision, prosecutors not only have to prove one of the crimes that are defined as "criminal profiteering activity" but they also have to prove a *pattern* of such activity, and that it was an *activity of organized crime*.

> "Pattern of criminal profiteering activity" means engaging in at least two incidents of criminal profiteering, as defined by this chapter, that meet the following requirements:
>
> (A) Have the same or a similar purpose, result, principals, victims, or methods of commission, or are otherwise interrelated by distinguishing characteristics.
>
> (B) Are not isolated events.
>
> (C) Were committed as a criminal activity of organized crime.

(Pen. Code Sec. 186.2(b)(1)).

The two prior acts must also occur within 10 years of the offense being prosecuted, excluding any period of imprisonment. A prior act that resulted in an acquittal cannot be counted. (Pen. Code Sec. 186.2(b)(2)).

The statute defines "organized crime" as

> crime that is of a conspiratorial nature and that is either of an organized nature and seeks to supply illegal goods or services such as narcotics, prostitution, pimping and pandering, loan-sharking, counterfeiting of a registered mark in violation of Section 350, the piracy of a recording or audiovisual work in violation of Section 653w, gambling, and pornography, or that, through planning and coordination of individual efforts, seeks to conduct

> the illegal activities of arson for profit, hijacking, insurance fraud, smuggling, operating vehicle theft rings, fraud against the beverage container recycling program, embezzlement, securities fraud, insurance fraud in violation of the provisions listed in paragraph (34) of subdivision (a), grand theft, money laundering, forgery, or systematically encumbering the assets of a business for the purpose of defrauding creditors.

(Pen. Code Sec. 186.2(d)). Organized crime also includes criminal street gang crimes (Pen. Code Sec. 186.22(f)); welfare fraud offenses (Welf. &: Inst. Code Sec. 14107, and identity theft (Pen. Code Sec. 530.5). (Pen. Code Sec. 186.2(d)).

2. Property that may be forfeited

Under Pen. Code Sec. 186.3(a), when a defendant is convicted of engaging in a pattern of criminal profiteering activity in violation of Pen. Code Sec. 186.2(a), they forfeit all property acquired through the pattern of criminal profiteering activity (Pen. Code Sec. 186.3(b)), all proceeds of the pattern of criminal profiteering activity, and all things received in exchange for proceeds immediately derived from the activity. (Pen. Code Sec. 186.3(c)).

3. Procedures

The prosecutor must file a forfeiture petition in the same court as the criminal proceeding and serve it by personal service or registered mail (publication notice is permitted only if the other two methods are impossible). The notice must state the deadline for filing a claim. (Pen. Code Sec. 186.4).

The deadline for filing a claim is 30 days from receipt of actual notice (or publication date if applicable). Third party claimants who miss that deadline are in default, and lose their interests in the property upon the government's proof of the elements of Sec. 186.5(d).

If the defendant fails to admit or deny that the property is forfeitable the court must enter a response of denial on his behalf. (Pen. Code Sec. 186.5(b)(2)).

If the property is real property a lis pendens must be filed. A forfeiture judgment does not affect the interests of a third party who acquired an interest prior to the filing of the lis pendens. (Pen. Code Sec. 186.4).

The government must prove beyond a reasonable doubt that the defendant engaged in a pattern of criminal profiteering and that the property is forfeitable under Pen. Code Sec. 186.3(b) or (c). (Pen. Code Sec. 196.5).

D. Computer hacking & other computer related crimes

1. Triggering offenses

a. Unauthorized access to computer systems (hacking)

Pen. Code Sec. 502 et seq. make it a forfeiture-triggering offense to knowingly access a computer or computer system or network, and, without permission...:

(1) alter, damage, delete or destroy any data, computer, computer system or network in order to (A) defraud, deceive or extort, or (B) wrongfully control or obtain money, property, or data;

(2) take, copy, or use any data;

(3) use computer services;

(4) add, alter, damage, or delete any data or software;

(5) disrupt computer services or cause a denial of computer services to authorized users;

(6) provide a means of accessing a computer or network;

(7) access or cause to be accessed any computer or network;

(8) introduce any computer contaminant into the computer or system;

(9) use the internet domain name of another in sending email (phishing) or cause damage to a computer or network;

(10) disrupt government computer services or cause denial of computer services to an authorized user;

(11) add, alter, damage, delete, or destroy any data, software on the system;

(12) disrupt a public safety infrastructure computer system or cause the denial of computer services to an authorized user;

(13) provide a means of accessing a computer or system; or

(14) introduce a computer contaminant into a public safety infrastructure computer.

(Pen. Code Sec. 502(c)(1)-(14)). See Pen. Code Sec. 502(b) for definitions. The penalties are in Pen. Code Sec. 502(d). Forfeiture is authorized under Pen. Code Sec. 502(g).

At sentencing the judge may also impose prohibitions on access to and use of computers and may consider alternative sentencing including community service. (Pen. Code Sec. 502(k)(1) & (2)).

The statute of limitations for forfeiture under this provision is three years from the illegal act or the date of discovery of the damage, whichever is later. (Pen. Code Sec. 502(e)(5)).

b. Crimes involving telecommunications and computer equipment/software

Note: The description of the offenses in parenthesis in the next paragraph were added by the author to give a general idea of what the section prohibits, but the section may be much broader than that. See the actual statute for details.

Under Pen. Code Sec. 502.01(a)(1): computer equipment and software and illegal telecommunications equipment can be forfeited for violations of Pen. Code: Sec. 272 (improper contact with a minor); Sec. 288 (lewd acts with minor); Sec. 288.2 (child porn); Sec. 311.1 (child porn); Sec. 311.2 (child porn); Sec. 311.3 (child porn); Sec. 311.4 (child porn); Sec. 311.5 (writing, publishing, distributing obscene matter); Sec. 311.10 (advertising for sale child porn); Sec. 311.11 (possession of child porn); Sec. 422 (criminal threats); Sec. 470 (forgery & counterfeiting); Sec. 470a (counterfeiting ID cards); Sec. 472 (forgery of document under seal of government or corporation); Sec. 475 (forged or counterfeit checks); Sec. 476 (passing forged or counterfeit check); Sec. 480 (counterfeit coin and currency); Sec. 483.5 (deceptive ID document); Sec. 484g (use of invalid credit card); Sec. 484e(a), (b), or (d) (unauthorized use of credit card); Sec. 484f(a) (counterfeit credit card); Sec. 484i(b) or (c) (altering a credit card with intent to defraud); Sec. 502(c) (use of computer system in fraud scheme); Sec. 502.7 (unauthorized use of phone system); Sec. 502.8 (advertising illegal communications equipment); Sec. 529 (false impersonation of officer of court); Sec. 529a (counterfeit birth certification); Sec. 530.5 (identity theft); Sec. 537e (possession of item with obliterated serial number); Sec. 593d (unauthorized access to cable); Sec. 593e (unauthorized access to cable); Sec. 646.9 (threats); or Sec. 647(j) (surreptitious spying on dressing rooms and restrooms).

However, no property can be forfeited under Pen. Code Sec. 502.01(a)(1) for an infraction. (Pen. Code Sec. 502.01(a)(1)).

If the defendant is a minor, the parents' property may be forfeited. (Pen. Code Sec. 502.01(a)(1)).

The definitions are set out in (Pen. Code Sec. 502.01(a)(2)-(5)).

2. Property that may be forfeited

a. Forfeiture under Pen. Code Sec. 502

Under Pen. Code Sec. 502(g) the following are forfeitable: any computer, computer network, software, or data owned by the defendant that is used to commit a public offense (defined in Sec. 502(c)); and any computer owned by the defendant which is used as a repository for the storage of software or data obtained by hacking.

This statute has additional financial penalties uncommon to criminal cases. Under Pen. Code Sec. 502(e)(1) the owner or lessee of any computer or network, program or data who suffers damages from computer hacking may sue the hacker for compensatory damages and injunctive relief. The conduct of an un-emancipated minor is imputed to the minor's parent or legal guardian. (Pen. Code Sec. 502(3)(1)). The court may award the victim punitive damages if the defendant is proven, by clear and convincing evidence, to have committed oppression, fraud, or malice (as defined in Civil Code Sec. 3294). (Pen. Code Sec. 502(e)(4)). The court may award the victim attorney's fees under Pen. Code Sec. 502(e)(2). The statute of limitations for bringing the action is 3 years from the date of the hacking or the date of discovery of the damage, whichever is later. (Pen. Code Sec. 502(e)(5)).

For purposes of a civil or criminal action under this section, a person who causes access of a computer or network in one jurisdiction from another jurisdiction is deemed to have personally accessed the computer in each jurisdiction. (Pen. Code Sec. 502(j)).

b. Forfeiture under Pen. Code Sec. 502.01

Under Pen. Code Sec. 502.01(a)(1) the following are forfeitable: computer equipment and software and illegal telecommunications equipment.

> For purposes of this section, "illegal telecommunications equipment" means equipment that operates to evade the lawful charges for any telecommunications service; surreptitiously intercept electronic serial numbers or mobile identification numbers; alter electronic serial numbers; circumvent efforts to confirm legitimate access to a telecommunications account; conceal from any telecommunications service provider or lawful authority the existence, place of origin, or destination of any telecommunication; or otherwise facilitate any other criminal conduct. "Illegal telecommunications equipment" includes, but is not limited to, any unauthorized electronic serial number or mobile identification number, whether incorporated into a wireless telephone or other device or otherwise. Items specified in this subdivision shall be considered illegal telecommunications equipment notwithstanding any statement or disclaimer that the items are intended for educational, instructional, or similar purposes.

(Pen. Code Sec. 502.8(g)).

3. Procedures

The procedures for forfeiture under Pen. Code Sec. 501 and 502.01(a)(1) are more like criminal forfeiture than other California forfeiture statutes. There is no separate civil forfeiture case – the forfeiture is conducted inside the criminal case.

If the defendant is convicted, the criminal sentencing judge conducts a hearing at or after sentencing. The prosecutor has the burden of proving by a preponderance of the evidence that the property is subject to forfeiture. (Pen. Code Sec. 502.01(b)).

Prior to the forfeiture hearing the prosecutor shall conduct an investigation to determine whether other persons own interests in the property, and send them notice at least 30 days before the hearing. (Pen. Code Sec. 502.01(c)(1)). Any persons claiming interests in the property must file a motion for redemption of their interest at least 10 days before the hearing, and send a copy of the motion to the prosecuting agency and the probation department. (Pen. Code Sec. 502.01(c)(2)).

There is no mention in the statute of a right to a jury trial on the forfeiture issue, or the third party's motions for redemption.

The prosecutor may defeat the interests of third parties who filed motions for redemption if he/she proves by a preponderance of the evidence that

> the person knew or should have known the property was being used in violation of [one of the specified statutes] and that the person did not take reasonable steps to prevent that use, or if the interest is a security interest, the person knew or should have known at the time that the security interest was created that the property would be used for a violation.

(Pen. Code Sec. 502.01(c)(3)).

If the court finds that one or more persons own a valid interest in the property, it must determine the value of the property and the value of each valid interest in the property. If the property is worth more than the value of a valid interest, the person may pay the difference and take ownership of the property. If they decline to do that the property will be sold and the person will be paid from the proceeds of sale, up to the value of his/her interest. (Pen. Code Sec. 502.01(d)(3)).

If the property is worth less than the value of the valid interest, the agency must sell the property and pay the proceeds to that person, up to the value of his/her interest. (Pen. Code Sec. 502.01(d)(4)).

If the defendant was a minor at the time of the offense, the forfeiture provisions are applied to property of the parents or guardians. (Pen. Code Sec. 502.01(e)). Parents or guardians must be notified at least 30 days before the hearing. (Pen. Code Sec. 502.01(e)(1)). The parents or guardians may avoid forfeiture if, at least 10 days before the hearing, they file a signed statement that the minor will not have access "to any computer or telecommunications device owned by the parent or guardian for two years" after sentencing. (Pen. Code Sec. 502.01(e)(2)).

If, within 2 years, the minor is convicted of a new offense involving the parents' or guardians' computer or telecommunications equipment, the property involved in the original offense and the property involved in the new offense are subject to forfeiture. (Pen. Code Sec. 502.01(e)(3)). If the parent or guardian makes full restitution to the victim, they can avoid forfeiture of their equipment if the parents' or guardians' equipment was located in the family's primary residence during the crime. (Pen. Code Sec. 502.01(e)(4)).

Notwithstanding these forfeiture provisions, the court has discretion to deny forfeiture if it finds that the defendant "is not likely to use the property otherwise subject to forfeiture for future illegal acts." (Pen. Code Sec. 502.01(f)).

If the convicted defendant is the only person owning a valid interest in the forfeited property, the victim may elect to take the property as full or partial restitution. If he/she elects to do so the court must determine the value of the property and credit that amount against the restitution owed by the defendant. (Pen. Code

Sec. 502.01(g)(1)). The victim cannot be penalized for refusing to accept the equipment as restitution. (*Id.*)

If the property is sold, the proceeds are distributed first to bona fide or innocent purchasers or encumbrancers up to the amount of his/her interest. (Pen. Code Sec. 502.01(h)(1)).

E. Dogfighting, cockfighting, bullfighting

1. Triggering offenses

Pen. Code Sec. 597.5 makes it a felony to own, possess, keep, or train a dog for dogfighting (Pen. Code Sec. 597.5(a)(1)); or to cause dogs to fight or injure another dog for amusement or gain (Pen. Code Sec. 597.5(a)(2)); or to allow dogfighting on any premises under his/her control or to aid or abet dogfighting (Pen. Code Sec. 597.5(a)(3)). It is a misdemeanor to knowingly be a spectator at such an event. (Pen. Code Sec. 597.5(b)). Nothing in this section prohibits using dogs in managing livestock or hunting, or training dogs for any other purpose. (Pen. Code Sec. 597.5(c)).

Pen. Code Sec. 598.1(a) authorizes forfeiture for defendants convicted of Pen. Code Sec. 597.5.

Pen. Code Sec. 597b makes it illegal to cause animals to fight with other animals or persons – or to "worry" or "injure" any animal – for amusement or personal gain. The first offense is a misdemeanor under Pen. Code Sec. 597b(a), but a second or subsequent offense may be a felony. (Pen. Code Sec. 597b(b)). Aiding and abetting such an offense is also a misdemeanor, but merely being a spectator is not aiding and abetting. (Pen. Code Sec. 597b(c)).

Forfeiture is authorized for "animal fighting other than dog" only for defendants convicted a second or subsequent time of Pen. Code Sec. 597b(b) – not first offenses or aiders and abettors. (Pen. Code Sec. 598.1(a)).

2. Property that may be forfeited

If the prosecutor has filed a petition for forfeiture and the person is convicted of a violation of Pen. Code Sec. 597.5 or 597b(b), the court may forfeit:

> [a]ny property interest, whether tangible or intangible, that was acquired through the commission of any of the crimes listed in subdivision (a) of Section 597.5 or subdivision (b) of Section 597b shall be subject to forfeiture, including both personal and real property, profits, proceeds, and the instrumentalities acquired, accumulated, or used by cockfighting or dogfighting participants, organizers, transporters of animals and equipment, breeders and trainers of fighting birds or fighting dogs, and persons who steal or illegally obtain dogs or other animals for fighting, including bait and sparring animals.

(Pen. Code Sec. 598.1(b)(1)).

Pen. Code Sec. 598.1(b)(2) contains several exceptions to that provision. Property owned solely by a bona fide purchaser for value who had no knowledge that the property was used or intended to be used, in violation of that statute is exempted by Pen. Code Sec. 598.1(b)(2)(A). Family residences owned by two or more people, one of whom has no knowledge of its illegal use are exempted by Pen. Code Sec. 598.1(b)(2)(B).

> [V]ehicles that are used merely to transport fighting birds and equipment to the site of the fight – and that are not directly used in animal or bird fighting, or in a fighting exhibition, or in the training of animals or birds to fight, or to inflict pain or cruelty upon animals or birds in respect to such fighting – cannot be seized (other than

for standard evidentiary purposes) or forfeited under section 599aa.

(*People v. Blue Chevrolet Astro* (2000) 83 Cal.App.4th 322, 99 Cal.Rptr.2d 609, 610).

3. Procedures

If the prosecutor chooses to pursue forfeiture he/she must file a forfeiture petition in the court where the defendant is charged with an offense under Pen. Code Sec. 597b. Pen. Code Sec. 598.1(c)(1). The petition must be served upon every person who may have a property interest in "the alleged proceeds." (Pen. Code Sec. 598.1(c)(2)). Service must be by registered mail or personal delivery unless they cannot be served that way, in which case service is by publication. (Pen. Code Sec. 598.1(c)(3)).

If the property for which forfeiture is sought is real estate, the prosecutor must file a lis pendens on the property at the recorder of deeds. (Pen. Code Sec. 598.1(c)(4)). The forfeiture judgment does not affect the interests third parties own in real estate acquired prior to the recording of the lis pendens. (Pen. Code Sec. 598.1(c)(5)).

Any person claiming an interest in the property must file a verified claim within 30 days of service (or the date of first publication, if notice is by publication), and must serve a verified copy of the claim on the prosecutor. (Pen. Code Sec. 598.1(d)). Anyone who fails to file a verified claim within that time is in default and his/her interest in the property is forfeited upon proof of the elements of Pen. Code Sec. 598.1(b). (Pen. Code Sec. 598.1(e)(1)). However if the criminal defendant defaults in failing to file a claim the court will enter a claim of denial on his/her behalf. (Pen. Code Sec. 598.1(e)(2)).

If the defendant is convicted, the forfeiture case is tried before the same jury or a different jury unless waived by consent of all parties. (Pen. Code Sec. 598.1(f)(2)).

F. Unlicensed driver

1. Triggering offenses

Veh. Code Sec. 14607.6(a), subjects to forfeit the vehicle of an unlicensed driver or person driving on suspended or revoked license, if the driver is the registered owner of the vehicle, and he/she has a previous misdemeanor conviction under Veh. Code Sec. 12500(a) (driving without a license), 14601 (driving while suspended or revoked license for reckless driving), 14601.1 (driving while suspended or revoked), 14601.2 (Driving Under Influence of alcohol or drugs or DUI causing injury), 14601.3 (driving after accumulating driving record history), 14601.4 (illegal act using vehicle while driving suspended or revoked), or 14601.5 (refusal to take DUI test or DUI).

The vehicle forfeiture statute is based on a nuisance theory.

2. Property that may be forfeited

Vehicles driven by persons who are not licensed to drive or whose license has been suspended or revoked can be forfeited as a nuisance – including vehicles belonging to persons other than the unlicensed driver, under certain circumstances. (Veh. Code Sec. 14607.6(a)).

3. Procedures

Note: The procedures are often more complicated than the explanations of them set out in this section. Please read the cited statutory provisions for more detail.

a. Reduced constitutional protections

Forfeiture procedures for driving without a license offenses differ dramatically from the fairly standard procedures used for other California forfeiture statutes.

By using the legal term "nuisance" this forfeiture statute triggers a different type of constitutional analysis than most forfeiture statutes. In the U.S. Supreme Court case *Bennis v. Michigan* (1996) 516 U.S. 442, the Court held that under nuisance forfeiture statutes, innocence of the property owner is irrelevant unless there is a statutory defense for innocent owners. Chief Justice Rehnquist, writing the opinion of the court, cited "a long and unbroken line of cases" dating back to forfeiture of pirate ships which held that "an owner's interest in property may be forfeited by reason of the use to which it is put even though the owner did not know that is was put to such use." (*Bennis v. Michigan,* supra, 516 U.S. at 449).

Fortunately the unlicensed driver forfeiture statute generally protects innocent third parties, with exceptions as noted in the section below.

Labeling this type of forfeiture a "nuisance forfeiture" allows the procedures to provide less due process to the claimant than other California forfeiture statutes.

Most California forfeiture statutes now have a requirement that the defendant be convicted of the triggering offense. For unlicensed driver forfeitures, the conviction is not required for the presently charged offense. (Veh. Code Sec. 14607.6(e)(5)). Instead, it relies on a previous conviction followed by a new charge of driving on a suspended or revoked license or without a license. The first conviction cannot by itself trigger a forfeiture. (Veh. Code Sec. 14607.6(a)).

This is one of only two California forfeiture statutes where the government's burden of proof at the forfeiture hearing is a preponderance of the evidence. (Veh. Code Sec. 14607.6(e)(5)). (The other exception is forfeiture of computers, devices, and software for computer crimes. See Chapter 3 Section D.) In other forfeiture statutes the burden of proof is clear and convincing evidence or beyond a reasonable doubt.

Since the statute was designed to serve a remedial purpose – removing the unregistered, suspended, or revoked driver's access to the vehicle – vehicles are immediately impounded but can be redeemed by owners or lienholders if they comply with the procedures.

b. procedure for first conviction for driving without a license

Upon a defendant's first conviction for Veh. Code Sec. 12500(a) (driving without a license); Sec. 14601 (driving while suspended or revoked license for reckless driving); Sec. 14601.1 (driving while suspended or revoked); Sec. 14601.2 (Driving Under Influence of alcohol or drugs or DUI causing injury); Sec. 14601.3 (driving after accumulating driving record history); Sec. 14601.4 (illegal act using vehicle while driving suspended or revoked); or Sec. 14601.5 (refusal to take DUI test or DUI) the court must inform the defendant that his car is subject to forfeiture as a nuisance if driven on a highway again by a driver with a suspended or revoked license. (Veh. Code Sec. 14607.8).

A vehicle is subject to forfeiture as a nuisance if: (1) a registered owner has a previous misdemeanor conviction for one of these offenses – Veh. Code Sec. 12500(a), Sec. 14601, Sec. 14601.1, Sec. 14601.2, Sec. 14601.3, Sec. 14601.4, or Sec. 14601.5, and (2) is caught again driving the vehicle on a highway in the state while unlicensed or on a revoked or suspended license. (Veh. Code Sec. 14607.6).

c. Impoundment

If a driver is unable to produce a valid driver's license the vehicle must be impounded, regardless of ownership, unless the officer is reasonably able to verify that the driver is properly licensed. The officer must attempt to verify license status before impounding. (Veh. Code Sec. 14607.6(c)(1)).

An officer may not impound a vehicle if the driver's license expired within the previous 30 days if driver would otherwise have been properly licensed. (Veh. Code Sec. 14607.6(c)(2)).

The officer may exercise discretion not to impound vehicles if the driver is an employee driving in the course of employment, if the driver is an employee of a business that services or parks vehicles and the owner relinquished possession solely for parking or servicing and did not agree to let the driver use it for any other purpose. In such a case the registered owner may be permitted to obtain its release. (Veh. Code Sec. 14607.6(c)(3)).

The vehicle shall be released and not forfeited: (1) if the driver of the impounded vehicle was not a registered owner at the time of its impoundment; or (2) if the driver was a registered owner but does not have a previous conviction for violation of Veh. Code Sec. 12500(a) (driving without a license), Sec. 14601 (driving while suspended or revoked license for reckless driving), Sec. 14601.1 (driving while suspended or revoked), Sec. 14601.2 (Driving Under Influence of alcohol or drugs or DUI causing injury), Sec. 14601.3 (driving after accumulating driving record history), Sec. 14601.4 (illegal act using vehicle while driving suspended or revoked), Sec. or 14601.5 (refusal to take DUI test or DUI). (Veh. Code Sec. 14607.6(c)(5)).

d. Getting the vehicle released from impoundment

If the driver who is driving without a license was a registered owner when the vehicle was impounded, the vehicle can be released if, within 3 days of impoundment, the driver presents a valid driver's license, including a valid temporary California license, and pays towing and storage charges and any administrative charges authorized by Veh. Code Sec. 22850.5. (Veh. Code Sec. 14607.6(d)(1)).

If someone other than the driver owns a community property interest in the vehicle, and that is the only vehicle available to the immediate family that may be operated with a Class C (basic, non-commercial) driver's license, the vehicle can be released if: the registered owner or community property interest owner proves ownership of that interest, that he/she has a valid license, and that the vehicle is properly registered; pays all towing, storage, and administrative fees; signs a stipulated vehicle release agreement in consideration for non-forfeiture of the vehicle; and if the driver requests release. (Veh. Code Sec. 14607.6(d)(2)). If the driving record of a registered owner of the vehicle shows a registered owner had previously signed a vehicle release agreement the vehicle can't be released again. (Veh. Code Sec. 14607.6(d)(5)).

In a stipulated vehicle release agreement the signers of the agreement consent to automatic forfeiture of the vehicle if it is driven by an unlicensed driver or someone driving on a suspended or revoked license. (Veh. Code Sec. 14607.6(d)(3)).

A stipulated release agreement must be reported to the DMC within 10 days. (Veh. Code Sec. 14607.6(d)(4)). The stipulated release agreement is effective only as long as it is noted on a driving record under Veh. Code Sec. 1806.1. (Veh. Code Sec. 14607.6(d)(3)).

A vehicle that is determined to have been stolen may be claimed by the registered owner at any time after impoundment, provided the registration is current and the registered owner has no outstanding traffic violations or parking tickets on his driving record, nor on the record of any other vehicle he/she owns. (Veh. Code Sec. 14607.6(l)).

Registered owners who suffer losses due to impoundment or forfeiture may recover the amount from the unlicensed driver. If the vehicle had been turned over to a business establishment in good faith and an unlicensed driver employed by the business causes it to be impounded, the owner may recover damages from the business. (Veh. Code Sec. 14607.6(m)).

e. Post-impoundment hearing

A registered or legal owner of an impounded vehicle may request a hearing pursuant to Veh. Code Sec. 14607.6(n). (Veh. Code Sec. 14607.6(c)(4)).

Registered and legal owners may request a hearing to determine the validity of the storage, if they request the hearing within 10 days after impoundment (within 3 days if personal service was provided to a registered owner.) (Veh. Code Sec. 14607.6(n)(1)). The hearing must be held within 2 days after being requested. (Veh. Code Sec. 14607.6(n)(2)). For purposes of this section, days means work days, not counting weekends and holidays. (Veh. Code Sec. 14607.6(o)).

The agency employing the person directing the storage is liable for costs of towing and storage if it is determined the driver had a valid license. (Veh. Code Sec. 14607.6(n)(3)).

Vehicles cannot be impounded if the driver has a valid license but for a different class of vehicle other than the one driven. (Veh. Code Sec. 14607.6(s)).

f. Forfeiture process

If the vehicle is not redeemed under Veh. Code Sec. 14607(d), the impounding agency must send notice, within 2 days of impoundment, to all legal and registered owners of the vehicle at the addresses on file with the DMV, informing them the vehicle is subject to forfeiture, with instructions for filing a claim and of its right to conduct a sale under subdivision (g). (Veh. Code Sec. 14607.6(e)(2)). If a registered owner was served at the time of impoundment with that information, no further notice is required to a registered owner, but notice must be sent to all the legal owners. (Veh. Code Sec. 14607.6(e)(2)). If notice is not sent to the legal owner within 2 working days, the legal owner does not have to pay for more than 15 days' impoundment when redeeming the vehicle. A legal owner who redeems the vehicle within 15 days of impoundment does not have to pay processing charges. (Veh. Code Sec. 14607.6(e)(3)).

Any owner of the vehicle who wishes to contest the forfeiture must file a claim and pay a $100 filing fee, but the filing fee is reimbursed by the government if the owner wins. (Veh. Code Sec. 14607.6(e)(4)).

If no claims are filed and served within 15 days after mailing of notice – or 5 days after personal service – the vehicle is declared forfeited. A declaration of forfeiture gives title to the state. (Veh. Code Sec. 14607.6(e)(3)).

If a claim is timely filed and served, the prosecutor must file a petition of forfeiture within 10 days of receipt of the claim, and set an expedited hearing date. (Veh. Code Sec. 14607.6(e)(4)). To the extent practicable the civil and criminal cases are heard together in a consolidated proceeding. (Veh. Code Sec. 14607.6(e)(4)).

Only claimants who filed a timely claim may defend the forfeiture action. (Veh. Code Sec. 14607.6(e)(5)).

A vehicle forfeiture case under Veh. Code Sec. 14607.6(e)(4) is treated as a limited civil case under Code Civ. Proc. Sec. 85, regardless of the value of the car. Sec. 85 normally requires the amount at issue to be less than $25,000. (Code Civ. Proc. Sec. 85(a) and Sec. 85(c)(20)).

Limited cases may be brought in the small claims division if the case meets the jurisdictional amount requirement of Code Civ. Proc. Sec. 87(a) – that is, if the vehicle is worth $5,000 or less. (Code Civ. Proc. Sec. 116.220).

Under the small claims rules, the filing fee is cheaper. If a party has filed 12 or fewer small claims in the state within the past year, the filing fee is $30 for property worth $1,500 or less, $50 for property worth $1,500 to $5,000, and $75 if it is worth more than $5,000. (Code Civ. Proc. Sec. 116.230(b)). If the person has filed more than 12 other small claims cases in the past year the fee is $100. (Code Civ. Proc. Sec. 116.230(c)). Additional filing fees of $20 to $45 are assessed when filing amendments to claims. (See Code Civ. Proc. Sec. 116.230(d)(1) – (4)).

If a vehicle code forfeiture claim is filed under both the limited civil case and small claims designation, the applicable small claims rules apply. (Code Civ. Proc. Sec. 87(a)).

At the forfeiture hearing the prosecutor has the burden of proof by a preponderance of the evidence. (Veh. Code Sec. 14607.6(e)(5)). There is no requirement that the defendant be convicted of the new offense. (Veh. Code Sec. 14607.6(e)(5)), but he/she must have a prior misdemeanor conviction for a violation of Veh. Code Sec. 12500(a) (driving without a license), Sec. 14601 (driving while suspended or revoked license for reckless driving), Sec. 14601.1 (driving while suspended or revoked), Sec. 14601.2 (Driving Under Influence of alcohol or drugs or DUI causing injury), Sec. 14601.3 (driving after accumulating driving record history), Sec. 14601.4 (illegal act using vehicle while driving suspended or revoked), or Sec. 14601.5 (refusal to take DUI test or DUI). (Veh. Code Sec. 14607.6(a)).

When the legal owner is a car dealer or financial institution, it may take possession of the forfeited vehicle and sell it, if they notify the impounding agency within 15 days of the mailing of notice. They can give notice to the agency in person, or by certified mail, fax or email. (Veh. Code Sec. 14607.6(g)). The sale must be conducted in the same manner as that used for repossessed or surrendered vehicles. Proceeds of sale are distributed according to Veh. Code Sec. 14607.6(i). (Veh. Code Sec. 14607.6(g)).

If the legal owner dealer or financial institution does not notify the agency within 15 days of its intent to conduct the sale, the forfeited vehicle will be sold at public auction within 60 days after the government receives title. (Veh. Code Sec. 14607.6(h)). The proceeds of sale are distributed according to Veh. Code Sec. 14607.6(j).

Low value vehicles that are not of a type that are generally sold to the public will be scrapped. (Veh. Code Sec. 14607.6(k)).

G. Human trafficking

If a defendant is charged with human trafficking involving a sex act with a victim under 18, the prosecutor may file a petition to forfeit "the alleged proceeds or instruments" of the crime. (Pen. Code Sec. 236.8(a)).

1. Triggering offenses

Note: the explanatory matter in parenthesis after the section numbers below was added by the author to give a basic idea of what the statute prohibits, but the statutes are much more detailed than these descriptions.

Human trafficking is defined as depriving another person of personal liberty:

(a) "with the intent to obtain forced labor or services," (Pen. Code Sec. 236.1(a));

(b) depriving another of personal liberty with the intent to commit any of the crimes codified in Pen. Code Sec. 266 (enticing a minor female into prostitution), Sec. 266h (pimping), Sec. 266i (pandering, persuading another person into prostitution), Sec. 266j (child prostitution), Sec. 267 (kidnaping for purpose of prostitution), Sec. 311.1 (child pornography), Sec. 311.2 (child pornography), Sec. 311.3 (child pornography), Sec. 311.4 (engaging a minor in the business of selling child pornography), Sec. 311.5 (advertising or publishing child porn), Sec. 311.6 (presenting live obscene conduct for public view), or Sec. 518 (extortion). (Pen. Code Sec. 236.1(b)); and

(c) persuading or attempting to persuade a minor to engage in a commercial sex act with the intent to violate Pen. Code Sec. 266 (enticing a minor female into prostitution), Sec. 266h (pimping), Sec. 266i (pandering, persuading another person into prostitution), Sec. 266j (child prostitution), Sec. 267 (kidnaping for purpose of prostitution), Sec. 311.1 (child pornography), Sec. 311.2 (child pornography), Sec. 311.3 (child pornography), Sec. 311.4 (engaging a minor in the business of selling child pornography), Sec. 311.5 (advertising or publishing child porn), Sec. 311.6 (presenting live obscene conduct for public view), or Sec. 518 (extortion). (Pen. Code Sec. 236.1(c)).

2. Property that may be forfeited

The human trafficking statutes authorize forfeiture of any interest in any vehicle, boat, plane, money, negotiable instruments, securities, real property or other thing of value used to facilitate a crime of human trafficking involving a commercial sex act where the victim is under 18 years of age at the time of the crime; all proceeds of the crime; and all things of value "received in exchange for the proceeds immediately derived from the act." (Pen. Code Sec. 236.7(b)).

3. Procedures

a. Petition and claim process

The prosecutor must send notice by personal service or registered mail to "every person who may have an interest in the property" and must also publish notice for at least three successive weeks in a newspaper of general circulation in the county where the property was located. The notice must state the deadline for filing claims. (Pen. Code Sec. 236.6(b)).

b. Pretrial restraining orders and release of property

Property of a criminal defendant charged with human trafficking can be restrained immediately following the filing of the complaint or indictment. (Pen. Code Sec. 236.6(a)).

If the property sought to be forfeited is real estate, the prosecutor must file a lis pendens with the county recorder pursuant to Code Civ. Proc. Sec. 405.2. (Pen. Code Sec. 236.6(c)).

The prosecutor must apply for a court order to freeze bank accounts. (Pen. Code Sec. 236.6(d)).

> No preliminary injunction shall be granted or receiver appointed without notice to the interested parties and a hearing to determine that the order is necessary to preserve the property or assets, pending the outcome of the criminal proceedings.

(Pen. Code Sec. 236.6(g)(1)).

A person claiming an interest in the restrained assets has 30 days from first publication of notice or actual notice, whichever is later, to file a verified claim in court "stating the nature and amount of his or her interest in the property or assets." The claimant must serve a verified copy of the claim on the prosecutor. (Pen. Code Sec. 236.6(e)).

A defendant or claimant who has filed a verified claim has the right to request a show cause hearing within 10 days of service of the request on the prosecutor. (Pen. Code Sec. 236.6(g)(2)). The purpose of the hearing is

> to determine whether the temporary restraining order should remain in effect, whether relief should be granted from a lis pendens..., or whether an existing order should be modified in the interests of justice. Upon a showing of good cause, the hearing shall be held within two days of

> the service of the request for a hearing upon the prosecuting agency.

(Pen. Code Sec. 236.6(g)(2)).

A petition to show cause is part of the criminal proceedings for purposes of appointment of counsel. (Pen. Code Sec. 236.6(g)(7)).

At the hearing the court "may consider any matter that it deems reliable and appropriate, including hearsay…." (Pen. Code Sec. 236.6(g)(3)).

> The court shall weigh the relative degree of certainty of the outcome on the merits and the consequences to each of the parties of granting the interim relief. If the prosecution is likely to prevail on the merits and the risk of the dissipation of assets outweighs the potential harm to the defendants and the interested parties, the court shall grant injunctive relief.

(Pen. Code Sec. 236.6(g)(3)).

The court must consider the public interest in preserving property and in compensating victims and paying fines; the difficulty of preserving property; the fact that the relief was requested by the prosecutor on behalf of victims; and the likelihood substantial public harm has occurred. (Pen. Code Sec. 236.6(g)(3)).

The court may consider a defendant's request for release of some of the restrained assets to pay criminal counsel, bail, or living expenses while the case is pending. (Pen. Code Sec. 236.6(g)(4)). The court must weigh the needs of the public against the defendant's needs in making the decision, (*Id.*) and must seek to protect innocent third parties such as spouses, who were not involved in the crime. (Pen. Code Sec. 236.6(g)(5)).

> The orders shall be no more extensive than necessary to effect the remedies available for the crime. In determining

> the amount of property to be held, the court shall ascertain the amount of fines that are assessed for a violation of this chapter and the amount of possible restitution.

(Pen. Code Sec. 236.6(g)(6)).

A court-appointed receiver may move for an interlocutory sale of any property that is liable to perish or be significantly reduced in value, or if the expenses of maintaining the property are disproportionate to the value of the property. The proceeds of interlocutory sale are deposited with the court pending the outcome of the case. (Pen. Code Sec. 236.6(g)(8)). The court may appoint a receiver to dispose of or protect the value of an asset. (Pen. Code Sec. 236.6(g)(10)).

> A preservation order shall not be issued against an asset of a business that is not likely to be dissipated and that may be subject to levy or attachment...

(Pen. Code Sec. 236.6(g)(11)).

c. Trial and judgment

The prosecution's burden of proof in the forfeiture trial is beyond a reasonable doubt. (Pen. Code Sec. 236.9(d)).

"The judgment of forfeiture shall not affect the interest in real property of a third party that was acquired prior to the recording of the lis pendens." (Pen. Code Sec. 236.8(a)).

However, real estate may be vulnerable to fines and restitution unless the third party can show they were bona fide purchasers for value: "The order imposing fines and restitution shall not affect the interest in real property of a third party that was acquired prior to the recording of the lis pendens, unless the property was obtained from the defendant other than as a bona fide purchaser for value." (Pen. Code Sec. 236.6(i)(2)).

If the prosecution loses or dismisses the criminal case, the injunction or restraining order must be dissolved. (Pen. Code Sec. 236.6(h)). If the defendant is convicted the court will make a finding at sentencing of the portion of the restrained assets to be applied to pay fines and restitution. The fines and restitution orders may exceed the amount of assets restrained. (Pen. Code Sec. 236.6(i)(1)(A)). The court may order an immediate transfer of assets to satisfy a restitution order, (*Id.*) or may stay the judgment pending appeal, in which case the injunction or restraining order remains in effect. (Pen. Code Sec. 236.6(i)(1)(B)).

After the court appointed a receiver and entered an order imposing fines and restitution the receiver is empowered to liquidate all assets and distribute them in this order of priority: (1) to pay receiver or court appointed appraiser for all expenditures in connection with the sale and for repairs, storage, and transportation of the property; (2) to valid lienholder, up to the value of his/her interest; (3) to victims as restitution for the human trafficking that was proven at trial; and (4) for payment of fines. (Pen. Code Sec. 236.6(j)).

4. Defenses to forfeiture

A. Innocent owner or bona fide purchaser for value

1. Protection for innocent owners or co-owners

In federal forfeiture cases, the innocent owner defense is an affirmative defense, meaning property owners have the burden of proving their innocence and lack of knowledge and consent to the illegal act that tainted the property.

Under California forfeiture statutes where a third party's "innocence" (i.e. lack of knowledge and consent to the illegal use) is a defense, the government has the burden of proving that they are *not* innocent. And the government usually has a high burden of proof – usually beyond a reasonable doubt or at least clear and convincing evidence.

Some California forfeiture statutes automatically protect persons other than the defendant from forfeiture of their interests. Under those statutes all the third party has to prove is their interest in the property.

Under most state statutes and for most categories of property, a criminal conviction is required in the underlying offense before property can be forfeited at all.

a. Drug cases

In drug cases, for third parties who own interests in the property, the burden of proof is on the government to show that the owner knew and consented to the illegal use of the property in the forfeiture-triggering offense.

> (d)(1) At the hearing, the state or local governmental entity shall have the burden of establishing, pursuant to subdivision (i) of Section 11488.4, that the owner of any interest in the seized property consented to the use of the property with knowledge that it would be or was used for a purpose for which forfeiture is permitted, in accordance with the burden of proof set forth in subdivision (i) of Section 11488.4.
>
> (2) No interest in the seized property shall be affected by a forfeiture decree under this section unless the state or local governmental entity has proven that the owner of that interest consented to the use of the property with knowledge that it would be or was used for the purpose charged. Forfeiture shall be ordered when, at the hearing, the state or local governmental entity has shown that the assets in question are subject to forfeiture pursuant to Section 11470, in accordance with the burden of proof set forth in subdivision (i) of Section 11488.4.

(Health & Saf. Code Sec. 11488.5(d)(1)-(2)).

When the property is cash or negotiable instruments totaling $40,000 or more, no conviction is required, but the government must prove a non-defendant's knowledge and consent by clear and convincing evidence. (Health & Saf. Code Sec. 11488.4(i)(4)).

For all other categories of property the government's burden of proof is beyond a reasonable doubt. (Health & Saf. Code Sec. 11488.4(i)(1)-(2)).

If the jury finds the property is forfeitable but one or more owners of interests in the property (including lienholders) did not have actual knowledge of, and consent to, the illegal use, their property interest is not forfeited. If the value of their interest is less than the equity in the property, the person may pay the government the difference between the appraised value and his/her property interest and take possession of the property. If the person elects not to buy out the government's interest, the property will be auctioned and the person will be paid the appraised value of his/her own interest. (Health & Saf. Code Sec. 11488.6).

b. Banking forfeitures

In banking forfeiture cases, a conviction is required. The forfeiture must be tried before the same jury or a new jury unless waived by all parties. (Fin. Code Sec. 5322(c)(2)). The government has the burden of proving grounds for forfeiture beyond a reasonable doubt. The verdict must be unanimous. (Fin. Code Sec. 5322(d)).

If property is found to be forfeitable under Fin. Code Sec. 5320 but the jury "does not find that [a lienholder] or owner of an interest under a conditional sale contract acquired that interest with actual knowledge that the property was to be used for a purpose for which forfeiture is permitted," then the person's interest is protected. The person can pay the difference between the appraised value of the property and his/her lien and the state will sign over the property to him/her. (Fin. Code Sec. 5324(b)). If the person doesn't want to buy the government out, the government will sell the property and pay him/her the appraised value of the lien. (Fin. Code Sec. 5324(c)). Lienholders are compensated before any proceeds are distributed to victims, law enforcement, or the general fund. (Fin. Code Sec. 5325(a)-(c)).

c. Criminal profiteering

In forfeitures brought under the California criminal profiteering law (similar to federal RICO), when the property is real estate, a forfeiture judgment does not affect a third party's interest in real property acquired prior to recording of the lis pendens. (Pen. Code Sec. 186.4(a)).

However, the third party may lose the right to contest the forfeiture by missing the deadline for filing a claim. A third party claimant who misses the deadline will be declared in default and his/her property interests will be forfeited if the government proves the elements of Sec. 186.5(d). (Pen. Code Sec. 186.5(b)(1)). Defaults may be vacated under the procedures set out in Chapter 14 Section C.

Section 186.5(d) requires the prosecutor to prove beyond a reasonable doubt that the defendant engaged in a pattern of criminal profiteering activity and that the property was "acquired through a pattern of criminal profiteering activity" (Pen. Code Sec. 186.3(b)) or "things of value that may have been received in exchange for the proceeds immediately derived from the pattern of criminal profiteering activity" (Pen. Code Sec. 186.3(c)). (Pen. Code Sec. 186.5(d)).

When property is forfeited for criminal profiteering, the proceeds are distributed first to any bona fide or innocent purchasers and lienholders. The court must seek to locate all lienholders and may hold the proceeds in escrow for up to 60 days to accomplish that. (Pen. Code Sec. 186.8(a)).

d. Human trafficking

In human trafficking forfeiture cases against real estate, third parties who own interests in the property are exempted from forfeiture of their interests. "The judgment of forfeiture shall not affect the interest in real property of a third party that was acquired prior to the recording of the lis pendens." (Pen. Code Sec. 236.8(a)). However, the third party's interest may be wiped out when the defendant's seized assets are levied to pay fines and restitution if they were not bona fide purchasers.

> The order imposing fines and restitution shall not affect the interest in real property of a third party that was

> acquired prior to the recording of the lis pendens, unless the property was obtained from the defendant other than as a bona fide purchaser for value.

(Pen. Code Sec. 236.6(i)(2)).

> In making its final order, the court shall seek to protect the legitimately acquired interests of innocent third parties, including an innocent spouse, who were not involved in the commission of criminal activity.

(Pen. Code Sec. 236.6(i)(3)).

Under Pen. Code Sec. 236.7(a)-(c), some innocent owners' property is protected even if it means the defendant's interest is not forfeited.

> Real property that is used as a family residence or for other lawful purposes, or that is owned by two or more persons, one of whom had no knowledge of its unlawful use, shall not be subject to forfeiture.

(Pen. Code Sec. 236.7(d)). Forfeiture under Pen. Code Sec. 236.7 also protects persons "holding a valid lien, mortgage, security interest, or interest under a conditional sales contract" unless the prosecutor shows they "acquired that interest with actual knowledge that the property was to be used for a purpose for which forfeiture is permitted." (Pen. Code Sec. 236.11(b)).

e. Animal-fighting cases

In forfeitures for animal fighting under Pen. Code Sec. 597b, the statute exempts from forfeiture

> [p]roperty used as a family residence and owned by two or more inhabitants, one of whom had no knowledge of its unlawful use.

(Pen. Code Sec. 598.1(b)(2)(B)).

f. Computer crimes

Pen. Code Sec. 502(g) authorizes the forfeiture of computer equipment owned by the defendant who is convicted of the computer crime. There is no separate forfeiture case – the forfeiture hearing is done at or before sentencing in the criminal case, like federal criminal forfeitures. When third parties own interests in the computer or equipment, they have a separate process to redeem their interests. This is similar to the third party process in federal criminal forfeitures.

Before the forfeiture trial, the prosecutor must make an investigation to determine whether anyone other than the defendant owns an interest in the property, and they must send notice to the third parties 30 days before the forfeiture hearing.

> A person claiming an interest in the property shall file a motion for the redemption of that interest at least 10 days before the hearing on forfeiture, and shall send a copy of the motion to the prosecuting agency and to the probation department.

(Pen. Code Sec. 502.01(c)(2)).

The standards for redemption are similar to the innocent owner defense except the government has the burden of proof. The prosecutor must show "by a preponderance of the evidence, ...that the person knew or should have known that the property was being used" in one of the specified computer related crimes. (Pen. Code Sec. 502.01(c)(3)).

When the defendant is a minor at the time of the offense, the parent's property may be forfeited. (Pen. Code Sec. 502.01(e)). The parents must be notified at least 30 days before the hearing. The parent or guardian may avoid forfeiture by filing a signed statement, at least 10 days before the hearing, indicating the minor will not have access to the computer or telecommunication devices for two years after the sentencing. (Pen. Code Sec. 502.01(e)(2)).

The court has discretion to deny forfeiture if it finds that the convicted defendant, or minor is not likely to use the property for future illegal acts. (Pen. Code Sec. 502.01(f)).

2. Subsequent purchasers protected if "bona fide purchaser for value"

When a person acquires his or her interest in property after the forfeiture-triggering crime, they may still have a defense.

a. Drug cases

In drug cases, the Health and Safety Code exempts bona fide purchasers from the special vesting rule of the "relation back doctrine" – the legal fiction that "all right title and interest" in forfeitable personal property vests in the government at the time of the illegal act, subject to it later being proven forfeitable.

> The operation of the special vesting rule established by this subdivision shall be limited to circumstances where its application will not defeat the claim of any person, including a bona fide purchaser or encumbrancer who, pursuant to Section 11488.5, 11488.6, or 11489, claims an interest in the property seized, notwithstanding that the interest in the property being claimed was acquired from a defendant whose property interest would otherwise have been subject to divestment pursuant to this subdivision.

(Health & Saf. Code Sec. 11470(h)(2)).

b. Banking offenses

In forfeitures for banking offenses (Pen. Code Sec. 186.7(a)), "[n]o property solely owned by a bona fide purchaser for value shall be subject to forfeiture." (Fin. Code Sec. 5324(a)).

c. Criminal profiteering

In forfeitures for criminal profiteering, "[n]o property solely owned by a bona fide purchaser for value shall be subject to forfeiture." (Pen. Code Sec. 186.7(a)).

d. Human trafficking cases

The human trafficking forfeiture statute protects bona fide purchasers from levies to pay the convicted defendant's fines and restitution.

> The order imposing fines and restitution shall not affect the interest in real property of a third party that was acquired prior to the recording of the lis pendens, unless the property was obtained from the defendant other than as a bona fide purchaser for value. If any assets or property affected by this section are subject to a valid lien, mortgage, security interest, or interest under a conditional sales contract and the amount due to the holder of the lien, mortgage, interest, or contract is less than the appraised value of the property, that person may pay to the state or the local government that initiated the proceeding the amount of the difference between the appraised value of the property and the amount of the lien, mortgage, security interest, or interest under a conditional sales contract. Upon that payment, the state or local entity shall relinquish all claims to the property.

(Pen. Code Sec. 236.6(i)(2)).

"No property solely owned by a bona fide purchaser for value shall be subject to forfeiture." (Pen. Code Sec. 236.11(a)).

e. Animal-fighting cases

In forfeitures for animal fighting under Pen. Code Sec. 597b, the statute exempts from forfeiture

> [p]roperty solely owned by a bona fide purchaser for value, who was without knowledge that the property was intended to be used for a purpose which would subject it to forfeiture under this section....

(Pen. Code Sec. 598.1(b)(2)(A)).

3. Owners of interests acquired before the lis pendens was filed

Under some forfeiture statutes, third parties not charged with a crime who acquired their interests before the property was seized are exempted from forfeiture of their interests, and don't have to prove anything to protect their interests.

In forfeiture cases against real estate for human trafficking, "[t]he judgment of forfeiture shall not affect the interest in real property of a third party that was acquired prior to the recording of the lis pendens." (Pen. Code Sec. 236.8(a)). The same is true in banking offense forfeitures under Fin. Code Sec. 5320 and Sec. 5321; and criminal profiteering forfeitures. (Pen. Code Sec. 186.4(a)).

B. Statute of limitations

There are several statutes of limitation in forfeiture cases, as well as deadlines that look like – but don't necessarily act like – statutes of limitation.

1. Deadline after seizure for commencing forfeiture process

In drug cases

> [w]ithin 15 days after the seizure, if the peace officer does not hold the property seized pursuant to Section 11488 for evidence or if the law enforcement agency for which the peace officer is employed does not refer the matter in writing for the institution of forfeiture proceedings by the Attorney General or the district attorney pursuant to Section 11488.1, the officer shall comply with any notice to withhold issued with respect to the property by the Franchise Tax Board. If no notice to withhold has been issued with respect to the property by the Franchise Tax Board, the officer shall return the property to the individual designated in the receipt therefor or if the property is a vehicle, boat, or airplane, it shall be returned to the registered owner.

(Health & Saf. Code Sec. 11488.2).

The 15-day deadline of Health & Saf. Code Sec. 11488.2 is probably unenforceable under the reasoning of *People v. Property Listed in Exhibit One* (1991) 227 Cal. App. 3d 1, 7-8. There, interpreting a statute which has been repealed, the court held the 30-day limit for the filing of a petition for forfeiture under Health & Saf. Code Sec. 11488(j) was "directory" rather than "mandatory."

> A conclusion that section 11488.4, subdivision (a)'s one-year filing period provides the jurisdictional time limit does not render section 11488.4, subdivision (j)'s thirty-day period meaningless. The effect of the 30-day direction is: if 30 days pass after the filing of a claim and no petition is filed, the nonjudicial forfeiture proceeding terminates. At that time, the owner of the property is entitled to its

> return because the property is not being held pursuant to a forfeiture proceeding. Further, the time limit can be looked to as providing a starting point for a possible due process inquiry based on delay. (*People v. Echols* (1982) 138 Cal. App.3d 838, 842 [188 Cal. Rptr. 328].)

(*People v. Property Listed in Exhibit One* (1991) 227 Cal. App. 3d 1, 7-8).

The court's reasoning in *Exhibit One* would more aptly apply to the 15-day deadline of in the current statute, since instead of setting a deadline for filing the forfeiture petition – a matter like the filing of a complaint that traditionally satisfies the statute of limitations – Sec. 11488.2 merely requires the prosecutor to "refer the matter in writing for the institution of forfeiture proceedings." Referring a matter in writing for the institution of forfeiture proceedings does not traditionally satisfy the statute of limitations.

2. Forfeiture statutes of limitations

a. Government's statute of limitations running from seizure

In drug forfeiture cases there is a one-year statute of limitations.

The forfeiture petition must be filed as soon as practicable but within one year of seizure of the property or the filing of a lis pendens, whichever occurs earlier. (Health & Saf. Code Sec. 11488.4(a)(2)). This statute of limitations runs from the date of seizure. (*People v. Grant* (1942) 52 Cal.App.2d 794, 796.)

If the year passes and the government has not filed a forfeiture action, it has missed its statute of limitations. If the government files the forfeiture petition after the statute of limitations has run, the claimant may raise the statute of limitations defense in his/her answer, or file a demurrer arguing the forfeiture petition shows on its face that the statute of limitations has passed.

Claimants who don't want to wait any longer can file a motion for return of property. See Chapter 14 Section A below.

In *Ramirez v. Tulare County Dist. Atty. Office* (2017) 9 Cal.App.5th 911, the Court of Appeal held that, a year having passed since the seizure without the government filing a forfeiture petition, the claimant was entitled to the return of his property or payment of its value, because the statute of limitations had run and the government could no longer forfeit it.

b. Statute of limitations running from date of offense

The drug forfeiture statute also has a separate statute of limitations measured from the date of the offense. For all categories of property for which forfeiture is contested – other than cash and monetary instruments totaling $40,000 or more – the offense must have occurred within 5 years of the seizure of the property or 5 years of the notification of the intention to seek forfeiture (for property such as real estate, which is not seized.) (Health & Saf. Code Sec. 11488.4(i)(3)).

Where they apply, the government must comply with both statutes of limitation.

b. Claimants' statute of limitations for filing motion for return of property

A claimant's statute of limitations for filing motions for return of property is 3 years from the date of seizure of the property. Code Civ. Proc. Sec. 338(c)(1) applies since the complaint is "for the specific recovery of personal property." (*Ramirez v. Tulare County*

Dist. Atty. Office (2017) 9 Cal.App.5th 911 citing *Minsky v. City of Los Angeles* (1974) 11 Cal.3d 113, 119 fn. 6.)

3. Rules for computing statute of limitations

"When the last day to perform or complete any act provided for in [the Code of Civil Procedure] falls on a Saturday, Sunday, or holiday as specified in Section 10, the time limit is extended until the next court day." (Code Civ. Proc. Sec. 2016.060).

A document is deemed filed on the date it is received by the clerk. (Cal. Rule of Court Sec. 1.20). If it is filed on the deadline it is timely.

a. Discovery rule

In *People v. Ten $500 traveler's checks*, the government argued that the statute of limitations should be extended by the "discovery rule" – relying on federal forfeiture cases.

The court rejected that argument:

> The federal statute of limitations for forfeiture proceedings incorporates a discovery rule (*see U.S. v. James Daniel Good Property* (9th Cir. 1992) 971 F.2d 1376, 1379-1381), but no similar rule appears in this state's forfeiture scheme. The enactment of such a provision, even if advisable, is a legislative, not a judicial function. (*See Dept. of Social Welfare v. Stauffer* (1943) 56 Cal.App.2d 699, 704 [133 P.2d 692] [rejecting argument that court write a discovery rule into Code of Civil Procedure section 340].)"

(*People v. Ten $500 traveler's checks* (1993) 16 Cal.App.4th 475, 480).

b. Tolling the statute of limitations

There does not appear to be any authority allowing the government's statute of limitations to be tolled (suspended for a period of time until a disability is removed) so the 1-year statute of limitation is the definite deadline.

c. Pleading the statute of limitations defense

> In pleading the Statute of Limitations it is not necessary to state the facts showing the defense, but it may be stated generally that the cause of action is barred by the provisions of Section [citation for the applicable statute of limitations].

(Code Civ. Proc. Sec. 458).

C. Suppression of illegally seized evidence

1. Applicability of the exclusionary rule to forfeiture

The exclusionary rule, which is used in criminal cases to suppress evidence seized in violation of the Fourth Amendment, also applies to civil forfeiture cases. (*Plymouth Sedan v. Pennsylvania* (1965) 380 U.S. 693.) The *Plymouth Sedan* Court cited *Boyd v. United States* (1885) 116 U.S. 616 in stating that

> a forfeiture proceeding is quasi-criminal in character. Its object, like a criminal proceeding, is to penalize for the commission of an offense against the law.

(*Plymouth Sedan v. Pennsylvania* (1965) 380 U.S. 693, 700). Noting that forfeiting the property at issue would constitute a stiffer penalty than the maximum fine for the crime, the Court held:

> It would be anomalous indeed, under these circumstances, to hold that in the criminal proceeding the

> illegally seized evidence is excludable, while in the forfeiture proceeding, requiring the determination that the criminal law has been violated, the same evidence would be admissible. That the forfeiture is clearly a penalty for the criminal offense and can result in even greater punishment than the criminal prosecution has in fact been recognized by the Pennsylvania courts.

(*Plymouth Sedan v. Pennsylvania* (1965) 380 U.S. 693, 701).

In *People v. $241,600* (1998) 67 Cal.App.4th 1100, 79 Cal.Rptr.2d 588, 594-95, the Court of Appeal for the Fourth District questioned the continued validity of the *Plymouth Sedan* decision. It noted that the U.S. Supreme Court had based part of its logic on the statement in *Boyd v. United States* (1885) 116 U.S. 616, that, despite being a civil action, in substance and effect the forfeiture was a criminal proceeding. In distinguishing *Plymouth Sedan*, the Fourth Appellate District noted that the California forfeiture statute in effect then did not require a conviction of the underlying criminal offense. That is no longer the case. As was pointed out above, Health & Saf. Code Sec. 11488.4(i)(3) now requires a criminal conviction before property can be forfeited, with a few narrow exceptions.

However, the ruling in *Plymouth Sedan* was broader than that, and did not tie the applicability of the exclusionary rule to a conviction requirement.

The decision in *People v. $241,600* is also questionable because it relies on *United States v. Janis* (1976) 428 U.S. 433, which refused to apply the exclusionary rule to a civil suit to collect a tax refund from the IRS, when the allegedly illegal search was conducted by Los Angeles police officers. The Supreme Court held that

> the additional marginal deterrence provided by forbidding a different sovereign from using the evidence in a civil proceeding surely does not outweigh the cost to society of extending the rule to that situation.

(*United States v. Janis*, supra, 428 U.S. at 453-54).

The dual sovereign problem does not exist in most forfeiture cases.

Furthermore, forfeiture cases are not analogous to civil suits to collect tax refunds. For one thing, IRS refusal to issue tax refunds is not predicated on a crime. Secondly, unlike IRS agents, police officers who participate in arrests leading to forfeiture cases stand to reap a portion of the proceeds for their departments.

Finally, has there is no hint of any attempt by the Supreme Court to retreat from the *Plymouth Sedan* decision, and that case is still accepted precedent in federal courts. (See e.g. *United States v. $ 186,416* (2010) 590 F.3d 942, 949).

2. Procedure for suppressing evidence

The procedures for moving to suppress illegally seized evidence are codified in Pen. Code Sec. 1538.5 – the same provision that governs motions for the return of property. The motion must be in writing, supported by a memorandum of points and authorities and proof of service. (Pen. Code Sec. 1538.5(a)(2)).

If the search was warrantless, the motion should show the search and seizure was unreasonable under the Fourth Amendment to the U.S. Constitution. If the search and seizure was conducted pursuant to a warrant, grounds for suppression are: that the warrant was insufficient on its face, there was no probable cause for the issuance of the warrant, the property was not described in the warrant, the method of execution of the warrant violated federal or state constitutional standards, or any other violation of the federal or state constitution. (Pen. Code Sec. 1538.5(a)(1)).

The motion should be heard by the magistrate who issued the warrant, subject to the provisions of Code Civ. Proc. Sec. 170 through 170.6. The court must conduct an evidentiary hearing and receive evidence of any facts necessary to decide the motion. (Pen. Code Sec. 1538.5(c)(1)).

If the court grants the suppression motion, the property that was suppressed must be returned to the owner unless it is otherwise subject to lawful detention. (Pen. Code Sec. 1538.5(e)). If the property was seized for forfeiture, however, it is "otherwise subject to lawful detention."

The illegal seizure of the property targeted for forfeiture does not automatically immunize the property from forfeiture. The government may still be able to prove its forfeiture case with other evidence – as long as that evidence is not tainted by the illegal search and seizure.

The fruit of the poisonous tree doctrine may prevent the government from proving its case with a claimant's answers in civil discovery in the forfeiture case.

In *People v. Superior Court of Kern County* (*Brent)* (1992) 2 Cal.App.4th 675, after the claimant won the suppression motion in his criminal case, the government served requests for admission attempting to elicit an admission that the money was furnished or intended to be furnished in a drug transaction. When he failed to answer the requests for admission the court deemed them admitted and sanctioned the claimant for failing to answer discovery. The claimant hired a lawyer to file a motion for return of property, arguing the admissions were "the fruit of the poisonous tree" (i.e., evidence flowing from the illegal search and seizure). The trial court judge agreed with the claimant that "the request for admissions [was] derived directly from an illegal search and seizure." Finding "no way to break the continuum between the tainted evidence and the request for admissions themselves" the court dismissed the forfeiture action. The government filed a writ of mandate, but the Court of Appeal never reached this issue because it found the government's petition for a writ of mandate was filed late.

The standards and constitutional concepts applicable to suppression motions in forfeiture cases are the same as those in criminal cases. Search and seizure law is too extensive and complex to be covered in this book. Consult a treatise on search and seizure law.

D. Undue delay and the right to speedy trial

The statute of limitations and the government's statutory deadlines for commencing a forfeiture action both serve to move the forfeiture case forward in a timely fashion, but the Due Process clause of the U.S. Constitution also limits the amount of time the government may delay the forfeiture process.

In *United States v. $8,850* (1983) 461 U.S. 555, the Supreme Court held that the Due Process clause prohibits unreasonable delays in commencing a forfeiture action after detention of the property.

Finding an "apt analogy" to "to a defendant's right to a speedy trial once an indictment or other formal process has issued" the Court applied the balancing test for speedy trial articulated in *Barker v. Wingo*: "length of delay, the reason for the delay, the defendant's assertion of his right, and prejudice to the defendant." (*United States v. $8,850*, supra, 461 U.S. at 564, quoting *Barker v. Wingo* (1972) 407 U.S. 514, 530.)

1. Length of the delay

There is no specific time limit when a delay becomes constitutionally unreasonable.

> Little can be said on when a delay becomes presumptively improper, for the determination necessarily depends on the facts of the particular case. Our inquiry is the constitutional one of due process; we are not establishing a statute of limitations. Obviously, short delays — of perhaps a month or so — need less

> justification than longer delays. We regard the delay here – some 18 months – as quite significant.

(*United States v. 1985 Cadillac Seville* (9th Cir. 1989) 866 F.2d 1142, 1147).

"The overarching factor is the length of the delay." (*United States v. $8,850,* 461 U.S. 555, 564.)

In *$8,850,* the Supreme Court upheld an 18 month delay in commencing a forfeiture action, saying it was justified by the Government's diligent efforts to process the administrative petition for remission (an administrative process that does not exist under California law) and to prosecute the related criminal case. The Court also took into account the claimant's failure to assert the right to the prompt institution of court proceedings, and inability to show prejudice from the delay. (*United States v. $8,850,* 461 U.S. 555, 569-70.)

Most of the federal forfeiture cases that have been dismissed under *$8,850* had a delay of over a year. (*See United States v. $7,990* (8th Cir. 1999) 170 F.3d 843, *cert. denied sub nom. Fiorentino v. United States* (1999) 528 U.S. 1041.)

In Health & Safety Code forfeiture cases, there is a statutory deadline of one year after seizure to commence the proceedings. (Health & Saf. Code Sec. 11488.4(a)(2)). That deadline is a statute of limitations, so all forfeiture petitions must be filed within a year of the property's seizure or the forfeiture is forever be time barred.

State forfeiture case can still be dismissed for delays shorter than one year but under *$8,850* shorter delays require a substantial showing of prejudice, assertion of the right, and a lack of justification for the delay.

Undue delay analysis doesn't end when the forfeiture petition is filed. If prosecutors continue to delay the process up to and through trial, claimants should continue asserting the right — which may mean filing successive motions to dismiss as circumstances change. At some point the combination of *Barker v. Wingo* factors may tip the scale, and require dismissal.

2. Justification for the delay

> Closely related to the length of the delay is the reason the Government assigns to justify the delay. The Government must be allowed some time to decide whether to institute forfeiture proceedings. The customs official's decision to seize property is of necessity a hasty one. Both the Government and the claimant have an interest in a rule that allows the Government some time to investigate the situation in order to determine whether the facts entitle the Government to forfeiture so that, if not, the Government may return the money without formal proceedings. Normally, investigating officials can make such a determination fairly quickly, so that this reason alone could only rarely justify a lengthy delay.

(*United States v. $8,850,* supra, 461 U.S. at 565-66).

When relying on *$8,850* analysis from federal cases, keep in mind that the systems vary greatly, and those differences may skew the balancing test.

On motion of either party, the forfeiture trial may be postponed until after the conviction in the related criminal case. (Health & Saf. Code Sec. 11488.5(e)). If the defendant asks for the postponement, that delay will count against the defendant in the balancing of factors. If the parties both agree to the delay, that delay would not count against either party in the undue delay analysis.

Sometimes prosecutors use the excuse that the property is being held as evidence to justify holding property without filing forfeiture proceedings. If the evidence is not of the type that is typically physically brought into court and introduced at trial, or if the property could be returned after photographing and forensic testing, challenge that excuse by offering to stipulate to the substitution of photographs instead of the actual seized item as an exhibit.

Another complicating factor occurs when the property owner is someone other than the criminal defendant and the forfeiture case is postponed until after the criminal trial. The prejudice is to the third party, who did not cause the delay in the criminal trial. But the delay probably would not be counted against the prosecution unless they asked for the delay. All of these factors are relevant in balancing the interests.

3. Assertion of the right

Delays are waived if you don't complain about them. Make a record of asserting the right to filing of a speedy trial beginning immediately after property is detained. Send letters (or emails) instead of calling the prosecutor, so you have written documentation.

Another way to assert the right to a prompt institution of forfeiture proceedings is to file a motion for return of property, as the Supreme Court recommended in *United States v. $8,850,* supra, 461 U.S. at 569. The California procedure for motions for return of property are discussed in Chapter 14 Section A.

4. Prejudice to the property owner

> The final element is whether the claimant has been prejudiced by the delay. The primary inquiry here is whether the delay has hampered the claimant in presenting a defense on the merits, through, for example, the loss of witnesses or other important evidence. Such prejudice could be a weighty factor indicating that the delay was unreasonable.

(*United States v. $8,850,* 461 U.S. at 569).

The Supreme Court also considered the prejudice to the owner from loss of use of his/her property:

> We regard the delay here – some 18 months – as quite significant. Being deprived of this substantial sum of money for a year and a half is undoubtedly a significant burden.

(*United States v. $8,850,* 461 U.S. at 565). This "substantial sum of money" was a mere $8,850!

In one of my cases local cops seized $2 million from my client's bank accounts. He was a lawyer and had a clear paper trail showing the cases in which he earned his money. When we got to court for a hearing in the state forfeiture case, the county DA told the judge they had handed off the case to the federal government under the federal adoption program, and the state judge said there was nothing he could do. I began submitting documentation to the Assistant U.S. Attorney showing the money was all legitimate proceeds of my client's law practice. The AUSA declined to file a forfeiture complaint on the first $500,000 seized from one account and then resigned from the U.S. Attorney's Office. Her supervisor took over the case and refused to give the rest back, but continued stalling on filing a forfeiture complaint, then, when a year had passed since the seizure, he stated he intended to turn the money over to the local cops that had originally seized it, so they could forfeit it under state law.

I moved for a temporary restraining order to stop them from returning my client's money to the state cops, along with a motion for the return of property under Federal Rule of Criminal Procedure Rule 41(g). The federal judge granted the TRO, stating:

> The $1.5 million dollars has been seized and detained for one entire year, without any hearing on the merits under

> either state or federal forfeiture law. With so large a sum detained for so long without any showing of probable cause for the detention, Claimants have shown irreparable harm.

(*United States v. Approximately $20,725 in U.S. Currency*, etc., E.D. Cal. # 11-mc-00003-JAM-EFB (filed 6/27/2011) (unpublished). The judge issued a temporary restraining order and set a hearing on my Federal Rule 41(g) motion for return of property. The prosecutor immediately agreed to give the rest of the money back with interest.

When the detained property is a vehicle needed for the family to get to work, school, and doctor's appointments, the claimants' hardship presents good arguments for prejudice. However, the Supreme Court said

> [t]he primary inquiry here is whether the delay has hampered the claimant in presenting a defense on the merits, through, for example, the loss of witnesses or other important evidence.

(*United States v. $8,850,* supra, 461 U.S. at 569). If the government raises that argument, remind them that the Supreme Court did not say that deprivation of the use of one's property for that length of time, and hardships flowing from the detention, could not count toward prejudice.

Few cases are won on litigated motions to dismiss for undue delay, but many cases are settled by presenting undue delay arguments along with arguments that the government doesn't really have a case. If you file a motion for return of property, be sure to include all of your undue delay arguments.

Now that most California forfeiture provisions require a criminal conviction, if property is detained a long time with no forfeiture proceedings and no criminal case either, that would be a prime target for an *$8,850* motion.

E. Eighth Amendment Excessive Fines clause

The defense of "gross disproportionality" or "excessive punishment" has only been around since 1993.

Before that, courts said there was nothing they could do when forfeiture of a very valuable asset was triggered by a minor offense. Disproportionality was an intentional feature of the War on Drug's "zero tolerance" program.

In 1974, the Supreme Court upheld the forfeiture of a leased pleasure yacht when the lessee was found to be in possession of marijuana. (*Calero-Toledo v. Pearson Yacht Leasing Co.* (1974) 416 U.S. 663). The yacht's owner raised other arguments and did not question the constitutionality of such a disproportionate forfeiture. They lost, ushering in two decades of "zero tolerance" to drug offenses, citing *Calero-Toledo* as justification.

Times changed over the following 20 years and, thanks to the widespread publicity and public criticism over seizures under the "zero tolerance" program, the mood of the U.S. Supreme Court changed.

In the 1993 case *Austin v. United States* (1993) 509 U.S. 602, the U.S. Supreme Court held that modern civil forfeiture under federal drug law is "punitive" and therefore the Eighth Amendment's Excessive Fines clause prohibits excessive forfeitures. A companion case, *Alexander v. United States* (1993) 509 U.S. 544, held that excessive forfeitures are unconstitutional in criminal forfeiture cases.

The California Constitution, Article I, Section 17, also prohibits "excessive fines."

1. When forfeitures are "punishment" for Eighth Amendment purposes

The question of whether the Eighth Amendment applies to a forfeiture turns on whether is it "punishment" or "remedial" – but those labels are not easy to define.

> [T]he forfeiture of contraband itself may be characterized as remedial because it removes dangerous or illegal items from society. *See United States v. One Assortment of 89 Firearms*, 465 U. S. 354, 364 (1984). The Court, however, previously has rejected government's attempt to extend that reasoning to conveyances used to transport illegal liquor. *See One 1958 Plymouth Sedan v. Pennsylvania*, 380 U. S. 693, 699 (1965). In that case it noted: "There is nothing even remotely criminal in possessing an automobile." *Ibid*. The same, without question, is true of the properties involved here, and the Government's attempt to characterize these properties as "instruments" of the drug trade must meet the same fate as Pennsylvania's effort to characterize the 1958 Plymouth Sedan as "contraband."

(*Austin v. United States* (1993) 509 U.S. 602, 618).

In *Austin* the Court rejected the government's argument that the federal drug forfeiture statute was remedial because it removed the instruments of the drug trade, thereby protecting the community from the threat of continued drug dealing. It also rejected the argument that it was remedial because forfeiture revenue compensates the government for the expense of drug law enforcement.

Even if it has some remedial features, a forfeiture statute is punitive if it is not solely remedial, the Supreme Court held.

> [A] civil sanction that cannot fairly be said solely to serve a remedial purpose, but rather can only be explained as also serving either retributive or deterrent purposes, is punishment, as we have come to understand the term.

(*Austin v. United States* (1993) 509 U.S. 602, 618, quoting *United States v. Halper* (1989) 490 U.S. 435, 448).

In concluding that the federal drug forfeiture statute was punishment for Eighth Amendment purposes, the Supreme Court relied on these factors:

(1) the statute contained an innocent owner defense,

(2) it "ties forfeiture directly to the commission of drug offenses," and

(3) the legislative history showed the purpose of the statute was to deter crime.

Applying the analysis of *Austin*, it appears that most California forfeiture statutes exact "punishment," and the proportionality defense would apply.

a. Most California forfeiture statutes are primarily punitive

(i). Innocence is a defense

Unlike the federal innocent owner defense – which requires owners to prove their innocence and lack of negligence in entrusting their property – California forfeiture law does not require claimants to prove their innocence. The government has to prove the owner knew of and/or consented to the illegal use – generally, by proof beyond a reasonable doubt. These features make California forfeiture laws more punitive.

(ii). Forfeiture is tied directly to a criminal offense

Generally California forfeiture statutes require a separate criminal prosecution before or soon after a forfeiture petition is filed. The two cases are generally filed in the same court and track each other. Guilt is proven in the criminal case. In the forfeiture cases where a criminal conviction is required, if the defendant isn't convicted the forfeiture case is dismissed. If the defendant is convicted the forfeiture trial begins, preferably before the same jury that heard the criminal trial.

Under California law, forfeiture is more tied to the commission of an offense than under the federal statutes.

(iii). The stated rationale is deterrence

All of the California forfeiture statutes have a stated legislative intent of deterring crime. Furthermore, the same statute includes criminal penalties as well as forfeiture provisions.

Except for the provisions regarding contraband (which may be strictly remedial) and the unlicensed driver forfeiture statute (which may be primarily remedial), California forfeiture statutes are primarily punitive.

The California Control of Profits of Organized Crime Act makes it clear the legislature intended the forfeiture to be punitive:

> The Legislature hereby finds and declares that an effective means of punishing and deterring criminal activities of organized crime is through the forfeiture of profits acquired and accumulated as a result of such criminal activities. It is the intent of the Legislature that the "California Control of Profits of Organized Crime Act"

> be used by prosecutors to punish and deter only such activities.

(Pen. Code Sec. 186.1).

Deterrence is one of the traditional goals of punishment, and it is a factor that weighs toward finding a forfeiture statute punitive instead of remedial.

The drug forfeiture statutes have language suggesting remedial intent, but features showing the intent to deter crime.

> Although civil forfeiture is intended to be remedial by removing the tools and profits from those engaged in the illicit drug trade, it can have harsh effects on property owners in some circumstances. Therefore, law enforcement shall seek to protect the interests of innocent property owners, guarantee adequate notice and due process to property owners, and ensure that forfeiture serves the remedial purpose of the law.

(Health & Saf. Code Sec. 11468(j)). However, the statute also says "[l]aw enforcement is the principal objective of forfeiture." (Health & Saf. Code Sec. 11468(a)). There, "law enforcement" is used in the sense of enforcement of the laws — in other words, deterrence.

To further illustrate the punitive intent of the drug law forfeiture provisions, the statute advises police to seek criminal prosecutions in tandem with any forfeitures. "Whenever appropriate, prosecutors should seek criminal sanctions as to the underlying criminal acts which give rise to the forfeiture action." (Health & Saf. Code Sec. 11468(c)). In all drug cases except forfeitures of over $40,000 in cash or monetary instruments, the forfeiture statute requires a criminal conviction of someone for the triggering offense.

b. A semi-remedial California forfeiture statute

The one exception where proportionality may not apply is the statute authorizing forfeiture of vehicles for second offense driving without a license. That statute is far more remedial. The statute specifically states that the forfeiture's purpose is to address a "nuisance" – a necessary measure to get the vehicle's driver off the roads. That factor makes it more "remedial" than the other forfeiture provisions.

But that alone does not mean it is not punishment for Eighth Amendment purposes. Remember *Halper* said "a civil sanction that cannot fairly be said *solely to serve a remedial purpose*, but rather can only be explained as also serving either retributive or deterrent purposes, is punishment" for proportionality defense purposes. Under that standard, even the vehicle code forfeiture provision for driving without a license may be sufficiently punitive to trigger excessiveness analysis.

In a prosecution under Fish and Game Code Sec. 8278, prohibiting crab fishermen from possessing a load containing more than 1% undersized Dungeness crab, the court found the forfeiture of the entire catch (worth $47,000) to be an excessive fine when only 2.2% of the crabs were under size. Despite finding Section 8278 to be a regulatory crime intended to protect the fishery and provide economic benefits to the state rather than punish violators, and despite the finding that strict liability applied, the court applied the standards of *Bajakajian* and found the statute to be punishment for excessive fines purposes. (*People v. Estes* (Cal. Super. Ct., 2013) 218 Cal.App.4th Supp. 14.)

There were no other published California cases citing *Bajakajian* that involved forfeiture.

2. Standards for proportionality

Forfeiture is unconstitutional if the forfeiture of the entire property would be "grossly disproportional to the gravity of the defendant's offense." (*United States v. Bajakajian* (1998) 524 U.S. 321, 336-37.)

The proportionality inquiry involves a balancing of factors:

> the nature and extent of the criminal activity, other related illegal activities (such as drug dealing, money laundering, or tax evasion), the extent of the harm caused by the offense, and the maximum penalties a court could have imposed for the offense.

(*United States v. Ahmad* (2000) 213 F.3d 805).

a. Nature and extent of criminal activity

In *United States v. Bajakajian,* the Supreme Court looked at the offense the defendant committed and the particular harms the statute was intended to address.

> Respondent's crime was solely a reporting offense. It was permissible to transport the currency out of the country so long as he reported it. Section 982(a)(1) orders currency to be forfeited for a "willful" violation of the reporting requirement. Thus, the essence of respondent's crime is a willful failure to report the removal of currency from the United States.

(*United States v. Bajakajian,* supra, 524 U.S. at 337).

b. Other related illegal activities

The *Bajakajian* decision noted that

> respondent's violation was unrelated to any other illegal activities. The money was the proceeds of legal activity, and was to be used to repay a lawful debt. Whatever his other vices, respondent does not fit into the class of persons for whom the statute was principally designed: he is not a money launderer, a drug trafficker, or a tax evader.

(*United States v. Bajakajian,* supra, 524 U.S. at 337-338).

Thus the court should take into consideration whether the offense that triggered forfeiture is part of a pattern or cluster of related criminal conduct. The fact that it was clean money that Bajakajian failed to report was significant in reducing the forfeiture in that case on proportionality grounds.

c. Extent of the harm caused by the offense

The *Bajakajian* court considered the dollar value of the harm caused by his crime.

> The harm that respondent caused was also minimal. Failure to report his currency affected only one party, the Government, and in a relatively minor way. There was no fraud on the United States, and respondent caused no loss to the public fisc. Had his crime gone undetected, the Government would have been deprived only of the information that $357,144 had left the country. The Government and the dissent contend that there is a correlation between the amount forfeited and the harm that the Government would have suffered had the crime gone undetected. We disagree. There is no inherent proportionality in such a forfeiture. It is impossible to

> conclude, for example, that the harm respondent caused is anywhere near 30 times greater than that caused by a hypothetical drug dealer who willfully fails to report taking $12,000 out of the country in order to purchase drugs.

(*United States v. Bajakajian,* supra, 524 U.S. at 338).

In a Ninth Circuit case the court noted that the offense – making a false statement on a loan application – did not cause any actual harm to creditors or the government, because the loan was repaid. (*United States v. 3814 N.W. Thurman St.* (1999) 164 F.3d 1191, amended on denial of rehearing (1999) 172 F.3d 689.)

d. Statutory penalties for the offense

Some courts have held that any forfeiture within the maximum statutory range of fines for the criminal statute violated would automatically be proportionate. The majority of the Court in *Bajakajian* rejected that analysis:

> Here, as the Government and the dissent stress, Congress authorized a maximum fine of $250,000 plus five years' imprisonment for willfully violating the statutory reporting requirement, and this suggests that it did not view the reporting offense as a trivial one. That the maximum fine and Guideline sentence to which respondent was subject were but a fraction of the penalties authorized, however, undercuts any argument based solely on the statute, because they show that respondent's culpability relative to other potential violators of the reporting provision – tax evaders, drug kingpins, or money launderers, for example – is small indeed.

(*United States v. Bajakajian,* supra, 524 U.S. at 339 n. 14).

The proportionality analysis should be personalized to *the claimant's* offense – not the statutory offense in general. The majority of the Court said in *Bajakajian:*

> [w]e now hold that a punitive forfeiture violates the Excessive Fines Clause if it is grossly disproportional to the gravity of *a defendant's* offense.

(*United States v. Bajakajian,* supra, 524 U.S. at 334 (emphasis added)).

In a very important opinion for proportionality analysis, the Ninth Circuit held:

> excessiveness review must consider the individualized culpability of the property's owner and, when analyzing the offending conduct, it must focus only on the conduct that actually gave rise to the forfeiture of the property at issue, not other criminal conduct by the same person.

(*United States v. Ferro* (2012) 681 F.3d 1105, 1107).

Ferro involved a wife's claim to the seizure of a huge and very valuable collection of antique guns purchased by her husband, a previously convicted felon. It was a felony for him to even possess guns, but it was not illegal for her to own guns, and he purchased them with marital property.

The Ninth Circuit reversed the district court's forfeiture, holding the district court erred by considering only the husband's culpability. The proper standard in the Ninth Circuit is the culpability of the property's owner. (The husband had relinquished his claims to the guns; only the wife's claim was being tried.)

The Court in *Bajakajian* looked first at the maximum sentence for the crime, then looked at what the maximum sentence and fine would be under the Federal Sentencing Guidelines and how that fit within the maximum punishment for the crime authorized by statute.

> [U]nder the Sentencing Guidelines, the maximum sentence that could have been imposed on respondent was six months, while the maximum fine was $5,000. Such penalties confirm a minimal level of culpability.

(*United States v. Bajakajian,* supra, 524 U.S. at 338-339).

California does not have sentencing guidelines, but it does have something similar. The legislature has set up three possible terms of sentence for each offense – the low-, mid-and high-term sentence, with judges choosing which one to impose based on the egregiousness of the crime and the defendant's prior record. Additionally some crimes are wobblers, and can be either misdemeanors or felonies depending on how they are charged and how the judge treats them. And of course there is the three strikes law which greatly enhances the length of the sentence for defendants with prior felony convictions. All of these factors can be relied on as guidance for determining whether a forfeiture would be grossly disproportionate punishment for the offense.

Proportionality is determined after trial. See Chapter 13 Sec. A.

5. Seizure & detention of property

A. Real estate can't be seized before trial

Forfeiture cases against personal property such as money and cars begins with the government seizing the property, and the property is generally detained until judgment in the forfeiture case. That is not true of real estate.

The Supreme Court held in *United States v. James Daniel Good Real Property* (1993) 510 U.S. 43, that, real estate cannot be seized prior to trial. Before that case was decided, property owners were usually ousted from possession of their homes as soon as the forfeiture case was filed. Homes and businesses were boarded up pending trial, falling victim to vandalism – unless the property owner negotiated an occupancy agreement with the government.

Now the government files a lis pendens on the title to the property to prevent real estate from being sold or mortgaged while the case is pending. Judges may also enter restraining orders prohibiting encumbering or transferring the property while the case is pending.

> If there is evidence, in a particular case, that an owner is likely to destroy his property when advised of the pending action, the Government may obtain an ex parte restraining order, or other appropriate relief, upon a proper showing in district court.

(*United States v. James Daniel Good Real Property*, supra, 510 U.S. at 58-59). See Chapter 5 Section C, below.

If the property has a mortgage and the owner/claimant ceases making payments, the government and/or lienholder can move for an interlocutory sale of the property. See Chapter 5 Section A-2 below.

1. Lis pendens

A "lis pendens" is a written notice filed in the chain of title to real estate at the recorder of deeds, informing anyone who conducts a title search that a lawsuit has been filed which could affect title to the property. Once that is filed, the world is on constructive notice that if they purchase the property before the lis pendens is removed their purchased interest is subject to the outcome of the lawsuit. If the seller of the property loses the forfeiture case, the buyer who purchased the property loses his/her interest.

The California statute now calls the lis pendens a "notice of pendency of action," (Code Civ. Proc. Sec. 405.2), but the document is still commonly referred to as a lis pendens in other statutes and in case law.

In drug case forfeitures, the government must file a lis pendens when trying to forfeit real estate in drug cases, (Health & Saf. Code Sec. 11488.4(a)(1)); banking offense forfeitures, (Fin. Code Sec. 5321(b)); and criminal profiteering forfeiture cases, (Pen. Code Sec. 186.4(a)).

California's lis pendens law applies to federal litigation too. (Code Civ. Proc. Sec. 405.5).

Third parties who acquire interests in real estate before the lis pendens is filed have the best protection. In banking forfeitures the statute says "[t]he judgment of forfeiture shall not affect the interest in real property of any third party which was acquired prior to the recording of the lis pendens." (Fin. Code Sec. 5321(b)). The same language appears in the criminal profiteering forfeiture statute (Pen. Code Sec. 186.4(a)); the human trafficking forfeiture statute (Pen.

Code Sec. 236.8(a)); and animal fighting forfeiture statute (Pen. Code Sec. 598.1(c)(5)).

Before recording the lis pendens at the Recorder of Deeds, the government must send a copy of the notice by registered or certified mail, return receipt requested, to all known addresses of the people who own interests in the property. (Code Civ. Proc. Sec. 405.22). A copy of the lis pendens must also be filed in the pending case. (*Id*).

> From the time of recording the notice of pendency of action, a purchaser, encumbrancer, or other transferee of the real property described in the notice shall be deemed to have constructive notice of the pendency of the noticed action as it relates to the real property and only of its pendency against parties not fictitiously named. The rights and interest of the claimant in the property, as ultimately determined in the pending noticed action, shall relate back to the date of the recording of the notice.

(Code Civ. Proc. Sec. 405.24).

> Any notice of pendency of action shall be void and invalid as to any adverse party or owner of record unless the requirements of Section 405.22 are met for that party or owner and a proof of service in the form and content specified in Section 1013a has been recorded with the notice of pendency of action.

(Code Civ. Proc. Sec. 405.23).

2. Interlocutory sale and lienholders' rights

If the claimant/property owner ceases making payments on the property while the case is pending, the mortgage holder can't just foreclose as they normally do. As long as the forfeiture case is pending, the lis pendens prohibits lienholders from enjoying their full foreclosure rights. With a lis pendens on the property, it would sell for a distressed price – if at all.

If the lienholder forecloses and sells the property at a non-judicial foreclosure sale, as they have the right to do under state law, the lis pendens on the title means the buyer buys the property subject to the outcome of the case. If the government wins the forfeiture case, the buyer loses the property.

In federal cases, in such circumstances the parties enter into a stipulation of interlocutory sale, meaning a sale while the case is pending. The stipulation of interlocutory sale includes a provision that the lis pendens will be removed when title transfers to the buyer. The property is sold through a real estate agent and agent commissions, fees, liens, and costs are paid off. The remainder of the proceeds of sale are paid into the seized assets fund, and the amount of money is substituted as the "res" (the property being forfeited). The case name is usually changed to reflect the new res.

Lienholders are paid off when title transfers unless the government challenges their claims. If the government disputes the claim, the lienholder remains a party and its claim is determined at trial.

There do not appear to be any state forfeiture cases involving the interlocutory sale of real estate, although there are plenty of cases of interlocutory sale of real estate in other civil litigation.

The lack of any state cases on this issue is probably the result of the small number of state forfeiture cases against real estate. Until recently, most real estate cases were handed over to the federal government for forfeiture under the federal adoption program, allowing the seizing agency to reap a larger share of the proceeds and making it easier to win a forfeiture judgment. Now that federal adoption has been curtailed, we will likely see more real estate forfeitures under state law.

When confronted with this issue, state courts will likely follow federal authorities and grant interlocutory sale to protect lienholders while preserving assets for forfeiture. State case law involving interlocutory sales of real estate in other civil litigation would also be instructive precedent.

B. Seizure of other types of property

1. Where warrants are required

Property subject to forfeiture may be seized on process issued by any court having jurisdiction over the property. (Health & Saf. Code Sec. 11471(drug cases)).

Seizure without a court order or warrant may be made under the circumstances listed in the next section.

When an officer seizes property with a warrant, he/she must give a receipt for it. (Pen. Code Sec. 1535). See Chapter 5 Section B-3 below.

2. Seizure without a warrant or seizure order

Under Health & Saf. Code Sec. 11471, property subject to forfeiture may be seized without judicial process under the following circumstances:

(a) seizure incident to arrest or search under a search warrant;

(b) property was subject of a prior judgment for the government in a criminal injunction or forfeiture proceeding;

(c) there is probable cause to believe the property is "directly or indirectly dangerous to health or safety;"

(d) there is probable cause to believe the property was used or intended to be used in violation of the drug laws. (Health & Saf. Code Sec. 11471(a) – (d)).

Absent exigent circumstances, real property may not be seized without prior notice and a hearing. The court must determine that seizure is necessary to preserve the property. The court may issue seizure orders or pendente lite orders to preserve the status quo or value of the property pending trial. (Health & Saf. Code Sec. 11471(e)).

3. Notice to Franchise Tax Board

When officers seize property they must notify the Franchise Tax Board if the value of the property exceeds $5,000. (Health & Saf. Code Sec. 11471.5 & 11488(a)). The purpose is to allow the tax board to check whether the owner owes the state money. If so the government can put a lien on the seized property. An owner who wins the forfeiture case will have the amount of their tax liens deducted from the proceeds before getting back the remainder.

4. Receipt for seized property

Any officer making a seizure under Health & Saf. Code Sec. 11488(a) is required to give a receipt to any person from whose possession the property was seized. If it was not seized from any person's possession the receipt is supposed to be delivered to the person in possession of the premises where it was seized. (Health & Saf. Code Sec. 11488(b)).

Giving a receipt creates a presumption that the person to whom a receipt was issued is the owner of the property. (Health & Saf. Code Sec. 11488(c)). In cases of warrantless seizures of property, the holder of the receipt is entitled to return of the property if the government does not refer the matter in writing to for the institution of a forfeiture proceeding within 15 days. (Health & Saf. Code Sec. 11488.2).

5. Seizure of business records

Where business records are seized in a drug case, the seizing agency must give the claimant copies of them upon request. (Health & Saf. Code Sec. 11470.4(f)).

Pen. Code Sec. 1536.5 contains detailed procedures for obtaining copies of one's own business records that were seized pursuant to a search warrant. See Chapter 14 Section B below.

C. Injunctions restraining property & receiverships

1. Drug offense forfeiture cases

In drug offense forfeiture cases, after filing of a petition for forfeiture the prosecutor may move for orders to preserve the value of the property, including: an injunction preventing transfer or encumbrance of property, the appointment of a receiver to manage the assets, or an order of interlocutory sale. (Health & Saf. Code Sec. 11492(a)). The court may require a surety bond. (Health & Saf. Code Sec. 11492(c)).

Before any preliminary injunction may be issued, interested parties must be given notice and a hearing and the government must show probable cause for forfeiture. (Health & Saf. Code Sec. 11492(b)).

2. Banking offenses

In forfeitures based on banking offenses, the Financial Code allows the court to enter orders to preserve property pending litigation, including injunctions prohibiting disposal of the property, and appointment of receivers. (Fin. Code Sec. 5323(a)). All interested parties including the defendant must be given notice of the request for an injunction or receivership, "including actual notice to targets of the anticipated criminal action."

A temporary restraining order may be issued without prior notice under the procedures set out in Code Civ. Proc. Sec. 527. (Fin. Code Sec. 5323(b)). At the hearing on the motion the court must determine that "an order is necessary to preserve the property" and that there is probable cause to believe that the property is forfeitable under Sec. 5320. (Fin. Code Sec. 5323(b)).

> [T]he court shall weigh the relative degree of certainty of the outcome on the merits and the consequences to each of the parties of granting the interim relief. If the prosecution is likely to prevail on the merits and the potential harm to the public outweighs the potential harm to the defendants and the interested parties, the court should grant injunctive relief.

(Fin. Code Sec. 5323(b)(1)).

These factors must be given "significant weight:" (A) the "public interest in preserving equity capital and other financial assets," (B) the difficulty of preserving assets where the alleged crimes involve fraud or moral turpitude; (C) the fact that the prosecution is brought on behalf of alleged victims of financial crimes; and (D) "the likelihood that substantial public harm has occurred." (Fin. Code Sec. 5323(b)(1)(A)-(D)).

If no criminal case is pending, court must weigh the relative degree of certainty of the outcome and the consequences to the parties of granting the relief. (Fin. Code Sec. 5323(b)(2)).

No injunction shall impair the defendant's ability to hire counsel for the criminal and forfeiture cases. (Fin. Code Sec. 5323(b)(3)).

The court may require a surety bond to preserve the property, "but the court shall give significant weight to the unique circumstances of public agencies, as opposed to private litigants, in determining whether to order a surety bond or undertaking." (Fin. Code Sec. 5323(c)).

The court must seek to protect interests of co-owners not involved in the crime. (Fin. Code Sec. 5323(d)).

3. Criminal profiteering cases

In criminal profiteering forfeiture cases, when a forfeiture petition is filed the prosecutor may request pendente lite orders to preserve the status quo, including an injunction restraining the transfer or encumbrance of the property or appointment of a receiver. (Pen. Code Sec. 186.6(a)). Before any injunction or receivership is granted the court must give interested parties notice and a hearing and must determine that restraint or receivership is "necessary to preserve the property, pending the outcome of the criminal proceedings, and that there is probable cause to believe that the property" is forfeitable under Pen. Code Sec. 186.3. (Pen. Code Sec. 186.6(b)). The court must "seek to protect the interests of those who may be involved in the same enterprise as the defendant, but who were not involved in" the profiteering activity. (Pen. Code Sec. 186.6(d)). The court may require a surety bond to assure preservation of the property. (Pen. Code Sec. 186.6(c)).

6. Commencement of the forfeiture process

Health & Saf. Code Sec. 11488.5(c)(3) makes the procedures in the Code of Civil Procedure applicable to forfeiture proceedings unless they are inconsistent with the forfeiture statute. The Code of Civil Procedure applies in all forfeiture cases, except that, when the Code of Civil Procedure provision conflicts with a provision in the forfeiture statute, the forfeiture statute overrides the Code of Civil Procedure provision.

Cross-complaints are not allowed in forfeiture cases, and related actions may not be joined with the forfeiture case (except other forfeiture cases). (Health & Saf. Code Sec. 11488.5(c)(3); *Jauregi v. Superior Court* (1999) 72 Cal.App.4th 931, 938).

In most forfeiture cases, the litigation is commenced with the prosecutor filing a civil forfeiture complaint in superior court of the county where the property was seized. However, in drug forfeiture cases involving property worth $25,000 or less, the case begins with an administrative forfeiture process. The administrative process precedes the judicial forfeiture process. If the claimant defaults by failing to file a timely claim in the administrative proceeding there will be no judicial proceedings.

The administrative forfeiture process is covered separately in Chapter 7. If your case was commenced with an administrative forfeiture notice instead of a judicial civil complaint filed in court, skip to chapter 7 for the administrative forfeiture procedures.

Most California forfeiture statutes follow the same judicial procedures set out in this chapter. These judicial procedures apply to all forfeiture statutes except Vehicle Code forfeiture cases and forfeiture of computer equipment used in computer crimes. See

Chapter 3 Section D-3 for computer crimes forfeiture procedures and Chapter 3 Section F-3 for Vehicle Code forfeiture procedures.

A. Government's petition for forfeiture

The government's first filing in court is called a "petition for forfeiture," rather than a "complaint." The general civil statute, Code Civ. Proc. 422.10, does not list "petition for forfeiture" among the pleadings allowed in civil actions, but petitions are treated like complaints when they are the first filings in a case.

Note that when administrative forfeiture procedures apply, the petition for forfeiture is not the first filing in the case — the claim is. In those cases the petition for forfeiture is filed after the claim. Maybe that is why the government's first filing is not called a complaint.

For forfeiture cases brought under the drug statutes, Health & Saf. Code Sec. 11470, *et seq.*, the prosecutor must file a petition for forfeiture in superior court in the county in which the defendant is charged, or where the property was seized or located. The petition must be filed within one year of seizure of the property, or in the case of real property, within one year of the filing of the lis pendens, whichever is earlier. (Health & Saf. Code Sec. 11488.4(a)(2)).

1. Contents of petition

In Vehicle Code forfeitures — which are limited civil cases — prosecutors have a Judicial Council form they use for the Petition for Forfeiture (Form MC-202).

Under all other forfeiture statutes, prosecutors draft the petition for forfeiture on a word processor in the same format as a standard civil complaint.

A complaint shall contain both of the following:

(1) A statement of the facts constituting the cause of action, in ordinary and concise language.

(2) A demand for judgment for the relief to which the pleader claims to be entitled.

(Code Civ. Proc. Sec. 425.10(a)).

In separate, numbered paragraphs the petition cites the forfeiture statute the case is brought under, describes the property, where and when it was seized, the current location of the property, the forfeiture theory the prosecutor alleges (e.g. traceable proceeds, or used or intended for use to facilitate the offense), and the facts allegedly justifying forfeiture.

In drug forfeiture cases brought under Health & Saf. Code Sec. 11488.4(a)(1), the petition for forfeiture must allege grounds for forfeiture meeting the elements of one or more of the provisions of Sec. 11470(a)-(g).

In banking offense forfeitures brought under Fin. Code Sec. 5320, the petition must allege offenses set out in Fin. Code Sec. 5303-5306, Corp. Code Sec. 25540 or 25541 relating to a lending institution, or felony violations of Pen. Code Sec. 487 or 504.

In criminal profiteering forfeitures, the petition must allege an offense from the list of offenses incorporated by reference in Pen. Code Sec. 186.2(a), as well as a pattern of criminal profiteering activity as defined in Pen. Code Sec. 186.2(b)(1). See Chapter 3 Section C above.

In computer hacking and computer related crimes forfeitures, the petition will allege a violation of Pen. Code Sec. 502 or 502.01(a)(1). Note that Sec. 502.01(a)(1) incorporates by reference a long list of statutes, including child pornography, unauthorized use of credit cards, counterfeiting, and identity theft. See Chapter 3 Section D above.

Forfeiture cases brought for dogfighting, cockfighting and animal fighting must allege violations of Pen. Code Sec. 597.5, 597b, or 598.1. See Chapter 3 Section E above.

2. Verification

The forfeiture statutes do not require the petition for forfeiture to be verified. However, forfeiture answers must be verified. Whenever the state or a county in its official capacity is the plaintiff, the answer must be verified even though complaint is not verified. (Code Civ. Proc. Sec. 446).

3. Documents required to be served

The petition for forfeiture must be served along with a claim form and directions for filing a claim. (Health & Saf. Code Sec. 11488.4(c)). It also must state the deadline for filing a claim. (Health & Saf. Code Sec. 11488.4(f)).

Under the California Rules of Court, service on a party represented by counsel must be on the party's attorney. (Cal. Rule of Court Sec. 1.21(a)).

4. Service of process requirements

a. Statutory requirements

In drug cases the forfeiture petition must be served on every individual designated in a receipt issued for the property seized. (Health & Saf. Code Sec. 11488.4(c)). If the agency determines the legal owner is someone different from the registered owner and that the ownership interest predated the seizure, it must send the notice to the legal owner. (Health & Saf. Code Sec. 11488.4(d)). In addition to personal service, notice must be published once a week for three weeks in a newspaper in the county. (Health & Saf. Code Sec. 11488.4(e)).

Known owners of interests in seized property are entitled to personal notice by registered mail or personal service, unless notice cannot be given that way, in which case published notice will suffice. (Fin. Code Sec. 5321).

b. Due process requirements for service

Due Process clause requires notice and an opportunity to be heard before anyone may be permanently deprived of their property. A forfeiture judgment obtained in violation of the statutory and constitutional notice requirements is void. (*United States v. Giraldo* (1st Cir. 1995) 45 F.3d 509, 512).

Due Process requires notice "reasonably calculated, under all the circumstances" to apprise interested parties of the pendency of a forfeiture action. (*Mullane v. Central Hanover Bank & Trust Co.* (1950) 339 U.S. 306, 313-14). "The means employed must be such as one desirous of actually informing the absentee might reasonably adopt to accomplish it." (*Id*).

In addition to the statutory requirements for giving notice, even if "statutory scheme is reasonably calculated to provide notice in the ordinary case" the government is "required to consider unique information about an intended recipient" in a good faith attempt to find the person and give them notice. (*Jones v. Flowers* (2006) 547 U.S. 220, 230).

"[A]ssessing the adequacy of a particular form of notice requires balancing the 'interest of the State' against "the individual interest sought to be protected by the [Due Process clause]." (*Jones v. Flowers* (2006) 547 U.S. 220, 229-30). When the stakes are high for the property owner, the government has a duty to take more extensive efforts to locate him and give notice. (See *Jones v. Flowers,* supra, 547 U.S. at 230 ("when, as here, the subject matter of the letter concerns such an important and irreversible prospect as the loss of a house" further efforts at giving notice are required when the government learns its initial attempt at giving notice was unsuccessful.))

> In *Mullane,* [the U.S. Supreme Court] stated that "when notice is a person's due... [t]he means employed must be such as one desirous of actually informing the absentee might reasonably adopt to accomplish it," 339 U.S., at 315, 70 S. Ct. 652, 94 L. Ed. 865, and that assessing the adequacy of a particular form of notice requires balancing the "interest of the State" against "the individual interest sought to be protected by the Fourteenth Amendment," *id.,* at 314, 70 S. Ct. 652, 94 L. Ed. 865. Our leading cases on notice have evaluated the adequacy of notice given to beneficiaries of a common trust fund, *Mullane, supra;* a mortgagee, *Mennonite [Bd. of Missions v. Adams,* 462 U.S. 791, 103 S. Ct. 2706, 77 L. Ed. 2d 180; owners of seized cash and automobiles, *Dusenbery [v. United States],* 534 U.S. 161, 122 S. Ct. 694, 151 L. Ed. 2d 597; *Robinson* v. *Hanrahan,* 409 U.S. 38, 93 S. Ct. 30, 34 L. Ed. 2d 47 (1972) (*per curiam);* creditors of an estate, *Tulsa Professional [Collection Svcs. V. Pope],* 485 U.S. 478, 108 S. Ct. 1340, 99 L. Ed. 2d 565; and tenants living in public housing, *Greene* v. *Lindsey,* 456 U.S. 444, 102 S. Ct. 1874, 72 L. Ed. 2d 249 (1982). In this case, we evaluate the adequacy of notice prior to the State extinguishing a property owner's interest in a home.
>
> We do not think that a person who actually desired to inform a real property owner of an impending tax sale of a house he owns would do nothing when a certified letter sent to the owner is returned unclaimed. If the Commissioner prepared a stack of letters to mail to delinquent taxpayers, handed them to the postman, and then watched as the departing postman accidentally dropped the letters down a storm drain, one would certainly expect the Commissioner's office to prepare a

new stack of letters and send them again. No one "desirous of actually informing" the owners would simply shrug his shoulders as the letters disappeared and say "I tried." Failure to follow up would be unreasonable, despite the fact that the letters were reasonably calculated to reach their intended recipients when delivered to the postman.

By the same token, when a letter is returned by the post office, the sender will ordinarily attempt to resend it, if it is practicable to do so. See *Small* v. *United States*, 329 U.S. App. D.C. 98, 136 F.3d 1334, 1337 (CADC 1998). This is especially true when, as here, the subject matter of the letter concerns such an important and irreversible prospect as the loss of a house. Although the State may have made a reasonable calculation of how to reach Jones, it had good reason to suspect when the notice was returned that Jones was "no better off than if the notice had never been sent." *Malone [v. Robinson]*, 614 A.2d [33,] 37. Deciding to take no further action is not what someone "desirous of actually informing" Jones would do; such a person would take further reasonable steps if any were available.

In prior cases, we have required the government to consider unique information about an intended recipient regardless of whether a statutory scheme is reasonably calculated to provide notice in the ordinary case. In *Robinson* v. *Hanrahan,* we held that notice of forfeiture proceedings sent to a vehicle owner's home address was inadequate when the State knew that the property owner was in prison. 409 U.S., at 40, 93 S. Ct. 30, 344 L. Ed. 2d 47. In *Covey* v. *Town of Somers*, 351 U.S. 141, 76 S. Ct. 724, 100 L. Ed. 1021 (1956), we held that notice of foreclosure by mailing, posting, and publication was inadequate when

> town officials knew that the property owner was incompetent and without a guardian's protection. *Id.*, at 146-147, 76 S. Ct. 724, 100 L. Ed. 1021.

(*Jones v. Flowers* (2006) 547 U.S. 220, 229-230).

B. Claimant's response to petition – verified claim and answer

Within 30 days of service, Claimants must respond to the petition for forfeiture by filing both a verified claim, and an answer or demurrer. At the time the claim and/or answer is filed (whichever is filed first), the claimant must pay the first paper filing fee. See Chapter 6 Section B-1-c below.

1. Verified claim

The claim process does not exist in ordinary civil cases. It is a requirement of the various forfeiture statutes, including federal statutes.

Persons who want to defend their property interests must file verified claims within 30 days of service of the notice or petition commencing the forfeiture process.

Use the Judicial Council claim form for the forfeiture statute the case was brought under. The clerk's office has copies of the claim form and they also may be downloaded from http://www.courts.ca.gov/forms. The claim must be verified – that is, declared under penalty of perjury.

> In all cases of a verification of a pleading, the affidavit of the party shall state that the same is true of his own knowledge, except as to the matters which are therein stated on his or her information or belief, and as to those matters that he or she believes it to be true; and where a pleading is verified, it shall be by the affidavit of a party,

> unless the parties are absent from the county where the attorney has his or her office, or from some cause unable to verify it, or the facts are within the knowledge of his or her attorney or other person verifying the same....
>
> ...A person verifying a pleading need not swear to the truth or his or her belief in the truth of the matters stated therein but may, instead, assert the truth or his or her belief in the truth of those matters "under penalty of perjury."

(Code Civ. Proc. Sec. 446).

A claim is not admissible in the criminal case. (Health & Saf. Code Sec. 11488.5(c)(1)). This is important for those with parallel criminal cases who fear admitting the seized property is theirs could be incriminating.

a. Deadline for filing a claim

Any person claiming an interest in the property has 30 days after being served with the petition for forfeiture to file a claim. (In those cases where administrative forfeiture applies and the claimant filed a claim in court to end the administrative process, they don't have to file a second claim in response to the forfeiture petition, but they do have to file an answer. See Chapter 8 Section A, below.

If service was by registered mail or personal service, the 30 days runs from the date of receipt of notice. (Health & Saf. Code Sec. 11488.5(a)(1); Fin. Code Sec. 5322(a)).

If the person was not personally served, the 30 day period runs from the date of last publication. (Health & Saf. Code Sec. 11488.5(a)(1)).

If no claims are timely filed the DA can prepare a written declaration of forfeiture. The declaration of forfeiture must be served on all persons listed in the receipt and any person served notice of the proceedings. (Health & Saf. Code Sec. 11488.4(j)(5)(B)).

A claim is deemed filed on the date it is received by the clerk. (Cal. Rule of Court Sec. 1.20).

b. How to file a claim

Claims must be filed by all persons claiming interests in the property, including persons who were assigned their interests prior to the property's seizure. (Health & Saf. Code Sec. 11488.5(a)(1)-(2)).

The claim must be filed in "the superior court of the county in which the defendant has been charged with the underlying or related criminal offense or in which the property was seized or, if there was no seizure, in which the property is located." (Health & Saf. Code Sec. 11488.5(a)(1)).

The Judicial Council has created claim forms which can be downloaded from its website at http://www.courts.ca.gov/forms. In drug cases use Form MC-200. Find the form online at http://www.courts.ca.gov/documents/mc200.pdf.

In Vehicle Code cases for driving without a license, use form MC-201. See http://www.courts.ca.gov/documents/mc201.pdf.

Save the downloaded form to your computer, then open it with Adobe Acrobat (or Acrobat Reader) and fill it out on your computer, save it, and then print it out.

In the "claimed property" field, use the description the prosecutor used in the notice of administrative forfeiture or describe it well enough that they can identify it.

In the value of claim boxes, don't overstate the value. If the property is worth less than $5,000 you don't have to pay a filing fee.

State your interest in the property by checking the appropriate boxes.

Make at least two copies before you sign it, because you'll need original signatures on two copies. Sign in the "signature of claimant" blank and also in the claimant signature blank beneath the verification.

Submit the signed claim form plus an additional copy to the clerk, along with a check or money order for the filing fee.

The clerk will give you back the extra copy as an "endorsed copy." You have to serve the endorsed copy on the District Attorney or Attorney General within 30 days after filing the claim. (Health & Saf. Code Sec. 11488.5(a)(1). Fin. Code Sec. 5322.)

The claim must be verified, and it must state the amount of their claimed interest and affirm or deny the allegations in the petition of forfeiture. (Health & Saf. Code Sec. 11488.5(1)(1); Fin. Code Sec. 5321(a)). The requirements of verification are set out in Code Civ. Proc. Sec. 446 and Chapter 8 Section A-4, below.

When a rule requires that a document be served and filed, it must be served on each party or their attorney. A proof of service must be filed with it. (Cal. Rule of Court Sec. 1.21(b)).

A proof of service is a declaration stating that service has been provided upon the each of the parties, naming them and stating which party each of the attorneys represents. (Cal. Rule of Court Sec. 1.21(c)).

c. Filing fees for claimant's first paper filed in the case

Filing fees for the first paper filed by a claimant in a forfeiture case are determined on a sliding scale, depending on the value of the property.

The fee structure for the first paper has three components – a uniform fee for the first paper fee, plus a supplemental fee, but the supplemental fee statute sunsets on July 1, 2018, unless the legislature extends it.

(i). Property worth less than $5,000

In drug forfeiture cases, if the property is worth less than $5,000 the claimant does not have to pay any filing fees to file a claim. (Health & Saf. Code Sec. 11488.5(a)(3)).

(ii). Property worth $5,000 to $10,000

For property worth more between $5,000 and less than or equal to $10,000, the filing fee is $225, computed as follows:

Uniform fee for filing first paper – $205 (Gov. Code 70614(b)).

Supplemental fee – $20 (Gov. Code Sec. 70602.5(c)).

(iii). Property worth $10,000 to $25,000

Forfeiture cases involving property worth more than $10,000 and less than or equal to $25,000, are limited civil cases. The filing fee to file a claim is currently $370, computed as follows:

Uniform fee for filing first paper – $330 (Gov. Code Sec. 70614(a)).

Supplemental fee – $40 (Gov. Code Sec. 70602.5(b)).

(iv). Property worth over $25,000

For property worth more than $25,000, the forfeiture case is an unlimited civil case. The filing fee for the first paper filed by claimants is currently $435, computed as follows:

Uniform fee – $355 (Health & Saf. Code Sec. 11488.5, incorporating the fee set in Gov. Code Sec. 70612).

First paper filing fee – $40 (Gov. Code Sec. 70602.5(a)).

Supplemental fee – $40 (Gov. Code Sec. 70602.6(a), effective until 7/1/2018).

(v). Vehicle Code forfeiture cases

In vehicle forfeiture cases for driving without a license, a claimant must pay a $100 filing fee to file a claim. (Veh. Code Sec. 14607.6(e)(4)).

d. Indigent claimants may qualify for a waiver of filing fees

Costs can very quickly add up to thousands of dollars. Indigent claimants should consider applying for fee waivers if they qualify. The court may grant a waiver of filing fees if the claimant meets the eligibility standards of Gov. Code Sec. 68632 and 68633, or it may order the applicant to make partial payments under Gov. Code Sec. 68632(d) or 68637(e).

See Chapter 9 Section B-2, below, for details on fee waivers.

2. Answer

The forfeiture statutes do not mention that a claimant has to file an answer in response to the government's petition for forfeiture, but the Code of Civil Procedure requires it. In judicial forfeiture cases the claim and answer are due at the same time (30 days after service of the petition for forfeiture). The filing fee for the first paper filed by a claimant covers the filing fees for both the claim and answer. See Chapter 7 Section B-3.

The requirements for filing an answer, demurrer, or other pleading in response to the forfeiture petition are the same in all forfeiture cases, including drug cases that begin with the administrative forfeiture process – but not Vehicle Code cases for driving without a license. See Chapter 3 Section F-3-f.

C. What if the D.A. doesn't file forfeiture petition?

In many cases property is seized and held a long time without the government filing anything to commence the forfeiture process.

If the prosecutor does not file a forfeiture petition within one year after seizure he/she has missed the statute of limitations. If the prosecutor does not voluntarily give the property back after the statute of limitations has run, the claimant can file a motion for return of property under Pen. Code Sec. 1538.5. See Chapter 14 Section A below.

The claimant does not have to wait until a year has passed to file a motion for return of property. It may be filed at any time. But if filed before the government's statute of limitations has run, the claimant will have to meet a burden of proof to win the motion. See Chapter 14 Section A below.

7. Administrative forfeiture

Administrative forfeiture (also known as "non-judicial forfeiture") is a process peculiar to drug cases under California state law. It was designed for create a quick way for the government to dispose of smaller cases that claimant don't find cost-effective to defend, by making the claimant file a claim and pay a filing fee – or lose their property by default.

> Under [Health & Saf. Code] section 11488.4, subdivision (j), if the property is within the jurisdictional amount, the district attorney may declare the property forfeit without a judicial proceeding. This procedure is known as nonjudicial or administrative forfeiture and was enacted to provide forfeiture without court involvement.

(*People v. Property Listed in Exhibit A* (1991) 227 Cal.App.3d 1).

> With nonjudicial forfeiture, if the district attorney provides the requisite notice and no claim is filed, the district attorney prepares a written declaration of forfeiture of the subject property to the state and disposes of the property in accordance with section 11489. (§ 11488.4, subd. (j).) The purpose of nonjudicial forfeiture is to save the government the time and expense of a judicial proceeding in cases where the value of the property seized is small.

(*Id*). The claimant can immediately take the case to court by filing a claim and paying the required filing fee (unless it is waived or doesn't apply).

> Once the claim is filed, nonjudicial forfeiture terminates and forfeiture can only be achieved through the judicial forfeiture procedure.

(*People v. $400* (1993) 17 Cal.App.4th 1615, 1619).

Under state law, administrative forfeiture only applies in drug cases involving property worth $25,000 or less, and vehicle forfeiture cases for driving without a license/DUI offenses. No other California forfeiture statute includes an administrative forfeiture process.

Federal law also has administrative forfeiture procedures applicable to seizures of property worth $500,000 or less.

The administrative process under California law is much more abbreviated than the federal administrative forfeiture process. State law does not have separate administrative remedies like the petition for remission and mitigation used in federal administrative forfeiture cases.

A. Administrative forfeiture procedure

The administrative procedure is confusing because it occurs in a different order from the procedures used in judicial forfeitures.

Administrative or "non-judicial" forfeiture does not involve any proceedings in court. The government simply sends notice of the intent to forfeit and the claimant either responds within 30 days by filing a claim in Superior Court, or defaults.

If the claimant defaults, the prosecutor prepares a written declaration of forfeiture, which is sufficient to transfer title, without having to go to court. The declaration of forfeiture must be served on all persons listed in the receipt and any person served notice of the proceedings. (Health & Saf. Code Sec. 11488.4(j)(5)(B)). The defaulting claimant may be able to vacate the default judgment under the procedures set out in Chapter 14 Section C.

If the claimant files a claim in Superior Court, the statute says the District Attorney shall file a petition for forfeiture within 30 days of the receipt of the claim. (Health & Saf. Code Sec. 11488.4(j)(5)(C)). There are two cases saying that statutory deadline is "directory" and not mandatory, but those decisions seem to violate the rules of statutory interpretation. See Chapter 7 Sec. D.

Once the petition for forfeiture is served on the claimant, the claimant has 30 days to file an answer, demurrer, or other responsive pleading. See Chapter 8 Sec. A for the procedures that follow.

1. Maximum dollar amounts

In drug forfeiture cases administrative forfeiture process applies only to personal property valued at $25,000 or less. (Health & Saf. Code Sec. 11488.4(j)).

All forfeitures under the Vehicle Code – regardless of value – are administrative forfeiture cases, with the judicial case commenced by the claimant's filing of a claim in Superior Court. (Veh. Code Sec. 14607.6(e)(4)).

2. Approval of district attorney

The drug law forfeiture statute says "the Attorney General or the district attorney of the county in which property is subject to forfeiture... may... order forfeiture..." (Health & Saf. Code Sec. 11488.4(j)). *Only* the Attorney General or the county District Attorney can make a decision to pursue administrative forfeiture.

In *Ramirez v. Tulare County District Attorney's Office*, the Fifth Appellate District invalidated three cases where the administrative process was initiated by police officers instead of prosecutors as required by the statute.

> [A] nonjudicial forfeiture proceeding initiated by police officers was "invalid in the first instance" and, consequently, "there was no proper or valid forfeiture proceeding to which [the plaintiff] could make a claim." (*Cuevas [v. Superior Court* (2013)] 221 Cal.App.4th [1312,] 1327.) Thus, the trial court concluded plaintiffs were not barred on the ground that they failed to file timely claims under sections 11488.4 and 11488.5.

(*Ramirez v. Tulare County Dist. Attorney's Office* (2017) 9 Cal.App. 5th 911, 922).

3. Statutory notice requirements

In drug cases, the notice must include a description of the property, its value, date and place of seizure, and the violation of law alleged. It must also include instructions for filing a claim, the time limits and a claim form. (Health & Saf. Code Sec. 11488.4(j)).

In Vehicle Code cases, the impounding agency must send notice, within 2 days of impoundment, to all legal and registered owners of the vehicle at the addresses on file with the DMV, informing them the vehicle is subject to forfeiture, with instructions for filing a claim, and of the DMV's right to sell the vehicle under Veh. Code Sec. 14607.6(g) if they do not comply. (Veh. Code Sec. 14607.6(e)(2)). If a registered owner was served at the time of impoundment, no further notice is required to a registered owner, but notice must be sent to all the legal owners. (Veh. Code Sec. 14607.6(e)(2)).

B. Claim commences judicial process if administrative forfeiture applies

In those categories of cases for which non-judicial (administrative) forfeiture applies -drug forfeiture cases involving personal property worth $25,000 or less, and all Vehicle Code cases for driving without a license, etc. – the government commences the administrative process by simply serving a notice of forfeiture in compliance with the above requirements. The prosecutor does not have to file anything in court at that point. Then the onus shifts to claimants to file claims in court, or else lose their property by default.

When the claimant files a claim, that commences the judicial process, and the prosecutor must respond by filing a petition for forfeiture.

1. Property owner's deadline for filing a claim

Any person claiming an interest in the property has 30 days after being served the notice of administrative forfeiture to file a claim in Superior Court. If the person was served by registered mail or personal service, the 30-day period runs from the date of actual notice (the date the claimant received the notice). (Health & Saf. Code Sec. 11488.5(a)(1). Fin. Code Sec. 5322(a)).

If the person was not personally served, the 30 day period runs from the date of last publication. Notice by publication is not sufficient unless it was not possible to serve interested parties notice any other way. See Chapter 6 Section A-4-b above.

A claim is deemed filed on the date it is received by the clerk. (Cal. Rule of Court Sec. 1.20).

2. How to file a claim

All persons claiming interests in the property, including persons who were assigned their interests prior to the property's seizure, may file claims. (Health & Saf. Code Sec. 11488.5(a)(1)-(2)).

The claim must be filed in "the superior court of the county in which the defendant has been charged with the underlying or related criminal offense or in which the property was seized or, if there was no seizure, in which the property is located." (Health & Saf. Code Sec. 11488.5(a)(1)).

The Judicial Council has created claim forms which all claimants should use. They can be downloaded from http://www.courts.ca.gov/forms. In drug cases use Form MC-200. Find the form here: www.courts.ca.gov/documents/mc200.pdf. In Vehicle Code cases for driving without a license, use form MC-201: http://www.courts.ca.gov/documents/mc201.pdf.

Download the form and save it to your computer, then open it with Adobe Acrobat (or Acrobat Reader) fill it out on your computer, save it to your hard drive, and print it out.

In the "claimed property" field, use the description the prosecutor used in the notice of administrative forfeiture and any other identifying information the notice gives.

In the value of claim boxes, don't overstate the value. If the property is worth less than $5,000 you don't have to pay a filing fee.

State your interest in the property by checking the appropriate boxes.

Make at least two copies before you sign it, because you'll need original signatures on two copies. Sign in the "signature of claimant" blank and also in the claimant signature blank beneath the verification.

Submit the signed claim form plus an additional copy to the clerk, along with the filing fee. In administrative forfeiture cases, the claim is the initiating document in the case. There won't already be a case file — the clerk will open one when the claim is filed.

The clerk will give you back the extra copy as an "endorsed copy." You have to serve the endorsed copy on the District Attorney or Attorney General within 30 days after filing the claim. (Health & Saf. Code Sec. 11488.5(a)(1)).

The claim must be verified, and it must state the amount of their claimed interest and affirm or deny the allegations in the petition of forfeiture. (Health & Saf. Code Sec. 11488.5(1)(1); Fin. Code Sec. 5321(a)). A verified copy of the claim must be served on the prosecutor. (Fin. Code Sec. 5322).

See Code Civ. Proc. Sec. 446 and Chapter 8 Section A-4 for the requirements of verification.

When a rule requires that a document be served and filed, that means it must be served on each party or their attorney and that it be filed with a proof of service attached. (Cal. Rule of Court Sec. 1.21(b)).

A proof of service is a declaration stating that "service has been provided upon the following persons" (naming the parties or attorneys), and must state which party each of the attorneys is representing. (Cal. Rule of Court Sec. 1.21(c)).

3. Filing fees for filing the claim which commences a judicial proceeding

Filing fees are complicated. Besides being on a sliding scale based on the value of the property, there are also three basic fees — a uniform fee, plus a first paper fee, plus a supplemental fee. To add further confusion, the supplemental fee statute sunsets on July 1, 2018 unless it is extended by later legislation.

a. For property worth less than $5,000

In drug forfeiture cases, if the property is worth less than $5,000 the claimant does not have to pay a filing fee to file a claim commencing the action. (Health & Saf. Code Sec. 11488.5(a)(3)).

b. For property worth over $5,000 and up to $10,000

In drug forfeiture cases, for property worth more between $5,000 and less than or equal to $10,000, the filing fee is $225, computed as follows:

Uniform fee for filing first paper – $205 (Gov. Code 70614(b)).

Supplemental fee – $20 (Gov. Code Sec. 70602.5(c)).

c. For property worth over $10,000 and up to $25,000

Drug forfeiture cases involving property worth more than $10,000 and less than or equal to $25,000, are limited civil cases. The filing fee to file a claim is currently $370, computed as follows:

Uniform fee for filing first paper – $330 (Gov. Code Sec. 70614(a)).

Supplemental fee – $40 (Gov. Code Sec. 70602.5(b)).

d. For property worth over $25,000

For property worth more than $25,000, the case is an unlimited civil case. The filing fee for the first paper filed by claimants is currently $435, computed as follows:

Uniform fee – $355 (Health & Saf. Code Sec. 11488.5, incorporating the fee set in Gov. Code Sec. 70612).

First paper filing fee – $40 (Gov. Code Sec. 70602.5(a)).

Supplemental fee – $40 (Gov. Code Sec. 70602.6(a), effective until 7/1/2018).

e. Vehicle Code forfeiture cases

In vehicle forfeiture cases for driving without a license, a claimant must pay a $100 filing fee to file a claim – regardless of the vehicle's value. (Veh. Code Sec. 14607.6(e)(4)).

4. Indigent claimants may qualify for a waiver of filing fees

Costs can very quickly add up to thousands of dollars. Indigent claimants should consider applying for fee waivers if they qualify. Upon application, the court may grant a waiver of filing fees if the claimant meets the eligibility standards of Gov. Code Sec. 68632 and 68633. Alternatively, the court may order the applicant to make partial payments under Gov. Code Sec. 68632(d) or 68637(e).

See Chapter 9 Section B-2 for details on fee waivers.

C. Consequences of failing to file a claim in an administrative forfeiture case

In drug cases, seizures of personal property valued at $25,000 or less have special procedures, set out in Health & Saf. Code Sec. 11488.4(j). If the claimant defaults, the Attorney General or DA can declare forfeiture of such property without having to apply to a court for an order, provided they gave valid notice of the forfeiture proceeding with the description of the property, the date and place of seizure, the legal violation alleged, and instructions for filing a claim, including the deadline. They must also provide a claim form. (Health & Saf. Code Sec. 11488.4(j)).

If no claim is filed within 30 days of the date of last publication or within 30 days of actual service, the court, on motion by the prosecutor, shall declare the property forfeited, provided the government first establishes a prima facie case for forfeiture. There is no criminal conviction requirement in the event of default, but the government must show a prima facie case for forfeiture. (Health & Saf. Code Sec. 11488.5(b)(1)). Forfeiture proceeds are distributed according to Health & Saf. Code Sec. 11489. (Health & Saf. Code Sec. 11488.5(b)(1)).

Claimants who missed the deadline because they didn't received notice on time or because of excusable neglect can move to set aside a default under the procedures explained in Chapter 14 Section C below.

D. Consequences of filing a claim in an administrative forfeiture case

If a verified claim is filed in response to an administrative notice of forfeiture, the forfeiture proceeding is set for a hearing at least 30 days later. (Health & Saf. Code Sec. 11488.5(c)(1)).

Filing a forfeiture claim in response to an administrative forfeiture notice triggers the government's duty to file a petition for forfeiture, but it may not happen immediately.

Health & Saf. Code Sec. 11488.4(j)(5)(C) says "[i]f a claim is timely filed, the Attorney General or district attorney shall file a petition of forfeiture within 30 days of receipt of the claim." That seems pretty plain and straightforward, but some courts have held that the 30-day deadline for filing a petition of forfeiture was directory rather than mandatory, and that the government's only deadline for filing a petition for forfeiture is the one-year statute of limitations. (*People v. Property Listed in Exhibit One* (1991) 227 Cal.App.3d 1. *See also People v. Superior Court* (*Plasencia*) (2002) 103 Cal.App.4th 409). Someone should challenge these two precedents – they seem to violate the "plain meaning" rule for interpreting statutes, which requires courts to "presume that the Legislature intended 'every word, phrase and provision... in a statute ... to have meaning and to perform a useful function.'" (*Garcia v. McCutchen* (1997) 16 Cal.4th 469, 476, 66 Cal.Rptr.2d 319, 940 P.2d 906.) See Chapter 2 Section D-8.

When a petition for forfeiture is filed in response to a claim, the forfeiture case

> shall then proceed pursuant to other provisions of this chapter [Health & Saf. Code Sec. 11469 – 11495], except that no additional notice need be given and no additional claim need be filed.

(Health & Saf. Code Sec. 11488.4(j)(5)(C)).

A claim is not admissible in the criminal case. (Health & Saf. Code Sec. 11488.5(c)(1)).

8. Claimant's answer or other initial pleading

Whether a forfeiture case begins with an administrative notice or with the prosecutor filing a petition for forfeiture, the rule is the same. Once the government files a petition for forfeiture, a claimant has 30 days after "service" of the petition to file a "responsive pleading" responding to the allegations in the petition for forfeiture and asserting his/her defenses. This is in addition to the verified claim required by the forfeiture statute.

"Service" means the date of actual receipt of the petition if it is served by personal service or registered mail. In those narrow circumstances where notice by publication is authorized, the deadline is "30 days from the date of the last publication of the notice of seizure, if that person was not personally served or served by mail, or within 30 days after receipt of actual notice." (Health & Saf. Code Sec. 11488.5(a)(1)). See Chapter

Responsive pleadings authorized by the Code of Civil Procedure are answers, and demurrers. (Code Civ. Proc. Sec. 422.10).

In forfeiture cases that begin as judicial forfeitures (as opposed to administrative forfeiture), the claimant must file both a verified claim and an answer (or other responsive pleading) within 30 days after service of the forfeiture petition.

In cases that began as an administrative forfeiture (drug law forfeiture cases where the property is worth $25,000 or less) the claimant already filed a verified claim to commence the judicial proceedings, and they only have to file an answer by the 30 day deadline.

A. Answer

> The purpose of the statutorily mandated claim is different from that of the answer. The claim is intended to assert an interest in the property, confer standing to the claimant, and to terminate the administrative forfeiture procedure, thereby forcing judicial proceedings. The answer is filed in a judicial action and raises issues of fact for trial, places the allegations of the complaint at issue and raises any affirmative defenses. (Code Civ. Proc., Sec. 590; 5 Witkin, Cal. Procedure (3d ed. 1985) Pleading, Sec. 967, p. 400.) The purpose of verification is to assure good faith averments by the party. (*Frio v. Superior Court* (1988) 203 Cal. App.3d 1480, 1498 [250 Cal. Rptr. 819].) The purpose of either pleading, claim or answer, is well served by assuring the averments made in the context of a forfeiture proceeding are truthful. Requiring that the answer be verified is not inconsistent with the language of the statute or at cross-purposes with the statute's intent, which is to deprive drug dealers of the tools and profits of their illicit trade. (*People v. Superior Court* (*Clements*) (1988) 200 Cal. App.3d 491, 499 [246 Cal. Rptr. 122].)

(*People v. $400* (1993) 17 Cal.App.4th 1615, 1620).

Claimants have 30 days after service of the petition for forfeiture to file a verified answer. (Code Civ. Proc. Sec. 412.20(a)(3)).

If the petition for forfeiture is amended, answers to the amended petition must be filed within 30 days of service of the amended petition. (Code Civ. Proc. Sec. 471.5(a)).

1. Requirements for contents of the answer

Answers must contain a general or specific denial of each material allegation in the forfeiture petition that the claimant disputes, and a statement of any new matters that constitute a defense. (Code Civ. Proc. Sec. 431.30(b)).

The additional requirements for the contents of an answer vary depending on the value of the property.

Forfeiture cases where the property is valued at less than $25,000 are limited civil cases. (Code Civ. Proc. Sec. 85(a)). Vehicle code forfeitures are all limited cases regardless of the value of the property. (Veh. Code Sec. 14607.6(e)(4)).

Cases involving property worth more than $25,000 are unlimited civil cases. The civil case cover sheet filed with the government's petition for forfeiture will state whether the case is a limited or unlimited case.

There is no Judicial Council form for answers in forfeiture cases, except Vehicle Code cases and cases involving property worth $1,000 or less. For Vehicle Code cases use Judicial Council form MC-202. See http://www.courts.ca.gov/documents/mc202.pdf. In cases where the value of the property is $1,000 or less, use form PLD-050. See http://www.courts.ca.gov/documents/pld050.pdf.

For all other types of cases the answer must be drafted following the same basic format as answers in a general civil cases.

a. Where the property is worth $1,000 or less

In cases where the value of the property is $1,000 or less, instead of filing a formal answer the claimant "may file a general written denial and a brief statement of any new matter constituting a defense." (Code Civ. Proc. Sec. 431.40(a)). The general written denial should be on Judicial Counsel form PLD-050. It need not be verified. (Code Civ. Proc. Sec. 431.40(c)). Download form PLD-050 from http://www.courts.ca.gov/documents/pld050.pdf.

These forms are also available in print form from the clerk's office. There is no charge for the forms.

b. Limited civil cases (property worth less than $25,000)

Limited civil cases (involving property worth less than $25,000) are governed by abbreviated procedures set out in Code Civ. Proc. Sec. 91 through 100.

All Vehicle Code forfeiture cases (for driving without a license offenses) are limited civil cases, regardless of the value of the vehicle. (VEH Sec. 14607.6(e)(4)).

Generally, in limited civil cases the answer need not be verified. (Code Civ. Proc. Sec. 92(b)). However, this conflicts with the provision requiring verification of answers when the complaint is brought by a government agency. (Code Civ. Proc. Sec. 446). Case law establishes that Section 446 governs in forfeiture cases, and the answer must be verified. (*People v. $400* (1993) 17 Cal.App.4th 1615, 1619-1620).

General denials are permitted in limited civil cases. (Code Civ. Proc. Sec. 431.30(d)).

Special demurrers are not allowed in limited civil cases, and "[m]otions to strike are allowed only on the ground that the relief sought is not supported by the allegations in the complaint." (Code Civ. Proc. Sec. 92(c)-(d)).

Every case must contain a caption showing the court and county, and the title of the action. (Code Civ. Proc. Sec. 422.30(a)). In a limited civil case the caption must state that it is a limited civil case. (Code Civ. Proc. Sec. 422.30(b)).

Discovery is also limited in limited civil cases. See Chapter 10 Section A.

c. Unlimited civil cases (property worth $25,000 or more)

In unlimited civil cases, the answer must contain a general or specific denial of each material allegation in the forfeiture petition that the claimant disputes, and a statement of any new matters that constitute a defense. (Code Civ. Proc. Sec. 431.30(b)).

The answer must be drafted following the same basic format as answers in a general civil cases. It must contain a caption showing the court and county, and the title of the action. (Code Civ. Proc. Sec. 422.30(a)). The body of the answer should be in numbered paragraphs corresponding to the paragraph numbers in the petition. For each paragraph, the answer must either admit or deny, or state that the claimant lacks sufficient information to admit or deny, each allegation in the corresponding paragraph of the forfeiture petition.

"Every material allegation of the complaint... not controverted by the answer, shall, for the purposes of the action, be taken as true." (Code Civ. Proc. Sec. 431.20(a)). In other words, if you don't dispute any material allegation it is deemed admitted.

If a person "has no information or belief upon the subject sufficient to enable him or her to answer an allegation of the complaint, he or she may so state in his or her answer and place his or her denial on that ground." (Code Civ. Proc. Sec. 431.30(e)).

The claimant may deny allegations by stating he/she denies everything in paragraph X (referring to the specific paragraph by number), or may admit certain allegations and deny all of the remaining allegations in that paragraph. (Code Civ. Proc. Sec. 431.30(f)).

"Affirmative relief may not be claimed in the answer." (Code Civ. Proc. Sec. 431.20(c)). In other words, you can't include a claim against the police department for false arrest.

2. Listing defenses

"The defenses shall be separately stated, and the several defenses shall refer to the causes of action which they are intended to answer, in a manner by which they may be intelligibly distinguished." (Code Civ. Proc. Sec. 431.30(g)).

See Chapter 4 for the defenses that may be raised in forfeiture cases. You should raise all of those defenses that may arguably apply, including failure to state a claim upon which relief may be granted, illegal search and seizure, statute of limitations, Eighth Amendment disproportionality, innocent owner/bona fide purchaser, and undue delay – even if you don't yet know whether you have enough evidence to prove that defense.

> In pleading the Statute of Limitations it is not necessary to state the facts showing the defense, but it may be stated generally that the cause of action is barred by the provisions of Section ____ [giving the number of the section and subdivision thereof, if it is so divided, relied upon].

(Code Civ. Proc. Sec. 458).

If you don't discover a particular defense until later, you can add it then by amending the answer.

3. Counterclaims & crossclaims

Although forfeiture generally follows ordinary civil procedures, the forfeiture statutes state that cross-complaints and joinder of other actions are not allowed. However a forfeiture case can be joined with other related forfeiture cases (such as multiple items of property seized from one or more claimants based on the same alleged offense.) (Health & Saf. Code Sec. 11488.5(c)(3)).

4. Verification

Even though there is no specific provision in the forfeiture statute requiring claimants to file verified answers, the requirement is incorporated by reference from the Code of Civil Procedure. "[F]orfeiture proceedings are governed by the provisions of the Code of Civil Procedure unless otherwise inconsistent with the forfeiture statute." (Health & Saf. Code Sec. 11488.4(i)).

> There is no express provision in the forfeiture statute requiring a verified answer. The statute expressly requires only that the claim be verified. However, Health and Safety Code section 11488.4, subdivision (i) provides that forfeiture proceedings are governed by the provisions of the Code of Civil Procedure unless otherwise inconsistent with the forfeiture statute.
>
> Section 446 of the Code of Civil Procedure provides that when a state or county, "or any officer of the state, or of any county thereof, . . . in his or her official capacity," (italics added) is the plaintiff in an action, the answer must be verified, unless the defendant is also a public official or the admission of the truth of the complaint might subject the answering defendant to a criminal prosecution.

(*People v. $400* (1993) 17 Cal.App.4th 1615, 1619 – 1620. See also Code Civ. Proc. Sec. 446).

> In all cases of a verification of a pleading, the affidavit of the party shall state that the same is true of his own knowledge, except as to the matters which are therein stated on his or her information or belief, and as to those matters that he or she believes it to be true; and where a pleading is verified, it shall be by the affidavit of a party, unless the parties are absent from the county where the

attorney has his or her office, or from some cause unable to verify it, or the facts are within the knowledge of his or her attorney or other person verifying the same. When the pleading is verified by the attorney, or any other person except one of the parties, he or she shall set forth in the affidavit the reasons why it is not made by one of the parties.

When a corporation is a party, the verification may be made by any officer thereof. When the state, any county thereof, city, school district, district, public agency, or public corporation, or an officer of the state, or of any county thereof, city, school district, district, public agency, or public corporation, in his or her official capacity is plaintiff, the complaint need not be verified; and if the state, any county thereof, city, school district, district, public agency, or public corporation, or an officer of such state, county, city, school district, district, public agency, or public corporation, in his or her official capacity is defendant, its or his or her answer need not be verified.

When the verification is made by the attorney for the reason that the parties are absent from the county where he or she has his or her office, or from some other cause are unable to verify it, or when the verification is made on behalf of a corporation or public agency by any officer thereof, the attorney's or officer's affidavit shall state that he or she has read the pleading and that he or she is informed and believes the matters therein to be true and on that ground alleges that the matters stated therein are true. However, in those cases the pleadings shall not otherwise be considered as an affidavit or declaration establishing the facts therein alleged.

> A person verifying a pleading need not swear to the truth or his or her belief in the truth of the matters stated therein but may, instead, assert the truth or his or her belief in the truth of those matters "under penalty of perjury."

(Code Civ. Proc. Sec. 446).

Translating the above code section into simple English, the verification should read something like this:

Verification

> I [insert your name here], the claimant herein, hereby certify under penalty of perjury that the foregoing is true of my own knowledge, except as to the matters which I have stated on my information and belief, and as to those matters I believe them to be true.

Date: __________ Signature: __________________

If the verification is by an officer of a corporation or agency:

Verification

> I [insert your name here], am the [title or position of officer] for [corporation name], the claimant herein. I hereby certify under penalty of perjury that I have read the foregoing and I am informed and believe the matters herein to be true and on that ground allege that the matters stated herein are true.

Date: __________ Signature: __________________

5. Filing fees

The filing fees for filing the claimant's first paper in the case cover the fees for both the verified claim and answer, or any other first paper, such as a demurrer. These are explained in detail in Chapter 6 Section B-1-c.

6. Filing and service of the answer

> [A]ll pleadings subsequent to the complaint, together with proof of service unless a summons need be issued, shall be filed with the clerk or judge, and copies thereof served upon the adverse party or his or her attorney.

(Code Civ. Proc. Sec. 465).

When a rule requires that a document be served and filed, that means it must be served on each party (including other claimants who have filed claims in the case) — or, if they are represented by counsel, on their attorneys). It must be filed with a proof of service attached. (Cal. Rule of Court Sec. 1.21(b)).

A proof of service is a declaration stating that service has been provided by first class mail on such-and-such date, upon the following parties, naming the persons served and stating which party each of the attorneys is representing. (Cal. Rule of Court Sec. 1.21(c)).

7. Amending an answer

> A party may amend its pleading once without leave of the court at any time before the answer or demurrer is filed, or after a demurrer is filed but before the demurrer is heard if the amended complaint ... or answer is filed and served no later than the date for filing an opposition to the demurrer.

(Code Civ. Proc. Sec. 472(a)) Section 472 remains in effect until January 1, 2021, after which a different version takes effect.

The court may allow a party to amend any pleading by adding or striking out the name of any party, or correcting a mistake in the name of the party or other mistake, and may enlarge the time for answering or demurring to the amended pleading. (Code Civ. Proc. Sec. 473(a)(1)).

If the answer is amended the government has 10 days in which to file a demurrer to the amended answer, if it chooses to file one. (Code Civ. Proc. Sec. 471.5(a)).

8. Supplementing an answer

A claimant may file a supplemental answer "alleging facts material to the case occurring after the former ... answer." (Code Civ. Proc. Sec. 464(a)).

There is no deadline for a supplemental answer but you have to file a motion to supplement along with it. (Code Civ. Proc. Sec. 464(a)).

9. Responding to an amended petition for forfeiture

Petitions for forfeiture can also be amended to allege facts material to the case occurring after the initial petition was filed. It must be accompanied by a motion to amend. (Code Civ. Proc. Sec. 464(a)).

If the government amends its petition for forfeiture, the clerk issues a supplemental summons and the summons and the government must serve the amended petition and summons on all claimants. (Code Civ. Proc. Sec. 464(c)).

Claimants must answer the amended petition within 30 days or a default may be entered against them, even though they filed an answer to the original petition. (Code Civ. Proc. Sec. 471.5).

B. Demurrers

Demurrers are one of the devices that allow a court to terminate litigation early if a party has a defect in its case that prevents it from prevailing. They are the California equivalent of Rule 12(b)(6) motions to dismiss under the Federal Rules of Civil Procedure.

Failure to object to a complaint by demurrer or answer waives all objections except jurisdiction and failure to state a claim upon which relief may be granted. (Code Civ. Proc. Sec. 430.80(a)).

A claimant may demur and answer at the same time. (Code Civ. Proc. Sec. 430.30(c)). "A demurrer is not waived by an answer filed at the same time." (Code Civ. Proc. Sec. 472a(a)).

If the claimant files a demurrer to the complaint but not an answer, he/she still has to pay the first paper filing fee or obtain a waiver of filing fees. See Chapter 6 Section B-1-c.

Either party may demur to the opponent's pleadings. A demurrer to the complaint must be filed within 30 days after service. (Code Civ. Proc. Sec. 430.40(a)). A demurrer to a forfeiture petition can be to the entire petition or to individual causes of action. (Code Civ. Proc. Sec. 430.50(a)).

This section applies to demurrers filed by the government as well as demurrers filed by claimants.

A demurrer to the answer must be filed within 10 days after service of the answer. (Code Civ. Proc. Sec. 430.40(b)).

A demurrer to an answer can be to the entire answer or one or more defenses. (Code Civ. Proc. Sec. 430.50(b)). If the government fails to demur to a claimant's answer, all objections are waived except the failure to state facts sufficient to constitute a defense. (Code Civ. Proc. Sec. 430.80(b)).

1. Grounds for a demurrer

When any ground for objection to a petition for forfeiture or answer appears on the face of the pleading, and/or matters to which the court may take judicial notice, the opponent may demur. (Code Civ. Proc. Sec. 430.30(a)). The court may consider documents incorporated by reference in the Complaint. (*Mandel v. Municipal Court for Oakland-Piedmont Judicial Dist.* (1969) 276 Cal.App.2d 649, 653).

A demurrer is the state equivalent of a Federal Rule 12(b)(6) motion to dismiss for failure to state a claim upon which relief may be granted.

Demurrers cannot be accompanied by declarations, documents, or any other evidence. An objection that does not appear on the face of the complaint, but which requires evidence to prove may not be raised by demurrer.

> In ruling on a demurrer, courts must assume the truth of the allegations in the complaint. *Blank v. Kirwan* (1985) 39 Cal.3d 311, 318. We treat the demurrer as admitting all material facts properly pleaded, but not contentions, deductions or conclusions of fact or law. We also consider matters which may be judicially noticed.

(*Serrano v. Priest* (1971) 5 Cal.3d 584, 591).

Matters for which the court may take judicial notice are a very limited category of matters, generally limited to laws and procedures, but also including some universally known or widely accepted facts. (Code Civ. Proc. Sec. 430.30(b)). See Chapter 8 Section B-1-a, below, for the requirements of judicial notice.

Issues that require evidence outside the face of the complaint should instead be raised in the answer, but then they would not be resolved until summary judgment or trial. (Code Civ. Proc. Sec. 430.30(b)).

A court ruling on a demurrer is required to

> give the complaint [or other pleading] a reasonable interpretation, reading it as a whole and its parts in their context. (*Speegle v. Board of Fire Underwriters* (1946) 29 Cal.2d 34, 42 [172 P.2d 867].) When a demurrer is sustained, we determine whether the complaint states facts sufficient to constitute a cause of action. (See *Hill v. Miller* (1966) 64 Cal.2d 757, 759 [51 Cal. Rptr. 689, 415 P.2d 33].) And when it is sustained without leave to amend, [the appellate court must] decide whether there is a reasonable possibility that the defect can be cured by amendment: if it can be, the trial court has abused its discretion and we reverse; if not, there has been no abuse of discretion and we affirm. (*Kilgore v. Younger* (1982) 30 Cal.3d 770, 781 [180 Cal. Rptr. 657, 640 P.2d 793]; *Cooper v. Leslie Salt Co.* (1969) 70 Cal.2d 627, 636 [75 Cal. Rptr. 766, 451 P.2d 406].) The burden of proving such reasonable possibility is squarely on the plaintiff. (*Cooper v. Leslie Salt Co.*, supra, at p. 636.)

(*Blank v. Kirwan* (1985) 39 Cal.3d 311, 318).

> While courts may notice official acts and public records, "we do not take judicial notice of the truth of all matters stated therein." (*Love v. Wolf* (1964) 226 Cal.App.2d 378, 403 [38 Cal. Rptr. 183]; accord, *People v. Long* (1970) 7 Cal.App.3d 586, 591 [86 Cal. Rptr. 590].) "[T]he taking of judicial notice of the official acts of a governmental entity does not in and of itself require acceptance of the truth of factual matters which might be deduced therefrom, since in many instances what is being noticed, and thereby established, is no more than the existence of such acts and

> not, without supporting evidence, what might factually be associated with or flow therefrom." (*Cruz v. County of Los Angeles* (1985) 173 Cal.App.3d 1131, 1134 [219 Cal. Rptr. 661].) We therefore deny plaintiff's first two requests for judicial notice.

(*Mangini v. RJ Reynolds Tobacco Co.*, 7 Cal. 4th 1057, 1064 (taking judicial notice of the existence of a report, but not its contents or scientific opinions.))

a. Judicial notice

When the court takes judicial notice of something, a party does not have to submit evidence to prove its truth.

Under Evid. Code Sec. 451, the court *shall* take judicial notice of the following:

(a) case law, statutory law and constitutional law of the state and the United States;

(b) matters designated for judicial notice by Gov. Code Sec. 11343.6 (filing of certified copy of a regulation or order of repeal with Secretary of State), Gov. Code Sec. 11344.6 (publication of a regulation in the California Code of Regulations or its supplement), or Gov. Code Sec. 18576 (state Civil Service Board and department rules and regulations) or 44 U.S.C. Sec. 1507 (publication in Federal Register of presidential proclamation and executive orders, and documents designated for publication there by the President or an Act of Congress);

(c) matters from the state bar rules of professional conduct, Bus. & Prof. Code Sec. 6076, and the California Rules of Court; (d) Rules of procedure prescribed by the U.S. Supreme Court including the Federal Rules of Civil and Criminal Procedure and rules of other federal courts; (e) the definition of English words and phrases and legal expressions; (f) "Facts and propositions of generalized knowledge that are so universally known that they cannot reasonably be the subject of dispute." (Evid. Code Sec. 451(a)-(f)).

Under Evid. Code Sec. 452, courts *may* take judicial notice of the following:

(a) case law, statutory law and constitutional law of any state in the U.S., the resolutions and private acts of U.S. Congress and the state legislature. (Evid. Code Sec. 452(a)).

(b) federal regulations; (Evid. Code Sec. 452(b)).

(c) official acts of the legislative, executive, and judicial departments of the federal government or any state; (Evid. Code Sec. 452(c)).

(d) court records from any state or federal court; (Evid. Code Sec. 452(d)). These records include certified copies of criminal convictions (Evid. Code Sec. 452.5(a)(1)) and official records of any act, condition or event recorded in the record of the conviction, including service of a prison term. (Evid. Code Sec. 452.5(b)(1)).

(e) rules of court of any federal or state court; (Evid. Code Sec. 452(e)).

(f) the laws of foreign nations, or foreign entities, or any organization of foreign nations; (Evid. Code Sec. 452(f)).

(g) "Facts and propositions that are of such common knowledge within the territorial jurisdiction of the court that they cannot reasonably be the subject of dispute." (Evid. Code Sec. 452(g)).

(h) "Facts and propositions that are not reasonably subject to dispute and are capable of immediate and accurate determination by resort to sources of reasonably indisputable accuracy." (Evid. Code Sec. 452(h)).

A court shall take judicial notice of any matter specified in Section 452 if a party requests it and:

(a) Gives each adverse party sufficient notice of the request, through the pleadings or otherwise, to enable such adverse party to prepare to meet the request; and

(b) Furnishes the court with sufficient information to enable it to take judicial notice of the matter.

(Evid. Code Sec. 453(a)-(b)).

b. Demurrer to a forfeiture petition

A claimant responding to a petition for forfeiture may demur on the following grounds: (a) lack of jurisdiction; (c) another action is pending between the same parties on the same cause of action; (e) the pleading does not state a cause of action; (f) the pleading is "uncertain," that is, ambiguous and unintelligible. (Code Civ. Proc. Sec. 430.10(a), (c), (e) and (f)). Other grounds for demurrers in that section do not apply to forfeiture.

c. Demurrer to an answer

The government may demur to an answer on these grounds: (a) does not state facts sufficient to constitute a defense; (b) the answer is uncertain, e.g. ambiguous or unintelligible. (Code Civ. Proc. Sec. 430.20(a)-(b)).

d. Demurrers challenging claimants' standing

Prosecutors often use demurrers to challenge a claimant's standing.

In order to defend property against the forfeiture, claimants must have standing – that is, a recognizable legal or equitable interest in the property. If challenged, the claimant has the burden to establish "an interest in the seized property' sufficient to satisfy the court of his standing to contest forfeiture." (*Jauregi v. Superior Court* (1999) 72 Cal.App.4th 931, 938-939).

> The doctrine of standing seeks to insure that courts decide actual controversies and not abstract questions. Absent standing, the claimant in a forfeiture action cannot contest the government's decision to seek forfeiture; this is the rule in state and federal proceedings. (*People v. $ 28,500 United States Currency, supra,* 51 Cal.App.4th at p. 467 [involving a former version of section 11488.4].) If it were otherwise, "'persons with no interest whatsoever in seized property could make a handsome living filing claims.' "(*U.S. v. Certain Real Prop. Located at 16510 Ashton* (6th Cir. 1995) 47 F.3d 1465, 1473 (dis. opn. of Boggs, J.).) Thus, "a claimant [in a civil forfeiture proceeding] must show he has a recognizable legal or equitable interest in the seized property" in order to establish standing; it is the claimant's burden to establish an "interest in the seized property" sufficient to satisfy the court of his standing to contest forfeiture. (*People v. $ 28,500 United States Currency, supra,* 51 Cal.App.4th at p. 467.) This is a threshold legal issue. (Id. at pp. 466-467; *People v. $ 241,600 United States Currency* (1998) 67 Cal.App.4th 1100, 1107-1108 [79 Cal. Rptr. 2d 588]; § 11488.4, subd. (g).)

(*Jauregi v. Superior Court* (1999) 72 Cal.App.4th 931).

Standing is a "threshold legal issue." (*Jauregi, supra,* 72 Cal.App.4th at p. 939; *People v. $ 28,500* (1996) 51 Cal.App.4th 447, 466-467; *People v. $ 241,600* (1998) 67 Cal.App.4th 1100, 1107-1108). "Absent standing, the claimant in a forfeiture action cannot contest the government's decision to seek forfeiture; this is the rule in state and federal proceedings." (*Jauregi v. Superior Court, supra,* 72 Cal.App.4th at 938; *People v. $ 28,500, supra,* 51 Cal.App.4th at 467)).

Standing is a concept arising from Article III of the U.S. Constitution, which requires litigants to have a concrete stake in the outcome of the lawsuit in order to participate in the litigation. To demonstrate standing the claimant must show an ownership, possessory, or other financial interest in the property sufficient to create "a case or controversy." The burden is not a heavy one in the early stages of the litigation. (*See United States v. 5208 Los Franciscos Way* (9th Cir. 2004) 385 F.3d 1187, 1191).

In federal cases, courts have often granted motions to dismiss claims for lack of standing, and thereby denied the claimant of the right to a jury trial on forfeitability of the property.

This issue usually arises when a very large amount of cash is seized from someone traveling on the highway, and that person does not have a history of employment or a paper trail showing sufficient income to have amassed that amount of money. If the person claimed it was his/hers, the federal courts have often scrutinized claims like that for evidence of straw ownership and dismissed the claim on standing grounds. The practice of judges weighing the credibility of the claimant's claim and dismissing the claim before trial has come under fire in federal cases. (See *United States v. 5 S 351 Tuthill Road* (7th Cir. 2001) 233 F.3d 1017, *amended on denial of rehearing,* 201 U.S. App. Lexis 4250).

Under state law, courts are more protective of claimants' trial rights. In a 2002 case the Second Appellate District held:

> [T]he question of standing is one of law, and is properly determined by the trial court when the material facts underlying the standing inquiry are undisputed. However, when the determination of standing is intertwined with the merits of the forfeiture proceeding and turns upon factual disputes or witness credibility evaluations, we hold that the jury must determine the underlying facts, unless the claimant waives his or her

> right to a jury. Otherwise, a claimant's statutory and constitutional right to a jury trial in a forfeiture proceeding would be meaningless. The claimant, however, bears the threshold burden of proving, by a preponderance of the evidence, his or her legally cognizable interest in the seized property at the forfeiture hearing, before the People are required to prove the merits of the forfeiture action. Because the determination of Plascencia's ownership of the seized currency requires the resolution of disputed facts and evaluations of witness credibility, a jury must make the factual findings underlying the trial court's ultimate determination of whether Plascencia has standing to challenge the forfeiture.

(*People v. Superior Court* (*Plascencia)* (2002) 103 Cal.App.4th 409).

2. Contents and filing requirements for demurrers

A claimant can demur to all of a complaint or individual causes of action. (Code Civ. Proc. Sec. 430.50(a)). A demurrer to an answer can be to the entire answer or one or more defenses. (Code Civ. Proc. Sec. 430.50(b)).

Failure to object to a complaint by demurrer or answer waives all objections to it except jurisdictional defects and failure to state a claim. (Code Civ. Proc. Sec. 430.80(a)).

If the government fails to demur to a claimant's answer, all objections are waived except the failure to state facts sufficient to constitute a defense. (Code Civ. Proc. Sec. 430.80(b)).

When a demurrer is based on matter for which the party is requesting judicial notice pursuant to Evid. Code Sec. 452 or 453, that matter must be specified in the demurrer and/or points and authorities in support thereof. (Code Civ. Proc. Sec. 430.70).

a. Deadline

A demurrer to the complaint must be filed within 30 days after service of the complaint. (Code Civ. Proc. Sec. 430.40(a)).

A demurrer to the answer must be filed within 10 days after service of the answer. (Code Civ. Proc. Sec. 430.40(b)).

b. Filing a demurrer and an answer

"A demurrer is not waived by an answer filed at the same time." (Code Civ. Proc. Sec. 472a(a)).

If the claimant files a demurrer but not an answer, and the demurrer is overruled, the court will set a deadline for filing an answer. (Code Civ. Proc. Sec. 472a(b)).

c. Meet and confer requirement

Before filing a demurrer the party must meet and confer, in person or by phone, with the party who filed the pleading, and try to resolve the objections by agreement. If the other party files an amended pleading in response to the meet and confer conference, the parties must meet and confer again before filing a demurrer to the amended pleading. (Code Civ. Proc. Sec. 430.41(a)).

As part of the meet and confer process the demurring party must identify the specific causes of action he/she believes to be subject to demurrer and provide legal authority to support his/her argument about the deficiencies. The party who filed the allegedly deficient pleading must provide legal support for its argument that the pleading is not deficient or come up with a way the pleading could be amended to cure the problem. (Code Civ. Proc. Sec. 430.41(a)(1)).

The parties must meet and confer again at least 5 days before the responsive pleading is due. If the parties are unable to meet before that deadline, the demurring party may get one automatic 30 day extension to file a response, if he/she files a declaration under penalty of perjury stating that they made a good faith attempt to meet and confer, and explaining why they could not meet and confer. The declaration must be filed by the date the response was due. The demurring party is not subject to default during that 30-day extension. Any further extensions require a court order, on a showing of good cause. (Code Civ. Proc. Sec. 430.41(a)(2)).

When the demurrer is filed it must be accompanied by a declaration stating either that they met and conferred and did not reach agreement, or that the party who filed the pleading failed to respond or otherwise failed to meet and confer in good faith. (Code Civ. Proc. Sec. 430.41(a)(3)(A)-(B)).

The judge's conclusion that the meet and confer process was insufficient is not proper grounds to overrule or sustain a demurrer. (Code Civ. Proc. Sec. 430.41(a)(4)).

If a court sustains a demurrer to one or more causes of action and grants leave to amend, the court may order the parties to confer before an amended pleading or a demurrer to an amended pleading may be filed. If the court holds a conference, the time for filing a demurrer does not begin to run until after the conference. (Code Civ. Proc. Sec. 430.41(c)).

This section does not apply if a party is incarcerated and not represented by counsel in the forfeiture action. (Code Civ. Proc. Sec. 430.41(d)(1)).

3. Responding to a demurrer

In response to a demurrer and prior to the case being at issue, a complaint may not be amended more than 3 times, absent an offer to the trial court as to additional facts to be pleaded that were reasonably likely to cure the defect. (Code Civ. Proc. Sec. 430.41(e)(1)).

This section does not affect a party's right to amend its pleading or respond to an amended pleading after the case is at issue. (Code Civ. Proc. Sec. 430.41(e)(2)). Nor does it affect appellate rights pursuant to Code Civ. Proc. Sec. 430.80. (Code Civ. Proc. Sec. 430.41(f)).

If a demurrer is overruled and that cause of action is not amended, the demurring party preserves the right to appeal after final judgment without filing a further demurrer. (Code Civ. Proc. Sec. 430.41(g)).

The current version of Code Civ. Proc. Sec. 430.41 sunsets on January 1, 2021 unless a later statute deletes or extends the date. (Code Civ. Proc. Sec. 430.41(h)).

4. Rulings on demurrers

If a demurrer to a complaint is overruled and no answer has been filed, the judge shall set a deadline for filing the answer. (Code Civ. Proc. Sec. 472a(b)).

When a demurrer is sustained, "the court shall include in its decision or order a statement of the specific ground or grounds upon which the decision or order is based" and may do so by reference to page and paragraph numbers in the demurrer. "The party against whom a demurrer has been sustained may waive these requirements." (Code Civ. Proc. Sec. 472d).

If a demurrer to a complaint is sustained the court may grant leave to amend and set a deadline. (Code Civ. Proc. Sec. 472a(c)).

When a demurrer is sustained or overruled and a time is set to file an amendment or answer, the time runs from the service of notice of the decision or order, unless notice is waived in open court and noted in the minutes. (Code Civ. Proc. Sec. 472b).

When a reviewing court reverses or otherwise remands an order granting or denying a demurrer, "any amended complaint shall be filed within 30 days after the clerk of the reviewing court mails notice of the issuance of the remittitur." (Code Civ. Proc. Sec. 472b). A remittitur is a notice issued by the Court of Appeal of a decision on the appeal. (Cal. Rules of Court Rule 8.272).

5. Appellate review of rulings on demurrers

When a court enters an order sustaining a demurrer without leave to amend, the question of whether the court abused its discretion is open on appeal even though no request to amend such pleading was made. (Code Civ. Proc. Sec. 472c(a)).

If an amended pleading is filed after the court's order, the following orders are deemed open on appeal:

> (1) An order sustaining a demurrer to a cause of action within a [forfeiture petition] where the order did not sustain the demurrer as to the entire [petition].
>
> (2) An order sustaining a demurrer to an affirmative defense within an answer where the order sustaining the demurrer did not sustain the demurrer as to the entire answer.
>
> (3) An order granting a motion to strike a portion of a pleading where the order granting the motion to strike did not strike the entire pleading.

(Code Civ. Proc. Sec. 472c(b)).

> "[O]pen on appeal" means that a party aggrieved by an order listed in subdivision (b) may claim the order as error in an appeal from the final judgment in the action.

(Code Civ. Proc. Sec. 472c(c)).

C. Motion to strike

Another kind of motion that is litigated during the pleading stage is the motion to strike. A claimant's motion to strike the forfeiture petition must be filed by the deadline for filing an answer. (Code Civ. Proc. Sec. 435(b)(1)).

The government may move to strike a claim or answer as well. (Code Civ. Proc. Sec. 436(a)-(b)).

Any party may file a motion to strike a pleading (petition for forfeiture, claim, answer, or demurrer) in whole or in part, to: "[s]trike out any irrelevant, false, or improper matter inserted in any pleading," or "any part of any pleading not drawn or filed in conformity with the laws of this state, a court rule, or an order of the court." (Code Civ. Proc. Sec. 436(a)-(b)).

A motion to strike must be filed within the time permitted to respond to the pleading the movant is attempting to strike. (Code Civ. Proc. Sec. 435(b)(1)).

Filing a motion to strike does not extend the time to demur. (Code Civ. Proc. Sec. 435(d)). Be sure to file a demurrer along with the motion to strike, or the demurrer will be waived.

Motions to strike can be used to strike answers, demurrers, or claims for not complying with the rules. Aggressive prosecutors may use this as a weapon of oppression against *pro se* litigants and novice forfeiture lawyers, or lawyers who are rusty at state civil litigation.

A motion to strike an answer must be filed within 10 days of service of the answer. (Code Civ. Proc. Sec. 435(b)).

A motion to strike a demurrer must be set for hearing on the hearing date for the demurrer. (Code Civ. Proc. Sec. 435).

The grounds for the motion to strike must appear on the face of the pleading, or from any matter which can be judicially noticed. (Code Civ. Proc. Sec. 437(a)).

Matters that may be judicially noticed are explained in Chapter 8 Section B-1-a, above.

The matter a party wants to have the court judicially notice must be specified in the supporting memorandum of points and authorities. (Code Civ. Proc. Sec. 437(b)).

If the motion requires a hearing, the filing fee is $60. (Gov. Code Sec. 70617(a)).

D. Motion for judgment on the pleadings

A party may move for judgment on the pleadings only on these grounds:

> (A) If the moving party is a plaintiff, that the complaint states facts sufficient to constitute a cause or causes of action against the defendant and the answer does not state facts sufficient to constitute a defense to the complaint.
>
> (B) If the moving party is a defendant [or claimant], that either of the following conditions exist:
>
> (i) The court has no jurisdiction of the subject of the cause of action alleged in the complaint.
>
> (ii) The complaint does not state facts sufficient to constitute a cause of action against that defendant [or claimant].

(Code Civ. Proc. Sec. 438(c)(1)). The motion may seek judgment on the entire petition for forfeiture or any of the causes of action raised, or on the entire answer or any of the affirmative defenses raised in the answer. (Code Civ. Proc. Sec. 438(c)(2)).

The court may on its own motion grant judgment on the pleadings, but only on one of these grounds: "the complaint states facts sufficient to constitute a cause or causes of action against the defendant and the answer does not state facts sufficient to constitute a defense to the complaint" (Code Civ. Proc. Sec. 438(c)(3)(A)), in which case the court may grant judgment for the plaintiff; or if the court finds it does not have jurisdiction or that the forfeiture petition does not state facts sufficient to state a cause of action against the claimant, the court may grant judgment for the claimant. (Code Civ. Proc. Sec. 438(c)(3)(B)).

The grounds for a motion for judgment on the pleadings must appear on the face of the pleadings and any matter for which the judge is required to take judicial notice, which matter the movant must specify in the points and authorities. (Code Civ. Proc. Sec. 438(d)).

A motion for judgment on the pleadings is not allowed after a pretrial conference order has been issued or within 30 days of the date set for trial, whichever is later. (Code Civ. Proc. Sec. 438(e)).

The motion may be made only after one of these conditions has occurred: (1) if the plaintiff makes the motion, after the defendant has filed an answer and the time for plaintiff to demur to the answer has expired; (2) if the claimant makes the motion, after the claimant has filed an answer and the time to demur to the complaint has expired. (Code Civ. Proc. Sec. 438(f)).

A motion for judgment on the pleadings may be made even if: (1) the movant has already demurred to the pleading on the same grounds and the demurrer has been overruled, provided "there has been a material change in applicable case law or statute since the ruling on the demurrer" or (2) the movant did not demur to the pleading on the same grounds as the motion for judgment on the pleadings. (Code Civ. Proc. Sec. 438(g)(1)-(2)).

The motion may be granted with or without leave to amend the pleading. (Code Civ. Proc. Sec. 438(h)(1)). If the court grants leave to amend the pleading it shall grant 30 days to file the amended pleading. (Code Civ. Proc. Sec. 438(h)(2)).

If the court grants a motion for judgment on the entire complaint without leave to amend, judgment shall be entered forthwith. (Code Civ. Proc. Sec. 438(h)(3)).

If the court grants judgment on a pleading with leave to amend, and the time expires without an amended pleading being filed, the court may strike the pleading and enter judgment for the adverse party. (Code Civ. Proc. Sec. 438(h)(4)(A)-(B)). In those circumstances, "judgment shall be entered forthwith in favor of the moving party." (Code Civ. Proc. Sec. 438(h)(4)(C)).

Where the court has granted judgment on a pleading with leave to amend, the court shall not enter judgment until the following occurs: (A) if an amended pleading if filed and the movant contends the amended pleading is filed late or that it violates the court's order, then the movant may move to strike the pleading; (B) if no amended pleading is filed the party may move for entry of judgment in its favor. (Code Civ. Proc. Sec. 438(i)(1)).

All motions for judgment on the pleadings must comply with Code Civ. Proc. Sec. 1010 which requires all notices to be in writing, and to state the grounds on which it is made and the documents on which it is based. If the documents have not been previously served, a copy must accompanying the notice. (Code Civ. Proc. Sec. 1010).

9. Miscellaneous procedural issues

A. Obtaining counsel and financing litigation

1. Right to court appointed counsel

Currently no court has recognized a federal constitutional right to court-appointed counsel for indigents in civil forfeiture cases. However, the California Supreme Court has come close.

a. U.S. Supreme Court

The right to court-appointed counsel for indigent defendants in criminal cases arises from the Sixth Amendment. (*Gideon v. Wainwright* (1963) 372 U.S. 335). By its terms, however, the Sixth Amendment only applies to criminal prosecutions.

> The Sixth Amendment provides, "In all criminal prosecutions, the accused shall enjoy the right . . . to have the Assistance of Counsel for his defence."

(*Gideon*, supra, 372 U.S. at 340).

Civil forfeiture has been characterized as "quasi-criminal" but it is not a criminal prosecution.

In recent decades the U.S. Supreme Court has extended the constitutional rights available to criminal defendants, and applied them to claimants in forfeiture cases. The Court reasoned that because forfeiture is punishment, Due Process requires some of the rights afforded criminal defendants. (*Austin v. United States* (1993) 509 U.S. 602).

Hopefully someday courts will expand the reasoning of *Gideon* to civil forfeiture cases, especially in statutory schemes like California's where there is a criminal conviction requirement.

If a right to counsel is recognized, it will probably be under the Fifth Amendment's Due Process clause rather than the Sixth Amendment.

Because forfeiture is punishment – and because it is so complex – the right to counsel seems necessary to guarantee the minimum due process.

In federal cases, the Civil Asset Forfeiture Reform Act of 2000 authorizes the appointment of counsel to defend indigent claimants in two very limited circumstances, but there is no equivalent California statute.

b. California Supreme Court

The most compelling case to require court appointed counsel is where the claimant is incarcerated and indigent. Being indigent he/she cannot hire an attorney to defend on his/her behalf. Being incarcerated he/she may lack the ability to appear in court to defend himself/herself in pro per, and may not have access to a law library and word processing equipment.

The California Supreme Court considered such a case in *Payne v. Superior Court of Los Angeles County* (1976) 17 Cal.3d 908. There, the prisoner was sued for the alleged theft of guard dogs, and because he was incarcerated and unable to appear, a default judgment was entered against him for $24,722. The California Supreme Court was sympathetic to his plight.

> [A]n indigent prisoner seeking to defend a civil suit, has a due process right of access to the courts which has been abridged. The state has the burden of demonstrating a compelling state interest to justify the infringement.
>
> The denial of access [to the courts] also constitutes a prima facie equal protection violation. Indigent prisoners are denied access to the courts to defend a civil suit, while

> free persons and prisoners possessing the means to hire counsel retain an access right.

(*Payne v. Superior Court of Los Angeles County,* supra, 17 Cal.3d at 919).

The Supreme Court stopped short of creating an absolute right to court appointed counsel. It provided instead that a court confronted with this dilemma should consider alternatives: allowing the prisoner the ability to appear in court to defend, deferring the trial until after the prisoner's release, or appointing counsel from one of the public or privately funded lawyers serving indigents. (*Payne,* supra, 17 Cal.3d at 924).

In 1979, the holding in *Payne* was extended to paternity suits against indigent inmates, with the California Supreme Court holding

> in proceedings to determine paternity in which the state appears as a party or appears on behalf of a mother or child, indigent defendants are constitutionally entitled to appointed counsel.

(*Salas v. Cortez* (1979) 24 Cal.3d 22, 34). That reasoning should apply to forfeiture cases, where the state appears as a party trying to take the property from the indigent defendant.

The California Supreme Court took up this issue again in *Yarbrough v. Superior Court* (1985) 39 Cal.3d 197, involving a civil suit for wrongful death brought against an indigent prisoner. It reaffirmed the holding in *Payne,*

> as a matter of due process and equal protection under both the federal and California Constitutions an indigent prisoner who is a defendant in "a bona fide legal action threatening his interests" is entitled to access to the courts to be heard in his defense.

(*Yarbrough,* supra, 39 Cal.3d at 200, quoting *Payne*, supra). The court clarified the standards to be applied:

> One of the criteria for appointment of counsel is that an adverse judgment will affect property rights....
>
> The court itself should evaluate the potential for loss to the prisoner, weighing such factors as age, term of incarceration, employment history, education, skills, family background and the likelihood of inheriting or otherwise obtaining property....
>
> In addition to finding a potential for loss that is not wholly ephemeral, the trial court must determine that counsel will be helpful to the prisoner under the circumstances of the case. The court should consider whether there are new questions of fact to be determined. The conviction itself will, of course, be admissible at the civil trial as an exception to the hearsay rule. (Evid. Code, § 1300.) Further, the doctrine of collateral estoppel will preclude relitigation of the issues decided in the criminal prosecution. (*Teitelbaum Furs, Inc. v. Dominion Ins. Co., Ltd.* (1962) 58 Cal.2d 601 [25 Cal. Rptr. 559, 375 P.2d 439].)

(*Yarbrough,* supra, 39 Cal.3d at 205).

> A determination by the trial court that counsel will not be helpful on the question of liability does not, however, foreclose the need for counsel on the issue of the amount of damages.

(*Yarbrough,* supra, 39 Cal.3d at 206).

Applying this principle to a forfeiture case, even if "liability" for forfeiture was established by the criminal trial, the claimant may have a proportionality defense which would reduce "the amount of damages."

The California Supreme Court noted that the trial court had failed to consider a necessary factor — the feasibility of postponing the civil case until Yarborough's release from imprisonment. (*Yarbrough,* supra, 39 Cal.3d at 206). This alternative will likely be relied on in forfeiture cases – since the plaintiff is the government, not a third party who could be substantially prejudiced by the postponement.

2. Release of seized funds to hire counsel

In bank offense forfeiture cases, when the prosecutor applies for a restraining order to keep property from being disposed of pending trial, the defendant may be able to get money released to hire counsel under Fin. Code Sec. 5323(b)(3), which provides "no injunction shall impair the defendant's ability to hire counsel for the criminal and forfeiture cases."

That is the only California forfeiture statute which includes such a provision.

3. Attorney's fees reimbursement

Some attorneys may be willing to take the case on a contingency – and get paid their fees out of the claimants' property when they get it back. But the claimant would need a strong case with a high likelihood of winning, and the property would have to be valuable enough to make it worth the attorney's risk.

Some attorneys will take strong cases on the hope of an attorney fee award, if there is a "fee shifting" statute that allows the court to order the government to pay the attorneys' fees of successful claimants.

Under the so-called "American rule," parties to litigation are required to pay their own attorneys' fees, unless a contract between the parties or a statute provides for attorney's fee reimbursement to the successful litigant ("fee shifting.") California law follows the American rule. (See Code Civ. Proc. Sec. 1021). There is no California fee shifting statute that applies to forfeiture cases.

In federal courts, the Civil Asset Forfeiture Reform Act of 2000 provides for attorneys' fee awards to successful claimants, though fee awards are rare.

Lienholder claimants usually have contractual provisions in their mortgages or financing agreements requiring payment of their attorneys' fees incurred in protecting their lien, so most lienholders' attorneys' fees are paid as part of resolving the lien.

B. Filing fees and costs

1. Budgeting for filing fees and costs

In addition to the filing fees for the initial pleadings filed by each party in a case (see Chapter 6 Section B-1-c), there are additional fees for motions and various other necessary court services throughout the litigation.

The filing fees for attorney applications to appear *pro hac vice* (representation by out of state attorney) are $500 initially and $500 for each year the litigation continues. (Gov. Code Sec. 70617(e)).

All motions requiring a hearing require a $60 filing fee. (Gov. Code Sec. 70617(a)). In addition there is a fee for the court reporter of $30 for hearings lasting less than an hour, $431 for 1/2 day, and $862 for a full day. (Gov. Code Sec. 68086(a)(1)-(2)).

A $60 filing fee also applies to motions for an order to attend a deposition more than 150 miles from deponent's residence under Code Civ. Proc. Sec. 2025.260; motions to set aside default or default judgment under Code Civ. Proc. Sec. 473.5; motions to set aside default and for leave to amend under Code Civ. Proc. Sec. 585.5; discovery motions under Code Civ. Proc. Sec. 2016.010; motions to continue the trial date; and motions for new trial. (Gov. Code Sec. 70617(a)).

Motions to continue hearings or case management conferences have a $20 filing fee. (Gov. Code Sec. 70617(c)(1)).

Motions for summary judgment or for summary adjudication have $500 filing fees. (Gov. Code Sec. 70617(d)).

Change of venue requires a $50 processing fee to the court from which the transfer is requested (for the cost of making up the record and sending it) – plus a separate check for the "uniform first paper filing fee" for the court to which the case will be transferred. (Gov. Code Sec. 70618). The Uniform fee for the first paper in each class of cases is explained in Chapter 6 Section B-1-c.

A stipulation and order requires a $20 filing fee. (Gov. Code Sec. 70617(c)(2)). A stipulation that does not require an order does not require a fee. (Gov. Code Sec. 70617(b)(5)).

No filing fees are required for civil case management statements. (Gov. Code Sec. GC 70617(b)(3)).

2. Obtaining a waiver of filing fees

As you can see from the section above, costs and fees mount very quickly and often add up to thousands of dollars.

If they qualify, claimants should immediately apply for fee waivers and save their funds for paying their attorneys.

Indigent claimants may apply for fee waivers if they meet the eligibility standards of Gov. Code Sec. 68632 and 68633. A fee waiver excuses the applicant from filing fees for the first pleading or other paper and other court fees and costs. The court may also order the applicant to make partial payments under Gov. Code Sec. 68632(d) or 68637(e).

Gov. Code Sec. 68636 allows the court to reconsider the waiver and withdraw it for future filings or deny it retroactively. At the end of the case the court may collect the previously waived fees under the circumstances outlined in Code Civ. Proc. Sec. 68637.

When an application for an initial fee waiver is granted, the following fees are waived: clerk's fees for filing papers, certifying or copying, issuing process or certificates, and transmitting papers; reporter's fees for attendance at hearings and trials if a reporter is provided by the court; court fee for a telephone appearance; clerk's fee for preparing, copying and transmitting the clerk's transcript on appeal to the reviewing court; the fee under Rule 8.130(b) or 8.834(b) for the deposit on a reporter's transcript on appeal; and the clerk's fee for preparing a transcript of an official electronic recording. (Cal. Rule of Court 3.55).

Additional fees that may be waived either in the initial fee waiver or in a later application, are jury fees, court interpreter's fees for witnesses, witness fees of police whose attendance is reasonably necessary, witness fees for court appointed experts, and other fees as itemized in the application. (Cal. Rules of Court 3.56).

A fee waiver does not mean that the claimant never has to pay the fees. If the claimant wins the case and gets back property worth more than $10,000, Gov. Code Sec. 68637(c) gives the court a lien for the waived fees and requires that they be paid out of the recovery. (Cal. Rules of Court 3.57).

In addition to the fees listed above, there will be court reporters' fees for depositions, and expert witness fees. Those cannot be waived by the clerk.

a. Fee waivers for indigents

The right of an indigent civil litigant to proceed *in forma pauperis* is grounded in a common law right of access to the courts and constitutional principles of due process. (*Earls v. Superior Court* (1971) 6 Cal.3d 109, 113-114, 98 Cal.Rptr. 302, 490 P.2d 814 [indigents are entitled not

> merely to access to the courts but to timely access]; *Ferguson v. Keays* (1971) 4 Cal.3d 649, 653-655, 658, fn. 8, 94 Cal.Rptr. 398, 484 P.2d 70 [appellate courts possess inherent power to waive filing fees for indigents; applicant need not establish total destitution to qualify for *in forma pauperis* relief].) "[R]estricting an indigent's access to the courts because of his poverty . . . contravenes the fundamental notions of equality and fairness which since the earliest days of the common law have found expression in the right to proceed *in forma pauperis*." (*Isrin v. Superior Court* (1965) 63 Cal.2d 153, 165, 45 Cal.Rptr. 320, 403 P.2d 728.)

(*Cruz v. Superior Court* (2004) 120 Cal.App.4th 175, 185).

Gov. Code Sec. 68632 says fee waivers shall be granted to:

(a) those receiving public benefits under SSI or SSP, CalWORKs, Tribal TANF, SNAP or the California Food Assistance Program, County Relief, General Relief (GR) or General Assistance (GA), CAPI (for aged, blind or disabled), IHSS, or Medi-Cal.

(b) an applicant whose monthly income is 125% or less of the current poverty guidelines of the US Department of Health and Human Services.

(c) an applicant that the court determines cannot pay the fees without using money needed for the "common necessaries of life" for the applicant and his/her family. If the court finds that the applicant can make a partial payment or a payment over time without using money needed for necessaries, the court may grant a partial waiver under Gov. Code Sec. 68634(e)(5). "Common necessaries of life" means

> the portion of the judgment debtor's earnings that the judgment debtor proves is necessary for the support of

> the judgment debtor or the judgment debtor's family supported in whole or in part by the judgment debtor

(Code Civ. Proc. Sec. 706.051(b)).

Use Judicial Council form FW-001 for the initial fee waiver and FW-002 for any request to waive additional fees. (Cal. Rules of Court 3.51(a)). They are available in several languages. Download these forms from http://www.courts.ca.gov/documents/fw001.pdf and http://www.courts.ca.gov/documents/fw002.pdf.

The clerk's offices are required to provide these forms free of charge. Court personnel are required to keep the information provided on the forms confidential. (Gov. Code Sec. 68633(f)).

The applicant applying for filing fee waivers under Gov. Code Sec. 68632 cannot be required to provide documents proving public benefits, provide proof of identity, submit to interviews concerning financial circumstances, be physically present, or fill out additional forms. Applicants seeking fee waivers under Sec. 68632(b) or (c) shall not be required to prove income, dependents, or expenses either. (Gov. Code Sec. 68633(a)-(c)).

An applicant shall indicate whether he/she has filed a prior application in the same case within the previous 6 months, and attach a copy if available. (Gov. Code Sec. 68634(h)).

The clerk shall inform the applicant that at a later date the court may require him/her to prove the financial information on the form, and that a trial court may seek reimbursement of waived fees. The clerk does not have to individually advise the claimant of that rule if it is stated on the form. It is stated on FW-001. (Gov. Code Sec. 68633(e)).

All applications for an initial fee waiver shall be accepted for filing. If the applicant submits the form without all the required information, the clerk may request that he/she supply the omitted information later, but may not refuse to file the application or the pleading for which the fee waiver was requested. (Gov. Code Sec. 68634(b)).

An applicant who submits a fee waiver form shall be allowed to immediately file the pleading without paying a fee. (Gov. Code Sec. 68634(c)).

If an application for an initial fee waiver is not ruled on within 5 days after it is filed, it is deemed granted. If the court denies it, it must give notice of the denial under Gov. Code Sec. 68634(e). (Cal. Rules of Court 3.53). Any delay by the court in processing an application does not count against any time limits for filing the pleading. (Gov. Code Sec. 68634(f)).

The court may delegate to a clerk the ability to approve a fee waiver, but not to deny one or to require a partial payment. (Gov. Code Sec. 68634(d)).

The fee waiver must be determined without regard to the substance of the filing. (Gov. Code Sec. 68634(e)). The court may grant the fee waiver, or deny it if the form is incomplete – if the court gives the reason and a reasonable time to complete it. (Gov. Code Sec. 68634(e)(1)-(2). If the information on the application conclusively establishes ineligibility, the court may deny the waiver, but the applicant must be given the specific reason for denial and an opportunity to request a hearing at which he/she may submit additional information. (Gov. Code Sec. 68634(e)(3)).

If the court has good reason to doubt the veracity of the factual information, the court shall set an eligibility hearing with 10 days' notice, and the specific reason the court doubts it. The court may require that specified information be presented at the hearing, but may not require the submission of information that is not related to the criteria for eligibility. (Gov. Code Sec. 68634(e)(4)).

After the hearing the court may require the applicant to pay a portion of the filing fees, or to pay them over time. If the application is denied in whole or part, the court must give a written statement of the reasons for denial. (Gov. Code Sec. 68634(e)(5)).

If the application is denied in whole or part, the applicant shall pay the fees or the portion ordered by the court, within 10 days after the court gives notice of the denial unless, before that time, the applicant submits a new application or requests a hearing under Gov. Code Sec. 68634(e). (Gov. Code Sec. 68634(g)).

b. Fee waivers for prisoners

Inmates may not be denied the ability to file papers solely because they have no assets or ability to pay even a partial fee. (Gov. Code Sec. 68635(h)).

To apply for an initial fee waiver the inmate must file a Judicial Council application giving his/her current address and stating he/she is incarcerated, plus an accounting of the money due the inmate over the preceding 6 months. The form must be certified by an official of the prison or jail. (Gov. Code Sec. 68635(c)).

An inmate incarcerated in state prison or the county jail must pay the full amount of the fees except as otherwise provided in Gov. Code Sec. 68635(b).

When pleadings or other documents are filed the court shall collect as partial payment a partial fee of 20% of the greater of either (1) average monthly deposits to the inmate account, or (2) average monthly balance of the inmate's account for the preceding 6 months. (Gov. Code Sec. 68635(d)).

After the initial filing fee is partially paid, the inmate must make partial payments of 20% of the preceding month's income credited to the account. The prison or jail forwards payments from this account to the clerk every time the amount in the account exceeds $10. (Gov. Code Sec. 68635(e)).

Since these fees are being automatically deducted from the inmate account, the inmate should watch the balance to make sure they stop the deductions when the amount is paid in full. The fees collected can't exceed the amount of the fees owed. (Gov. Code Sec. 68635(f)).

When an application for an initial fee waiver is granted, the following fees are waived: clerk's fees for filing papers, certifying or copying, issuing process or certificates, and transmitting papers; reporter's fees for attendance at hearings and trials if a reporter is provided by the court; court fee for a telephone appearance; clerk's fee for preparing, copying and transmitting the clerk's transcript on appeal to the reviewing court; the fee under Rule 8.130(b) or 8.834(b) for the deposit on a reporter's transcript on appeal; and the clerk's fee for preparing a transcript of an official electronic recording. (Cal. Rule of Court 3.55).

Additional fees that may be waived either in the initial fee waiver or in a later application, are jury fees, court interpreter's fees for witnesses, witness fees of police whose attendance is reasonably necessary, witness fees for court appointed experts, and other fees as itemized in the application. (Cal. Rule of Court 3.56).

c. Fee waiver may be reconsidered, and applicant made to pay the fees

Applicants who are granted a fee waiver must notify the court within 5 days of any change in financial circumstances that affects his/her ability to pay. (Gov. Code Sec. 68636(a)).

If the court obtains information that the applicant who was granted a fee waiver is not entitled to one, the court may summon the applicant to court on 10 days' notice, giving the specific reasons the fee waiver might be reconsidered. The court may require the applicant to provide evidence but shall not require submission of information unrelated to requirements of eligibility. The court may not conduct such a hearing more often than every 6 months. (Gov. Code Sec. 68636(b)).

At the final disposition of the case, the court may give the claimant notice to appear at a hearing no less than 10 days later, and may require reasonably available evidence to support his application, but may not require information not related to eligibility. (Gov. Code Sec. 68636(c)).

At the hearing the court may withdraw the waiver retroactively and order the waived fees paid immediately or over time, to begin no less than 10 court days later. (Gov. Code Sec. 68636(d)-(e)). If the court obtains evidence suggesting that the fee waiver was requested in bad faith, the court can order a hearing and determine whether limitations should be placed on court services. (Gov. Code Sec. 68636(f)).

Additional fees that may be waived either in the initial fee waiver or in a later application, are jury fees, court interpreter's fees for witnesses, witness fees of police whose attendance is reasonably necessary, witness fees for court appointed experts, and other fees as itemized in the application. (Cal. Rules of Court 3.56).

d. Court may collect the waived fees later

If a claimant whose fees were waived wins judgment or dismissal of the case, the judgment shall include an order requiring the party who lost (the government) to pay to the court the total amount of waived fees and costs. The court may refuse to enter a satisfaction of judgment until such an order to pay waived fees has been satisfied. (Gov. Code Sec. 68637(b)(1)).

A party petitioning the court to enter satisfaction of judgment shall declare under penalty of perjury that any order to pay waived fees have been paid. (Gov. Code Sec. 68637(b)(2)). This does not apply when the party whose fees were waived loses the case. (Gov. Code Sec. 68637(b)(3)).

If the party whose fees were waived recovers $10,000 or more in settlement or compromise of the case, the court shall have a lien for the waived fees and they shall be paid out of the recovery – before that party receives anything from the recovery. (Gov. Code Sec. 68637(c)(2)). The court may refuse to enter a dismissal in the case until the lien is satisfied. The party filing a petition for dismissal shall declare under penalty of perjury that the lien has been paid or that the recovery had a value of less than $10,000. (Gov. Code Sec. 68637(c)(4)).

C. Postponing the forfeiture case until after the criminal conviction

A defendant may have Fifth Amendment concerns when litigating a forfeiture case, but the pendency of a criminal case should not deter claimants from filing claims and defending their forfeiture case.

Claimants can file a claim and answer and then move for the forfeiture case to be continued until after the criminal conviction.

> The forfeiture hearing shall be continued upon motion of the prosecution or the defendant until after a verdict of guilty on any criminal charges specified in this chapter and pending against the defendant have been decided.

(Health & Saf. Code Sec. 11488.5(e)).

10. Discovery

Unless limited by another statute or a court order, "any party may obtain discovery regarding any matter, not privileged, that is relevant to the subject matter involved in the pending action or to the determination of any motion made in that action, if the matter either is itself admissible in evidence or appears reasonably calculated to lead to the discovery of admissible evidence.

Discovery may relate to the claim or defense of the party seeking discovery or of any other party to the action. Discovery may be obtained of the identity and location of persons having knowledge of any discoverable matter, as well as of the existence, description, nature, custody, condition, and location of any document, electronically stored information, tangible thing, or land or other property." (Code Civ. Proc. Sec. 2017.010).

Parties may obtain discovery by depositions, interrogatories, requests for the production of documents, requests to view tangible things and places, requests for admission, physical and mental examinations, and simultaneous exchanges of expert witness trial information. (Code Civ. Proc. Sec. 2019.010).

The methods of discovery may be used in any sequence. The fact that one party is conducting discovery shall not delay discovery of any other party. (Code Civ. Proc. Sec. 2019.020(a)). However the court may establish the sequence and timing of discovery. (Code Civ. Proc. Sec. 2019.020(b)).

The following types of discovery requests documents are served on the parties but not filed in court unless relevant to determination of an issue in a motion or hearing: subpoenas and subpoenas *duces tecum*; deposition notice and response; notice of intention to record testimony by audio or videotape or to take deposition by phone, videoconference or other electronic means; agreement to extend time for responding to discovery requests; interrogatories and responses and objections; demand for production of documents or things; requests for admissions and responses; agreement to do physical or mental examinations; demand for medical reports and response; demand for exchange of expert witnesses; demand for production of discoverable reports and writings of expert witnesses; list of expert witnesses a party intends to use at trial, or statement that a party does not intend to use an expert witness; declaration for additional discovery; stipulation to enlarge the number of discovery requests from that specified by statute; demand for bill of particulars and response; notice of deposit of jury fees; and notice to produce party, agent or tangible things before a court and response. (Cal. Rules of Court 3.250(a)).

The party who serves a discovery paper – except for a response – must retain the originals. (Cal. Rules of Court 3.250(b)(1)). "The original of a response must be served, and it must be retained by the person upon whom it is served." (Cal. Rules of Court 3.250(b)(2)). Originals must be retained in the format in which they were created or received. (Cal. Rules of Court 3.250(b)(3)). Originals must be retained for six months after the case closes unless the court orders a longer period. (Cal. Rules of Court 3.250(b)(4)).

A. Special discovery rules in limited civil cases

Forfeiture cases against property worth $25,000 or less are limited civil cases (Code Civ. Proc. Sec. 86(a)(1)), as are all Vehicle Code forfeitures (Veh. Code Sec. 14607.6(e)(4)).

The following rules apply to limited civil cases only.

In limited cases, discovery is limited to any combination of 35 of the following: interrogatories (with no subparts), demands for production of documents or things, and requests for admission. (Code Civ. Proc. Sec. 94(a)(1)-(3)).

Each party may have only one deposition, but when the deposition is of an organization, multiple people may be designated to testify at the one deposition. (Code Civ. Proc. Sec. 94(b)).

Any party may serve a deposition subpoena *duces tecum* requiring the person to mail copies of documents to the party's attorney along with an affidavit under Evid. Code Sec. 1561. (Code Civ. Proc. Sec. 94(c)). Any other party may obtain copies of the subpoenaed documents by tendering the cost of copying.

Discovery may include physical and mental examinations under Code Civ. Proc. Sec. 2032.10 et seq., (Code Civ. Proc. Sec. 94(d)); or requests of identity of expert witnesses under Code Civ. Proc. Sec. 2032.010 et seq. (Code Civ. Proc. Sec. 94(e)).

The parties may stipulate to additional discovery. (Code Civ. Proc. Sec. 95(b)). Otherwise, additional discovery is allowed only on motion and a showing that the moving party is unable to prosecute or defend the action effectively without additional discovery. The court may consider whether the parties used all applicable discovery in good faith and whether they attempted to obtain a stipulation or means other than formal discovery to obtain the evidence. (Code Civ. Proc. Sec. 95(a)).

Between 30 and 45 days before the first trial date set, a party may serve a request that the opponent produce a list of the names and addresses of their witnesses, and a description of the physical evidence and documents they intend to introduce (with a copy of documents). (Code Civ. Proc. Sec. 96(a)-(b)). The clerk's office has forms to use for these requests. (Code Civ. Proc. Sec. 96(f)).

The requests are served but not filed in court. (Code Civ. Proc. Sec. 96(e)). No additional, amended, or late statement is permitted except by stipulation or court order. (Code Civ. Proc. Sec. 96(d)).

The opposing party must respond within 20 days from service of the request. (Code Civ. Proc. Sec. 96(c)). The response is not filed in court. (Code Civ. Proc. Sec. 96(e)).

The request form must contain a notice that the party receiving the request may be prohibited from calling a witness or introducing evidence not disclosed in the response. (Code Civ. Proc. Sec. 96(a)). Exceptions to this rule are: witnesses or evidence used only for impeachment, which need not be disclosed (Code Civ. Proc. Sec. 97(a) and 97(b)(3)); a party who calls himself or an adverse party as a witness (Code Civ. Proc. Sec. 97(b)(1)-(2)); and documents obtained by discovery (Code Civ. Proc. Sec. 97(b)(4)). The court may permit a party to call a witness or introduce evidence not disclosed under this rule, if it finds the party made a good faith effort to comply or the failure was the result of mistake, inadvertence, surprise or excusable neglect. (Code Civ. Proc. Sec. 97(b)(5)). The court may award costs and expenses as a condition of granting the request. *Id.*

Be careful when computing the deadline for mailing the request or response – the rules for service by mail set out in Code Civ. Proc. Sec. 1013 apply. (Code Civ. Proc. Sec. 96(g)).

Under Code Civ. Proc. Sec. 1013, the time for responding to a discovery request served by mail is extended 5 days if both sender and recipient is located inside California, 10 days if either is located outside California but inside the United States, and 20 days if either is outside the U.S. If sent by Express Mail or other overnight delivery, add two court days to the time for responding. Parties may also serve discovery responses by fax if the parties have agreed in writing to service by fax. Add two court days to the time for responding to a document served by fax. (Code Civ. Proc. Sec. 1013, made applicable by Code Civ. Proc. Sec. 96(g)).

In limited civil cases, instead of presenting direct testimony, a party may offer affidavits or declarations under penalty of perjury – including expert witness testimony and testimony authenticating documents. (Code Civ. Proc. Sec. 98). The affiant must be located within 150 miles and be available for service of process for a reasonable time during the 20 days before trial.

The party wishing to introduce affidavits must serve them on the opposing party at least 30 day before trial.

Parties may also introduce all or part of a deposition at which the opposing party had an opportunity to participate. (Code Civ. Proc. Sec. 98(a)-(b)).

The general rules for format and content of these discovery devices are detailed in Chapter 10 Sections C through G below.

Note: *in limited civil cases, where the rules differ from the general rules in timing and number, the limited case rule applies.*

B. Discovery in unlimited civil cases

Forfeiture cases involving property worth $25,000 or more, are unlimited civil cases. Litigants in unlimited civil cases enjoy wider discovery, and parties may exceed the stated limit if they submit a declaration explaining why the additional discovery is needed.

The general limits on the number of questions in each discovery device in unlimited civil cases are set out in Chapter 10 Sections C through G below.

C. Interrogatories

Interrogatories are written questions which one party serves on an opposing party. The opposing party must answer them under oath, within 30 days of the date of service, but that period is extended if served by mail.

1. Form interrogatories vs. special interrogatories

Form interrogatories are boilerplate interrogatories created by the Judicial Council which apply to a wide variety of civil cases. You can download form interrogatories set DISC-001 (for unlimited civil cases) from http://www.courts.ca.gov/documents/disc001.pdf. In limited civil cases use set DISC-004, from this link http://www.courts.ca.gov/documents/disc004.pdf

Step-by-step instructions for form interrogatories can be found at http://saclaw.org/sbs-discovery-special-interrogatories-3/. I highly recommend all of the Sacramento County Public Law Library's website guides to discovery, even for experienced lawyers, because they are time-savers. Be sure to check your court's local rules for any requirements that differ from Sacramento County's rules and modify the template accordingly.

Special interrogatories are interrogatories you draft yourself, tailored to the issues in the case. The Sacramento County Public Law Library created a handy step-by-step guide to drafting special interrogatories, available on its website at http://www.saclaw.org/wp-content/uploads/sbs-discovery-special-interrogatories.pdf. A link in that page leads to a downloadable, customizable template with the legally required language, in Word format.

2. Timing and number

Interrogatories may be served any time that is at least 10 days after service of the summons or the entry of appearance of the party. (Code Civ. Proc. Sec. 2030.020(b)). Leave of court is not required to serve interrogatories. (Code Civ. Proc. Sec. 2030.020(a)).

A party may serve any number of official form interrogatories. (Code Civ. Proc. Sec. 2030.020(a)(2)). Form interrogatories are generic interrogatories created by the Judicial Council.

Litigants in unlimited civil cases are limited to 35 special interrogatories. (Code Civ. Proc. Sec. 2030.030(a)(1)-(2)). If the first set of interrogatories contains 35 or fewer questions, a second set may be served later. (Code Civ. Proc. Sec. 2030.030(b)).

In limited civil cases (where the property is worth $25,000 or less), special interrogatories, individual requests for production of documents, and requests for admission all count toward the limit of 35 discovery requests.

A party that wants to propound more than 35 interrogatories in an unlimited civil case may exceed that limit if they submit a declaration for additional discovery pursuant to Code Civ. Proc. Sec. 2030.050. If more than 35 interrogatories are served without that declaration, only the first 35 need be answered, but the answering party must state an objection to the balance under Sec. 2030.240. (Code Civ. Proc. Sec. 2030.030(c)).

A party who attaches a Sec. 2030.50 declaration may serve a greater number of interrogatories if it is warranted because of the complexity or quantity of the issues, the financial burden of a deposition, and the expedience of using interrogatories to allow the responding party to review its documents and interview its witnesses before answering. (Code Civ. Proc. Sec. 2030.040(a)).

The responding party may file a motion for a protective order if they believe the number of interrogatories is unwarranted. The propounding party has the burden of justifying the number. (Code Civ. Proc. Sec. 2030.040(b)).

3. Contents and service requirements

The first paragraph of a set of interrogatories must include the name of the propounding party and the responding party and the set number. (Code Civ. Proc. Sec. 2030.060(b)).

Sets of interrogatories must be numbered consecutively. (Code Civ. Proc. Sec. 2030.060(a)). Each set of interrogatories must contain separately numbered interrogatories. (Code Civ. Proc. Sec. 2030.060(c)).

Remember that in drafting interrogatory questions, subparts are not allowed, nor are compound, conjunctive or disjunctive questions. (Code Civ. Proc. Sec. 2030.060(f)).

a. Forms of the questions that may be asked

An interrogatory question may *not* impose a continuing duty to supplement an answer that was correct and complete when answered originally. (Code Civ. Proc. Sec. 2030.060(g)). Instead parties may serve supplemental interrogatories shortly before trial, asking for any additional information that has been acquired since the first set of interrogatories were answered. See Chapter 10 Section C-6, below.

Each interrogatory question must be complete in itself – no introductory instructions may be included. (Code Civ. Proc. Sec. 2030.060(d)). If an interrogatory defines any term, that term must appear in all capital letters. (Code Civ. Proc. Sec. 2030.060(e)).

In addition to questions asking for facts, interrogatories may ask for opinions or a party's contentions about a certain issue.

> An interrogatory may relate to whether another party is making a certain contention, or to the facts, witnesses, and writings on which a contention is based. An interrogatory is not objectionable because an answer to it involves an opinion or contention that relates to fact or the application of law to fact, or would be based on information obtained or legal theories developed in anticipation of litigation or in preparation for trial.

(Code Civ. Proc. Sec. 2030.010(b)).

b. Service of interrogatories

The interrogatories must be served on the party to whom they are directed and all other parties. (Code Civ. Proc. Sec. 2030.080(a)-(b)).

Interrogatories and interrogatory answers are not filed in the court docket. (Code Civ. Proc. Sec. 2030.280(a)). The propounding party must retain the original of the interrogatories with the original proof of service – and the originals of the responses – for 6 months after the case is closed, or longer if the court, on motion, rules that they must be preserved longer. (Code Civ. Proc. Sec. 2030.280(b)).

4. Responding to interrogatories

Each party must timely respond to interrogatories, either by answering them or objecting within 30 days after service, plus any additional days added for service by mail. For the consequences of missing this deadline, see Chapter 10 Section C-5, below.

The time for responding to a discovery request served by mail is extended by 5 days if both sender and recipient are located inside California, 10 days if either is located outside California but inside the United States, and 20 days if either is outside the U.S. (Code Civ. Proc. Sec. 1013(a)). If sent by Express Mail or other overnight delivery service, add two court days to the time for responding. (Code Civ. Proc. Sec. 1013(c)). Parties may also serve discovery responses by fax if the parties have agreed in writing to service by fax. Add two court days to the time for responding to a document served by fax. (Code Civ. Proc. Sec. 1013(e)).

A party may respond to interrogatories by answering the question, producing written documents that answer the question, or objecting to the interrogatory. (Code Civ. Proc. Sec. 2030.210(a)).

a. Protective order to avoid responding to interrogatories

If the proponent exceeded the permissible number of special interrogatories, or asked questions that would reveal trade secrets or privileged information, or if answering the interrogatories would be unduly burdensome and expensive, the responding party may move for a protective order. (Code Civ. Proc. Sec. 2030.090(a)).

A motion for a protective order must be accompanied by a meet and confer declaration under Code Civ. Proc. Sec. 2016.040, showing the parties made a reasonable and good faith attempt to resolve the dispute informally. See Chapter 11 Section A-4, below, for the requirements of a meet and confer declaration.

In ruling on a motion for a protective order the court may, for good cause, make any order necessary to protect a party or other person or organization from "unwarranted annoyance, embarrassment, or oppression, or undue burden and expense." This can include ordering that some of the interrogatories not be answered, that additional time is granted to answer, that a trade secret or other confidential commercial information not be disclosed, that the answers be sealed, or that the proponent conduct a deposition instead. (Code Civ. Proc. Sec. 2030.090(b)).

The court may impose a monetary sanction against the party that unsuccessfully makes or opposes a protective order. (Code Civ. Proc. Sec. 2030.090(d)).

b. Format of responses to interrogatories

The first paragraph of the answers to interrogatories must include the name of the responding party, the set number and the name of the propounding party. (Code Civ. Proc. Sec. 2030.210(b)).

The numbers in the answers to interrogatories must correspond to the numbers in the interrogatories, but the text of the interrogatory need not be quoted. (Code Civ. Proc. Sec. 2030.210(c)).

The responding party should answer the questions as completely as possible. If the answer cannot be answered completely, it should be answered to the fullest extent possible. (Code Civ. Proc. Sec. 2030.220(a)-(b)).

If the responding party does not have personal knowledge, he/she should so state, but still must make reasonable and good faith attempt to obtain the information by asking other people or organizations, unless the information is equally available to the propounding party. (Code Civ. Proc. Sec. 2030.220(c)). If the information is equally available to the propounding party, the responding party should raise that as an objection to the interrogatory.

If answering the interrogatory would require compiling or summarizing documents and if the burden or expense would be the same for the propounding party, the responding party may so state and instead identify the documents from which the information could be derived and allow the proponent a reasonable opportunity to view and inspect the documents and/or make copies of them. (Code Civ. Proc. Sec. 2030.230).

If part of an interrogatory is objectionable, the remainder of the question must be answered (Code Civ. Proc. Sec. 2030.240(a)), and the objection should be stated clearly. (Code Civ. Proc. Sec. 2030.240(b)). If the objection is the work product privilege, that must be expressly stated. (Code Civ. Proc. Sec. 2030.240(b)).

c. Signatures on the interrogatory answers

The answers to interrogatories must be signed by the responding party under penalty of perjury unless they contain only objections. (Code Civ. Proc. Sec. 2030.250(a)). Any interrogatory responses containing objections must be signed by the party's attorney. (Code Civ. Proc. Sec. 2030.250(c)).

When the responding party is a corporation, partnership, association or government agency, one of its officers must sign them under penalty of perjury. If the person signing them is an attorney for the party, that party waives attorney client privilege and work product privileges on any subsequent discovery regarding the source of the information contained in the response. (Code Civ. Proc. Sec. 2030.250(b)).

d. Service of answers to interrogatories

The answers and objections to interrogatories must be served within 30 days of service of the interrogatories, unless the court has shortened or lengthened the time for response. The original must be served on the propounding party. (Code Civ. Proc. Sec. 2030.260(a)). A copy must be served on all other parties unless it would be unduly burdensome or expensive. (Code Civ. Proc. Sec. 2030.260(c)).

The parties may agree to extend the time for responding, but it must be confirmed in writing, and must specify the new deadline. (Code Civ. Proc. Sec. 2030.270(a)-(b)). An extension under this section preserves the party's right to object or utilize one of the alternative responses of Sections 2030.210 through 2030.230. (Code Civ. Proc. Sec. 2030.270(c)).

The answers and objections to interrogatories are not filed in court. (Code Civ. Proc. Sec. 2030.280(a)). The answering party must serve the original of the answers and/or objections to interrogatories on the propounding party. (Code Civ. Proc. Sec. 2030.280(b)).

5. Late or unresponsive answers to interrogatories

a. Untimely answers

If a party fails to serve a timely response, he/she waives all right to produce documents instead of answering, and waives all objections including attorney client privilege and work product. (Code Civ. Proc. Sec. 2030.290(a)). The court may relieve that party from the waiver if the party serves a response in substantial compliance and shows their failure to serve a timely response was the result of mistake, inadvertence, or excusable neglect. (Code Civ. Proc. Sec. 2030.290(a)).

The propounding party may move for an order compelling a response. (Code Civ. Proc. Sec. 2030.290(b)). The court shall impose a monetary sanction under Code Civ. Proc. Sec. 2023.010 et seq., on a party or attorney who unsuccessfully makes or opposes a motion to compel, unless the court finds that person was substantially justified or other circumstances make imposing sanctions unjust. (Code Civ. Proc. Sec. 2030.290(c)).

If a party fails to obey an order compelling answers, the court may impose monetary sanctions – or an issue sanction, an evidence sanction, or a terminating sanction under Code Civ. Proc. Sec. 2023.010 et seq. (Code Civ. Proc. Sec. 2030.290(c)).

b. Incomplete or unresponsive answers

A propounding party may move for an order compelling a further response if an answer is evasive or incomplete, if an objection is without merit or too general, or if the respondent's exercise of the option to produce documents is unwarranted or inadequate. (Code Civ. Proc. Sec. 2030.300(a)).

Such a motion must include a meet and confer declaration under Sec. 2016.040. (Code Civ. Proc. Sec. 2030.300(b)). See Chapter 11 Section A-4 for the requirements for meet and confer declarations.

A motion to compel further response must be made within 45 days of service of the response or any supplemental response, or on a date to which the parties have agreed in writing -or the propounding party waives any right to further response. (Code Civ. Proc. Sec. 2030.300(c)).

The court may impose a monetary sanction upon any party who unsuccessfully makes or opposes a motion to compel further response. (Code Civ. Proc. Sec. 2030.300(d)).

If a party fails to obey an order compelling further response the court may issue a monetary sanction, an issue sanction, an evidence sanction, or a terminating sanction under Sec. 2023.010. (Code Civ. Proc. Sec. 2030.300(e)).

6. Supplemental interrogatories

Supplemental interrogatories are the same interrogatories served earlier, used to elicit further information obtained after the first answers to the interrogatories were served.

A party may propound a supplemental interrogatory to elicit additional information acquired after the first interrogatories were answered. Two sets of supplemental interrogatories are permitted before the first trial setting and one additional supplement after the initial trial date setting. (Code Civ. Proc. Sec. 2030.070(b)).

7. Amended and supplemental answers to interrogatories

A party may, without leave of court, serve an amended answer to any interrogatory if information is subsequently discovered, inadvertently omitted, or mistakenly stated in the original interrogatory. At trial any party may use the original answer, and the responding party may then use the amended answer. (Code Civ. Proc. Sec. 2030.310(a)).

The party who propounded the interrogatory may move that the original answer be deemed binding. The motion must include a meet and confer declaration. (Code Civ. Proc. Sec. 2030.310(b)).

The court may grant such a motion if it determines that the initial failure to answer correctly substantially prejudiced the propounding party, or the responding party failed to show substantial justification and the prejudice can't be cured by a continuance to permit further discovery, or by use of the initial answer under Code Civ. Proc. Sec. 2030.410. (Code Civ. Proc. Sec. 2030.310(c)).

The court shall impose a monetary sanction on the party who unsuccessfully makes or opposes such a motion unless it finds the one subject to the sanction was substantially justified or other circumstances make a monetary sanction unjust. (Code Civ. Proc. Sec. 2030.310(d)).

8. Use of interrogatory answers

Any party may use any answer to interrogatories against the responding party at trial or any hearing. It is not a valid objection that the party is available to testify or has testified. (Code Civ. Proc. Sec. 2030.410).

D. Requests for production of documents or things

Any party may obtain discovery within the scope of Code Civ. Proc. Sec. 2017.010 et seq., by "inspecting, copying, testing, or sampling documents, tangible things, land or other property, and electronically stored information in the possession, custody, or control of any other party to the action." (Code Civ. Proc. Sec. 2031.010(a)).

In limited civil cases each category of documents requested counts toward the maximum total of 35 requests, interrogatories, and requests for admission – combined. In unlimited cases parties may propound an unlimited number of requests for production of documents and tangible things. However – like all discovery, the documents request must be reasonably calculated to lead to the discovery of relevant, admissible evidence. If the number of demands are excessive, the opponent may seek a protective order. (CCP § 2031.060).

A party may demand that an opponent produce, and permit them to inspect, any document in the possession or control of that party (Code Civ. Proc. Sec. 2031.010(b)); or to inspect, photograph, test or sample any tangible things in their possession (Code Civ. Proc. Sec. 2031.010(c)); or to enter upon property to inspect, measure, survey, photograph, test, or sample any designated object or operation on it (Code Civ. Proc. Sec. 2031.010(d)); or to inspect, copy, test, or sample electronically stored data. (Code Civ. Proc. Sec. 2031.010(e)).

The demand shall not be filed in court. (Code Civ. Proc. Sec. 2031.290(a)). The party demanding an inspection "shall retain both the original of the demand, with the original proof of service affixed to it, and the original of the sworn response until six months after final disposition of the action." (Code Civ. Proc. Sec. 2031.290(b)).

The Sacramento County Public Law Library's website has a step-by-step guide for making requests for production, including a downloadable template in Word format and a sample request for production with easy to understand notes. See http://saclaw.org/sbs-discovery-request-for-production-of-documents-or-things-2/.

1. Timing of requests

A defendant may serve requests for production of documents and things at any time, without leave of court. (Code Civ. Proc. Sec. 2031.020(a)). A plaintiff may serve them without leave of court 10 days or more after service of the summons or entry of appearance by that party, whichever is earlier. (Code Civ. Proc. Sec. 2031.020(b)).

A plaintiff may serve requests for production of documents and things earlier that 10 days after service or entry of appearance – only with leave of court. (Code Civ. Proc. Sec. 2031.020(d)).

2. Format of requests

Each set of document requests must be numbered consecutively. (Code Civ. Proc. Sec. 2031.030(a)(1)). The first paragraph must identify the proponent, the responding party and the set number. (Code Civ. Proc. Sec. 2031.030(b)).

Each request for documents must: be separately numbered; describe the items requested either individually or by category, (Code Civ. Proc. Sec. 2031.030(c)-(c)(1)); specify a reasonable time for the inspection at least 5 days after service of the demand, unless a court orders otherwise, (Code Civ. Proc. Sec. 2031.030(c)(2)); specify the reasonable place for the inspection, (Code Civ. Proc. Sec. 2031.030(c)(3)); and specify what inspection, copying or testing will be performed and whether that will alter or destroy the item (Code Civ. Proc. Sec. 2031.030(c)(4)).

The requests must be served on all parties, not just the responding party.

3. Special rules for discovery of electronic data

If requesting electronically stored data, the proponent must specify the form in which he/she wants it produced. (Code Civ. Proc. Sec. 2031.030(a)(2)).

If a party objects to discovery of electronic information on the grounds that it is not reasonably accessible because of undue burden or expense and that that party will not search the source without an agreement or court order, it must identify the types or categories of information that it asserts are not reasonably accessible. (Code Civ. Proc. Sec. 2031.210(d)).

The court shall limit the frequency and extent of discovery of electronically stored information if it determines that: (1) the information is available from some other source that is more convenient or less burdensome or expensive; (2) the discovery is cumulative; (3) the party had the opportunity to get the information in other discovery that was conducted; (4) the burden or expense outweighs the likely benefit, considering the amount in controversy, the resources of the parties, the importance of the issues, and the importance of the requested discovery in resolving the issues. (Code Civ. Proc. Sec. 2031.310(g)).

The court shall not impose sanctions on a party for failure to provide electronically stored information that has been lost, damaged, altered, or overwritten as a result of a routine, good faith operation of the electronic information system. (Code Civ. Proc. Sec. 2031.310(j)(1)). This does not alter any obligation to preserve discoverable information. (Code Civ. Proc. Sec. 2031.310(j)(2)).

4. Responses to requests for production

A response to a demand for inspection, copying, testing, or sampling must state in the first paragraph the name of the responding party and demanding party and the set number. (Code Civ. Proc. Sec. 2031.210(b)).

The responses should be in separately numbered paragraphs, corresponding to the numbers in the demand, but the text of the demand need not be repeated. (Code Civ. Proc. Sec. 2031.210(c)).

The party to whom a demand for inspection, copying, testing, etc. has been directed must respond separately to each item or category of items by (1) stating he/she will comply, (2) stating he/she lacks the ability to comply, or (3) objecting to the demand. (Code Civ. Proc. Sec. 2031.210(a)).

A statement that the responding party will comply

> shall state that the production, inspection, copying, testing, or sampling, and related activity demanded, will be allowed either in whole or in part, and that all documents or things in the demanded category that are in the possession, custody, or control of that party and to which no objection is being made will be included in the production.

(Code Civ. Proc. Sec. 2031.220).

A representation of inability to comply "shall affirm that a diligent search and a reasonable inquiry has been made in an effort to comply with that demand" and shall

> specify whether the inability to comply is because the particular item or category has never existed, has been destroyed, has been lost, misplaced, or stolen, or has never been, or is no longer, in the possession, custody, or control of the responding party. The statement shall set forth the name and address of any natural person or organization known or believed by that party to have possession, custody, or control of that item or category of item.

(Code Civ. Proc. Sec. 2031.230).

The Sacramento County Public Law Library's website contains a step-by-step guide to responding to requests for production, including a link to a downloadable template in Word format. See http://saclaw.org/sbs-discovery-responding-to-requests-for-production-or-inspections-2/.

a. Objections

If only part of the demand is objectionable, the response must contain a statement of compliance or indicate inability to comply with the remainder of that item or category. (Code Civ. Proc. Sec. 2031.240(a)).

If the party objects, he/she must identify with particularity the document or thing falling within the demand to which he objects and state the specific ground for objection, naming the privilege or work product doctrine if that is the objection. (Code Civ. Proc. Sec. 2031.240(b)(1)- (2)). Enough factual information must be provided to enable the other party to evaluate the merits of that claim, including a privilege log as that term is defined in California case law. This statute does not change California case law. (Code Civ. Proc. Sec. 2031.240(c)(1)-(2)).

A privilege log is a list of all documents which the responding party believes are privileged or subject to the attorney work product doctrine.

> The information in the privilege log must be sufficiently specific to allow a determination of whether each withheld document is or is not fact privileged.

(Wellpoint Health Networks, Inc. v. Superior Court of Los Angeles County (McCombs) (1997) 59 Cal.App.4th 110, 130, citing Lipton v. Superior Court (1996) 48 Cal. App.4th at p. 1619.)

If a party objects to discovery of electronic information on the grounds that it is not reasonably accessible because of undue burden or expense and that the party will not search the source without an agreement or court order, it must identify the types or categories of information that it asserts are not reasonably accessible. (Code Civ. Proc. Sec. 2031.210(d)).

For the substantive law on discovery objections see Chapter 10 Sec. I, below.

b. Signatures

Responses to demands for inspection must be signed under penalty of perjury unless the response only contains objections. (Code Civ. Proc. Sec. 2031.250(a)).

If the responding party is a corporation, association, or government agency one of its officers or agents must sign it under oath. If the person signing on behalf of a corporation is an attorney, he/she waives attorney client privilege and work product protection during any subsequent discovery regarding the sources of information contained in the response. (Code Civ. Proc. Sec. 2031.250(b)).

If the response contains any objections the attorney for the party must sign it as well. (Code Civ. Proc. Sec. 2031.250(c)).

c. Deadlines for responses

Within 30 days of service of a demand for inspection, the responding party must serve the original of the response on the demanding party, with copies to all other parties. On motion the court may shorten or extend the time for responding. (Code Civ. Proc. Sec. 2031.260(a)).

The time for responding to a discovery request served by mail is extended 5 days if both sender and recipient are located inside California, 10 days if either is located outside California but inside the United States, and 20 days if either is outside the U.S. (Code Civ. Proc. Sec. 1013(a)). If sent by Express Mail or other overnight delivery, add two court days to the time for responding. (Code Civ.

Proc. Sec. 1013(c)). Parties may also serve discovery responses by fax if the parties have agreed in writing to service by fax. Add two court days to the time for responding to a document served by fax. (Code Civ. Proc. Sec. 1013(e)).

The parties may agree to extend the deadline, but it must be confirmed in writing. (Code Civ. Proc. Sec. 2031.270(a)-(b)). Unless the agreement states otherwise, the extension preserves the right to object. (Code Civ. Proc. Sec. 2031.270(c)).

d. Format of the documents production

Documents produced in response to a request for production of documents "shall either be produced as they are kept in the usual course of business, or be organized and labeled to correspond with the categories in the demand." (Code Civ. Proc. Sec. 2031.280(a)).

They must be produced on the date set in the demand unless the respondent objected to that date. (Code Civ. Proc. Sec. 2031.280(b)).

Electronic stored information should be produced in the format requested in the demand unless the responding party objects; if they object they must state in their responses the form in which they will produce them. (Code Civ. Proc. Sec. 2031.280(c)). If a demand does not state the form, "the responding party shall produce the information in the form or forms in which it is ordinarily maintained or in a form that is reasonably usable." (Code Civ. Proc. Sec. 2031.280(d)(1)). "A party need not produce the same electronically stored information in more than one form." (Code Civ. Proc. Sec. 2031.280(d)(2)).

"If necessary, the responding party at the reasonable expense of the demanding party shall, through detection devices, translate any data compilations included in the demand into reasonably usable form." (Code Civ. Proc. Sec. 2031.280(e)).

e. Supplemental demands for later acquired information

At a later time the proponent may serve a supplemental demand to inspect, copy, test, etc. any later acquired documents or tangible things pertaining to the earlier demand for production. (Code Civ. Proc. Sec. 2031.050(a)).

One supplemental demand is permitted before the initial setting of a trial date and one after a trial date is set, (Code Civ. Proc. Sec. 2031.050(b)), but the court may permit additional supplemental demands, (Code Civ. Proc. Sec. 2031.050(c)).

f. Special rules for claims of privilege or work product

If electronically stored data is produced in discovery before the party realizes it contains information subject to a privilege or work product protection, the party claiming the privilege may notify any party that received the information. After being notified of the claim of privilege the party receiving the information must immediately sequester the information and either return the information and any copies, or present the data to the court under seal for a determination of the validity of the claim of privilege. (Code Civ. Proc. Sec. 2031.285(a)-(b)).

The party receiving the privileged information is precluded from using or disclosing it until the claim of privilege is resolved. (Code Civ. Proc. Sec. 2031.285(c)(1)). If the party disclosed it before being notified of the claim of privilege, they must immediately take reasonable steps to retrieve it. (Code Civ. Proc. Sec. 2031.285(c)(2)).

If the receiving party contests the claim of privilege, he/she must file a motion. (Code Civ. Proc. Sec. 2031.285(d)(1)). Until that motion is resolved the receiving party shall preserve the information and keep it confidential, and must not use it in any manner . (Code Civ. Proc. Sec. 2031.285(d)(2)).

g. Protective orders

The responding party may move for a protective order. The motion must be filed promptly and must be accompanied by a meet and confer declaration pursuant to Code Civ. Proc. Sec. 2016.040. (Code Civ. Proc. Sec. 2031.060(a)).

The court may make any order that justice requires to protect the responding party from unwarranted annoyance, embarrassment, or oppression, or undue burden and expense, and may include ordering that some or all of the demanded items not be produced; that the time for producing be extended; that the place of production be changed; that the inspection or copying be under certain conditions; that confidential information not be disclosed; or that the item produced be sealed and only opened pursuant to court order. (Code Civ. Proc. Sec. 2031.060(b)).

A party who seeks a protective order on the ground that electronically stored information is not reasonably accessible because of undue burden or expense has the burden of demonstrating that the information is from a source not reasonably accessible because of undue burden or expense. (Code Civ. Proc. Sec. 2031.060(c)). The court may nonetheless order discovery if the demanding party shows good cause, subject to the limitations of Code Civ. Proc. Sec. 2031.060(f). (Code Civ. Proc. Sec. 2031.060(d). The court may impose reasonable conditions including making the demanding party pay part or all of the expense. (Code Civ. Proc. Sec. 2031.060(e)).

The court may limit the frequency or extent of discovery of electronic information if: (1) it is possible to obtain the information from another source that is more convenient or less expensive; (2) the discovery sought is unreasonably cumulative; (3) the party had ample opportunity to obtain the information from other discovery in the case; (4) the likely burden or expense outweighs the likely benefit, considering the amount in controversy, the resources of the parties, the importance of the issues and the importance of the information to the issues. (Code Civ. Proc. Sec. 2031.060(f)).

The court may impose monetary sanctions on the party who unsuccessfully makes or opposes a motion for protective order, (Code Civ. Proc. Sec. 2031.060(h)) but the court may not impose sanctions when the electronically stored information "has been lost, damaged, altered, or overwritten as the result of the routine, good faith operation of an electronic information system." (Code Civ. Proc. Sec. 2031.060(i)(1)).

h. Failure to timely or thoroughly respond and motions to compel

Failing to respond timely to a demand for production waives any objection to the demand including objections based on privilege or work product, but the court may relieve the party from the waiver if the responding party serves a response in substantial compliance with the requirements, and serves a timely response showing the delay was the result of mistake, inadvertence, or excusable neglect. (Code Civ. Proc. Sec. 2031.300(a)(1)-(2)).

The party serving the demand may move to compel a response. (Code Civ. Proc. Sec. 2031.300(b)).

Permissible grounds for a motion to compel are: (1) the statement of compliance with the demand is incomplete; (2) a representation of inability to comply is inadequate, incomplete, or evasive; or (3) an objection is without merit or too general. (Code Civ. Proc. Sec. 2031.310(a)).

The motion must set forth specific facts showing good cause justifying the discovery sought. (Code Civ. Proc. Sec. 2031.310(b)(1)).

The party must also file a meet and confer declaration under Sec. 2016.040. (Code Civ. Proc. Sec. 2031.310(b)(2)).

The motion to compel must be filed and served within 45 days of service of the response (or the date to which the parties have agreed in writing) – or else the right to compel a further response is waived. (Code Civ. Proc. Sec. 2031.310(c)).

If a party responding to a demand for inspection fails to permit the inspection in accordance with its statement of compliance, the demanding party may move to compel compliance. (Code Civ. Proc. Sec. 2031.320(a)). Except as provided in Code Civ. Proc. Sec. 2031.320(d), the court shall impose a monetary sanction unless there was substantial justification for the failure to comply or other circumstances make the sanction unjust. (Code Civ. Proc. Sec. 2031.320(b)).

If the party fails to comply with an order compelling the inspection, etc., the court may impose an issue sanction, evidence sanction, or terminating sanction, and/or a monetary sanction. (Code Civ. Proc. Sec. 2031.320(c)).

Absent exceptional circumstances the court shall not impose sanctions for failure to provide electronically stored information that has been lost, damaged, altered, or overwritten as the result of the routine, good faith operation of its electronics information system. (Code Civ. Proc. Sec. 2031.320(d)(1)). This does not alter the party's duty to preserve discoverable information. (Code Civ. Proc. Sec. 2031.320(d)(2)).

The party opposing a motion to compel further response may object "that the information is from a source that is not reasonably accessible because of the undue burden or expense," but they have the burden of proving that. (Code Civ. Proc. Sec. 2031.310(d)).

The court may nonetheless order discovery of the information if the demanding party shows good cause, subject to the limitations of Code Civ. Proc. Sec. 2031.310(g). (Code Civ. Proc. Sec. 2031.310(e)). In such cases the court may set conditions for discovery including allocating expenses of discovery. (Code Civ. Proc. Sec. 2031.310(f)).

The court may impose a monetary sanction on any party that unsuccessfully makes or opposes a motion to compel, unless it finds the party acted with substantial justification or other circumstances make a monetary sanction unjust. If a party fails to obey an order compelling a response the court may impose an issue sanction, an evidence sanction, or a terminating sanction. The court may also impose a monetary sanction, in lieu of or in addition to the other sanctions. (Code Civ. Proc. Sec. 2031.300(c)).

Unless there are exceptional circumstances, a court shall not impose sanctions for failing to provide electronically stored information that has been lost, damaged, altered or overwritten as a result of a routine, good faith operation of an electronic information system. (Code Civ. Proc. Sec. 2031.300(d)(1)). This section does not alter any obligation to preserve discoverable information. (Code Civ. Proc. Sec. 2031.300(d)(2)).

The court shall impose a monetary sanction against a party who unsuccessfully makes or opposes a motion to compel further response unless it finds the party acted with substantial justification or other circumstances make sanctions unjust. (Code Civ. Proc. Sec. 2031.310(h)).

If a party fails to obey such an order the court may impose an issue sanction, an evidence sanction, or a terminating sanction, and/or a monetary sanction. (Code Civ. Proc. Sec. 2031.310(i)).

E. Requests for admission

Any party may submit written requests for admission to any other party, requesting that they "admit the genuineness of specified documents, or the truth of specified matters of fact, opinion relating to fact, or application of law to fact. A request for admission may relate to a matter that is in controversy between the parties." (Code Civ. Prod. Sec. 2033.010).

A defendant may serve requests for admission at any time, without leave of court. (Code Civ. Proc. Sec. 2033.020(a)). A plaintiff may serve them, without leave of court, any time at least 10 days after service of the summons on a party or his/her appearance, whichever occurs first. (Code Civ. Proc. Sec. 2033.020(b)). They may be served earlier than that only with leave of court. (Code Civ. Proc. Sec. 2033.020(d)).

The Sacramento County Public Law Library's website has a step-by-step guide for making requests for admission, including links to the Judicial Council form coversheet (DISC-020), a downloadable pleading paper template in Word format, and a sample request for admissions with easy to understand explanatory notes. See http://saclaw.org/sbs-discovery-requests-for-admission-2/.

1. Limits on number

These are the rules for unlimited civil cases (involving property worth $25,000 or more). For the rules in limited civil cases, see Chapter 10 Section A.

No party may request admissions to more than 35 matters that do not relate to the genuineness of documents. If the initial set of admission requests does not exhaust the 35, the balance may be requested in later sets. (Code Civ. Proc. Sec. 2033.030(a)). If a party wants to serve more than 35 requests for admission he/she must serve a declaration pursuant to Code Civ. Proc. Sec. 2033.050. Otherwise the responding party may object by responding to only the first 35 requests that do not relate to the genuineness of documents. (Code Civ. Proc. Sec. 2033.030(b)). The number of admission requests relating to the genuineness of documents is unlimited. However the court may issue a protective order, as justice requires, to protect a party from "unwarranted annoyance, embarrassment, oppression, or undue burden or expense." (Code Civ. Proc. Sec. 2033.030(c)).

A party who attaches a Sec. 2033.050 declaration may request a greater number of admissions "if warranted by the complexity or quantity of existing or potential issues." The responding party may seek a protective order under Sec. 2033.080. (Code Civ. Proc. Sec. 2033.040(a)). The proponent has the burden of justifying the number of requests for admission. (Code Civ. Proc. Sec. 2033.040(b)).

2. Format of requests

Each set of requests for admission must be numbered consecutively. (Code Civ. Proc. Sec. 2033.060(a)). The first paragraph must state the name of the proponent and responding party and the set number. (Code Civ. Proc. Sec. 2033.060(b)).

Each request must be separately numbered, (Code Civ. Proc. Sec. 2033.060(c)), and must be complete in itself, with no preface or instruction unless that has been approved under Code Civ. Proc. Sec. 2033.710 et seq. (Code Civ. Proc. Sec. 2033.060(d)).

If any term is specially defined it must be typed in all capitals whenever the term appears in the document. (Code Civ. Proc. Sec. 2033.060(e)). Subparts are not allowed, nor are compound, conjunctive or disjunctive requests unless they occur in form requests for admission developed by the Judicial Council under Code Civ. Proc. Sec. 2033.710 et seq. (Code Civ. Proc. Sec. 2033.060(f)).

Requests seeking an admission of the genuineness of a document must attach copies of the documents to the requests. The original of the document must be made available for inspection on request. (Code Civ. Proc. Sec. 2033.060(g)).

Requests for admission may not be combined with any other method of discovery. (Code Civ. Proc. Sec. 2033.060(h)).

3. Declaration for additional discovery

In order to serve more than 35 requests for admissions, the proponent must attach a Declaration for Additional Discovery, containing substantially the following text:

DECLARATION FOR ADDITIONAL DISCOVERY

I, __________, declare:

1. I am (a party to this action or proceeding appearing in propria persona) (presently the attorney for __________, a party to this action or proceeding).

2. I am propounding to __________ the attached set of requests for admission.

3. This set of requests for admission will cause the total number of requests propounded to the party to whom they are directed to exceed the number of requests permitted by Section 2033.030 of the Code of Civil Procedure.

4. I have previously propounded a total of __________ requests for admission to this party.

5. This set of requests for admission contains a total of __________ requests.

6. I am familiar with the issues and the previous discovery conducted by all of the parties in this case.

7. I have personally examined each of the requests in this set of requests for admission.

8. This number of requests for admission is warranted under Section 2033.040 of the Code of Civil Procedure

because __________. (Here state the reasons why the complexity or the quantity of issues in the instant lawsuit warrant this number of requests for admission.)

9. None of the requests in this set of requests is being propounded for any improper purpose, such as to harass the party, or the attorney for the party, to whom it is directed, or to cause unnecessary delay or needless increase in the cost of litigation.

I declare under penalty of perjury under the laws of California that the foregoing is true and correct, and that this declaration was executed on __________.

____________(Signature)_____________
Attorney for John Doe

(Code Civ. Proc. Sec. 2033.050).

4. Service of requests

Copies of the requests for admission must be served on all parties, not just the responding party. (Code Civ. Proc. Sec. 2033.070).

5. Response to requests for admission

a. Format

The first paragraph of the response must state the name of the responding party, the requesting party, and the set number. (Code Civ. Proc. Sec. 2033.210(c)). Each answer should be set out in a separate paragraph, with paragraph numbers corresponding to the paragraph numbers of the request. The text of the request need not be repeated. (Code Civ. Proc. Sec. 2033.210(d)).

The responding party must respond separately to each request, (Code Civ. Proc. Sec. 2033.210(a)), answering the substance of each request or stating an objection to the request. (Code Civ. Proc. Sec. 2033.210(b)). The response to request for admissions must be sworn under oath. (Code Civ. Proc. Sec. 2033.210(a)).

Each answer should be as complete as the information reasonably available to the party permits. (Code Civ. Proc. Sec. 2033.220(a)).

Each answer should admit as much of the information as is true, deny the matter that is untrue, and state the matters for which the responding party lacks sufficient information to admit or deny. (Code Civ. Proc. Sec. 2033.220(b)(1)-(3)).

When responding parties state they lack sufficient information to admit or deny, they must state they made "a reasonable inquiry concerning the matter in the particular request" and that the information known or readily obtainable is insufficient to enable the party to admit or deny the matter. (Code Civ. Proc. Sec. 2033.220(c)).

The responding party must sign the responses under penalty of perjury unless they contain only objections. (Code Civ. Proc. Sec. 2033.240(a)). The attorney for the responding party must sign any responses that contain objections. (Code Civ. Proc. Sec. 2033.240(c)).

For corporations, partnerships or government agencies, an officer or agent must sign under oath on behalf of the party. If the signing officer is an attorney they waive attorney client privilege and work product protection during any subsequent discovery concerning the identity of sources of the information. (Code Civ. Proc. Sec. 2033.240(b)).

The Sacramento County Public Law Library website has a step by step guide to responding to requests for admissions, including links to a customizable template and sample response. See http://www.saclaw.org/respond-req-admissions.

b. Service of responses

Responses to requests for admission are not filed in court. (Code Civ. Proc. Sec. 2033.270(a)). The original of the responses must be served on the requesting party within 30 days of the date of service of the requests for admission, and a copy must be served on all other parties.

That deadline may be shortened or lengthened by order of the court. (Code Civ. Proc. Sec. 2033.250(a)). The parties may agree to extend the time, but the agreement must be in writing. (Code Civ. Proc. Sec. 2033.260(a)-(b)). An extension by agreement preserves the right to object. (Code Civ. Proc. Sec. 2033.260(c)). Notice of this agreement to extend the deadline must be served on all the parties. (Code Civ. Proc. Sec. 2033.260(d)).

The requesting party must retain the originals of all responses to requests for admission, with the original proof of service affixed, until after the final disposition of the case. (Code Civ. Proc. Sec. 2033.270(b)).

c. Consequences of failing to file timely and complete responses

If the responding party fails to file a timely response, he/she waives any objections including those based on privilege or work product, but on motion, the court may relieve him/her of that waiver if the party subsequently files a response and demonstrates that the failure to file a timely response was the result of mistake, inadvertence, or excusable neglect. (Code Civ. Proc. Sec. 2033.280(a)).

The requesting party may move for an order that the genuineness of any documents and the truth of any matters in the requests be deemed admitted, and monetary sanctions may be imposed. (Code Civ. Proc. Sec. 2033.280(b)). The court shall make such an order unless it finds the responding party has served a proposed response in substantial compliance with Sec. 2033.220. However the court must impose a monetary sanction on the party or attorney, or both, who failed to timely file the response. (Code Civ. Proc. Sec. 2033.280(c)).

6. Protective orders

After the requests are served the responding party may promptly move for a protective order. The motion must include a meet and confer declaration under Code Civ. Proc. Sec. 2016.040. (Code Civ. Proc. Sec. 2033.080(a)).

The court may make any order that justice requires to protect a party from unwarranted annoyance, embarrassment, oppression, or undue burden and expense. (Code Civ. Proc. Sec. 2033.080(b)). That order can specify that the requests not be answered at all, that the number is unwarranted, that the time be extended, that trade secrets or confidential information not be admitted or be admitted in a certain way, or that some or all of the answers be sealed and opened only on court order. (Code Civ. Proc. Sec. 2033.080(b)(1)-(5)).

The court shall impose a monetary sanction against any party who unsuccessfully makes or opposes a motion for a protective order unless it finds the person was substantially justified or other circumstances make a sanction unjust. (Code Civ. Proc. Sec. 2033.080(d)).

7. Motions to compel response or further response

If a party refuses to admit the genuineness of a document or the truth of a statement and the propounding party later proves the truth of the matter, the propounding party may move for an order requiring the responding party to pay the reasonable expenses incurred in proving it, including reasonable attorney's fees. (Code Civ. Proc. Sec. 2033.420(a)). The court shall make such an order unless it finds the objection was waived under Sec. 2033.290; the admission sought was not substantially important; the responding party had reasonable grounds to believe it would prevail on the issue; or there was another good reason for the failure to admit. (Code Civ. Proc. Sec. 2033.420(b)).

After receiving a response, the propounding party may move for an order compelling a further response if an answer is evasive or incomplete, or an objection is without merit or too general. (Code Civ. Proc. Sec. 2033.290(a)). A meet and confer declaration must be filed with it, stating "facts showing a reasonable and good faith attempt at an informal resolution of each issue presented by the motion." (Code Civ. Proc Sec. 2016.040 & 2033.290(b)).

Unless a motion compelling further response is filed within 45 days after service of the response (or a later date if agreed on by the parties) it is waived. (Code Civ. Proc. Sec. 2033.290(c)).

The court shall impose monetary sanctions against parties who unsuccessfully make or oppose such a motion unless it was substantially justified or other circumstances make an award unjust. (Code Civ. Proc. Sec. 2033.290(d)).

If a party fails to obey such an order, the court may order that the matters be deemed admitted, and/or impose a monetary sanction. (Code Civ. Proc. Sec. 2033.290(e)).

8. Uses and effects of requests for admission

Matters admitted pursuant to a request for admissions are conclusively established unless the court allows a withdrawal or amendment under Code Civ. Proc. Sec. 2033.300. (Code Civ. Proc. Sec. 2033.410(a)).

An admission is binding only on the party that made it, and for the pending action only. It may not be used against that party in any other proceeding. (Code Civ. Proc. Sec. 2033.410(b)).

9. Withdrawing or amending an admission

A party may withdraw or amend an admission only with leave of court, after a noticed motion served on all parties. (Code Civ. Proc. Sec. 2033.300(a)).

The court may permit withdrawal or amendment only if it determines the admission was due to mistake, inadvertence, or excusable neglect, and that the party that served the request for admissions would not be substantially prejudiced. (Code Civ. Proc. Sec. 2033.300(b)). The court may impose conditions including allowing the propounding party to pursue additional discovery relating to the withdrawn or amended admission, and may order the withdrawing party to pay the costs of the additional discovery. (Code Civ. Proc. Sec. 2033.300(c)(1)-(2)).

F. Depositions

The Sacramento County Public Law Library website has a handy guide to depositions, including links to deposition subpoena forms from the Judicial Council (SUBP-015 and SUBP-020); a downloadable customizable template for the notice of deposition; and a sample deposition notice with explanations of the features. See http://www.saclaw.org/deposition-guide.

1. Notice of deposition

Defendants may serve deposition notices at any time after being served or appearing in the action, without leave of court. (Code Civ. Proc. Sec. 2025.210(a)). Plaintiffs may serve deposition notices without leave of court beginning 20 days after service on, or appearance by, any defendant. On motion, the court may allow service on an earlier date. (Code Civ. Proc. Sec. 2025.210(b)).

The notice of deposition must state: the address where the deposition will be taken; the date and time; the name of each deponent; the name, address, and phone number of any non-party deponent; any intention to record the deposition by audio or videotape, and/or stenographically by instant visual display; any intention to use a video recording of a deposition of any expert witness at trial under Code Civ. Proc. Sec. 2025.620(d); the form in which electronically stored information is to be produced; disclosure of any contract between the noticing party or third party financing the litigation and the court reporter, and the court reporter's company; disclosure of any request by the party noticing the deposition (or third party financing the litigation) directing his/her attorney to use a particular deposition officer (court reporter). (Code Civ. Proc. Sec. 2025.220(a)).

2. Location of taking of deposition

The deposition of a natural person must be taken at a place within 75 miles of the deponent's residence, or within the county where the court is located and within 150 miles of the deponent's residence, unless the court orders otherwise. (Code Civ. Proc. Sec. 2025.250(a)).

The deposition of a corporation or organization that is a party must be taken within 75 miles of its executive or business office in California, or within the county where the case is pending and within 150 miles of that office. (Code Civ. Proc. Sec. 2025.250(b)).

The deposition of a non-party organization must be within 75 miles of the organization's principal executive or business office in California, unless the organization consents to a more distant place. (Code Civ. Proc. Sec. 2025.250(c)).

If an organization "has not designated a principal executive or business office in California" the deposition may be held either within the county where the action is pending or within 75 miles of any executive or business office of the organization in California. (Code Civ. Proc. Sec. 2025.250(d)).

If the deponent is a natural person and either a party or an officer, managing agent, director, or employee of a party the court, on motion, may allow the deposition to be further away. The motion must be accompanied by a meet and confer declaration under Code Civ. Proc. Sec. 2016.040. (Code Civ. Proc. Sec. 2025.260(a)).

The court must determine whether the interests of justice will be served by requiring a deponent's attendance at a more distant place, considering such factors as: whether the moving party selected the forum; whether the deponent will be a witness at trial; the deponent's convenience; feasibility of a deposition by written questions or another discovery method; the number of depositions conducted at a more distant place than allowed under Code Civ. Proc. Sec. 2020.250; the expense of requiring the deposition within the distance permitted under Code Civ. Proc. Sec. 2020.250; and the whereabouts of the deponent at the time the deposition is scheduled. (Code Civ. Proc. Sec. 2025.260(b)(1)-(7)).

The moving party may be ordered to advance the deponents' travel costs. (Code Civ. Proc. Sec. 2025.260(c)). The court may impose a monetary sanction on any party that unsuccessfully makes or opposes the motion to increase the travel limits for a deponent. (Code Civ. Proc. Sec. 2025.260(d)).

3. Service of deposition notice; timing

The notice of deposition must be served on the deponent as well as all of the parties who have appeared in the action. The proof of service must list the parties served. (Code Civ. Proc. Sec. 2025.240(a)).

The deposition must be scheduled at least 10 days after service of the deposition notice. (Code Civ. Proc. Sec. 2025.270(a)). But if the deponent was commanded by deposition subpoena to produce the "personal records of a consumer or employment records of an employee" the deposition must be scheduled at least 20 days after issuance of the subpoena. (Code Civ. Proc. Sec. 2025.270(c)).

The court may shorten or extend these deadlines on motion or may stay the taking of a deposition until after a motion for protective order under Code Civ. Proc. Sec. 2025.420 is decided. (Code Civ. Proc. Sec. 2025.270(d)).

4. Person most qualified deposition

When a party wants to conduct a deposition of an employee or officer of a corporation, partnership, government agency, or other organization, but does not know the name of the person who would have personal knowledge of the facts they need to elicit, they use a "person most qualified" deposition.

If the named deponent is not a natural person, but an agency, corporation, or other entity, the deposition notice must be directed to the corporation or other entity. The notice must demand that they produce the person most qualified to answer questions regarding the subject matter, describing with particularity the matters on which examination is requested. The corporation or agency will then designate and produce those "officers, directors, managing agents, employees, or agents who are most qualified to testify on its behalf as to those matters to the extent of any information known or reasonably available to the deponent." (Code Civ. Proc. Sec. 2025.230).

The Sacramento County Public Law Library website guide to depositions, includes in its sample notice of deposition instructions on how to draft the notice of deposition for a "person most qualified" deposition. See http://www.saclaw.org/deposition-guide.

5. Manner of taking depositions

If the deposition is to be conducted stenographically by instant visual display, the court reporter should be served a copy of the deposition notice. Any offer to provide the instant display or rough draft transcripts to any party which is accepted before or at the deposition must be extended to all parties. All parties must be charged the same for the service. (Code Civ. Proc. Sec. 2025.220(a)(5)).

Depositions may be taken by telephone, videoconference, or other remote electronic means, if: notice is served with the deposition subpoena; the party taking the deposition pays all expenses; and any party may be personally present at the deposition without giving prior notice. (Cal. Rules of Court 3.1010(a)).

If a party intends to use the video deposition of an expert witness at trial under Code Civ. Proc. Sec. 2025.620, the videographer must be authorized to administer oaths, and be a person with no financial interest in the lawsuit, with no blood ties to a relative or employee of any of the parties. (Code Civ. Proc. Sec. 2025.220(a)(6)).

6. Manner of attendance at deposition

Any party may appear at a deposition by phone, videoconference, etc. if that party gives notice of appearing in that fashion and pays all the expenses for the appearance. The notice must be served by personal delivery, fax, or email at least 3 court days before the deposition. (Cal. Rules of Court 3.1010(b)).

A deponent who is a party must appear at his deposition in person. (Cal. Rules of Court 3.1010(c)). A nonparty may appear by phone with court approval. The court must find good cause and no prejudice to any party. Any party may be personally present at the deposition. (Cal. Rules of Court 3.1010(d)).

7. Compelling deponents' attendance at deposition

A deposition notice must be served on all parties, not just the deponent. (Code Civ. Proc. Sec. 2025.240).

Service of a deposition notice under Code Civ. Proc. Sec. 2025.240 is sufficient to compel the appearance of a party or a party's officer, director, managing agent, or employee, and the production of any document, electronic evidence, or tangible thing by them. (Code Civ. Proc. Sec. 2025.280(a)).

Any other person must be served a deposition subpoena under Code Civ. Proc. Sec. 2020.010 et seq. (Code Civ. Proc. Sec. 2025.280(b)). The Sacramento County Public Law Library website's guide to depositions includes links to deposition subpoena forms from the Judicial Council (SUBP-015 and SUBP-020). See https://saclaw.org/sbs-discovery-depositions-2/.

A subpoena must be personally served on the deponent. Any person over 18 who is not a party may serve subpoenas. The Code of Civil Procedure does not specifically bar parties from serving subpoenas, but it is unwise to do so. If the deponent denies proper service it may be difficult for the party/process server to convince the judge he/she is an unbiased witness. With regard to service of the summons and complaint the Code provides "[a] summons may be served by any person who is at least 18 years of age and not a party to the action." (Cal. Civ. Proc. Code § 414.10).

After serving the subpoena, the process server must complete a proof of service (Judicial Council form POS-020). Download it here: http://www.courts.ca.gov/documents/pos020.pdf.

When serving a subpoena on a non-party witness, the witness fee and mileage to and from the place of the deposition should be tendered to the witness along with the subpoena and notice of deposition. Witness fees are $35 per day for non-expert witnesses plus $0.20 per mile for every mile between the witness's home and the place of the deposition. (Gov. Code Sec. 68093). Expert witnesses who are subpoenaed must be paid their hourly rate for the number of hours they will be deposed, but they may be paid on the day of the deposition. (Code Civ. Proc. Sec. 2034.430(b)).

When a deponent is required to produce electronically stored information they must provide a means of gaining direct access to any electronically stored information that is password protected or otherwise inaccessible, or provide a translation of it into a reasonably useful form. (Code Civ. Proc. Sec. 2025.280(c)).

Where a subpoena of a nonparty directs only the production of business records for copying, the deposition subpoena serves as the notice of deposition. (Code Civ. Proc. Sec. 2025.220(b)).

The Sacramento County Public Law Library website has an excellent guide for personal service, available here http://www.saclaw.org/personal-service. When using anyone other than an experienced process server, be sure your process server consults that guide to ensure service is proper.

8. Duration of depositions

As a general rule a deposition by all counsel, other than the witness' counsel, must be limited to 7 hours, but the court may order otherwise. (Code Civ. Proc. Sec. 2025.290(a)). The parties may stipulate to a longer deposition. (Code Civ. Proc. Sec. 2025.290(b)(1)).

This limit does not apply to expert witnesses. (Code Civ. Proc. Sec. 2025.290(b)(2)).

Nor does it apply to cases designated as complex under Cal. Rule of Court 3.400, unless a physician submits a declaration saying "the deponent suffers from an illness or condition that raises substantial medical doubt of survival of the deponent beyond six months." In that case the deposition is limited to 2 days of examination by all attorneys other than his/her own attorney, totaling no more than 7 hours of testimony per day, or 14 hours total testimony. (Code Civ. Proc. Sec. 2025.290(b)(3)).

The limit also does not apply to "most qualified person" depositions under Code Civ. Proc. Sec. 2025.230. (Code Civ. Proc. Sec. 2025.290(b)(5)).

If any party appears in an action after a deposition has concluded, the new party may notice another deposition. (Code Civ. Proc. Sec. 2025.290(b)(6)).

G. Discovery from third parties

Discovery may be obtained from non-parties by oral or written depositions, and subpoenas to produce business records and things (*subpoenas duces tecum*). (Code Civ. Proc. Sec. 2020.010(a)(1)-(3)).

A deposition subpoena must be served to compel attendance at depositions by third parties. (Code Civ. Proc. Sec. 2020.010(b)).

1. Subpoenas

A deposition subpoena may compel the testimony of the deponent, or the production of business records for copying, the production of tangible things or electronic information, or any combination of the above. (Code Civ. Proc. Sec. 2020.020(a)-(c)).

Code Civ. Proc. Sec. 1985 through 1987 and Evid. Code Sec. 1560 through 1567 apply to deposition subpoenas. (Code Civ. Proc. Sec. 2020.030).

The clerk of the court issues subpoena forms, signed and sealed but otherwise blank, to be filled out by the attorney for the party. (Code Civ. Proc. Sec. 1985(c)). The attorney of record for the party may also sign and issue subpoenas, without the seal. (*Id.*)

Under Code Civ. Proc. Sec. 1985(b), a subpoena *duces tecum* issued before trial must be served with an accompanying affidavit showing good cause for the production, and specifically describing the matters or things requested, the materiality of the things to the issues in the case, and stating the witness has the desired matters or things in his/her possession or control. This affidavit is *not* required if the subpoena is not requesting documents, but only the third party's attendance at a deposition. (*Id.*)

a. Service of subpoenas

Subpoenas may be served by delivering the subpoena and tendering the applicable witness fees. (Code Civ. Proc. Sec. 1987). If it is a subpoena *duces tecum,* a copy of the supporting affidavit must be served with it, and if the materials are to be produced at a deposition, it must be attached to the notice of deposition, and served on all the parties. (Code Civ. Proc. Sec. 1987.5).

Witness and mileage fees should be tendered to the witness along with the subpoena. The witness fees and mileage fees for a deposition subpoena to a non-party are the same as witness fees to attend court hearings. But if the subpoena only requires the production of documents and things and not to appear to testify or be deposed, the only fees owed are those under Evid. Code Sec. 1563. (Code Civ. Proc. Sec. 1986.5).

See Chapter 10 Section G-2-e for the copying fees for subpoenas *duces tecum.*

If a witness hides to avoid being served, on motion and with an affidavit describing the concealment and the materiality of the witness, the court may order the Sheriff to serve the subpoena. The Sheriff may break into a building to serve it. (Code Civ. Proc. Sec. 1988). Disobedience of subpoenas is punishable to contempt. (Code Civ. Proc. Sec. 1991 – 1991.2). A witness who hides to avoid service forfeits $500 and damages to the party that served the subpoena. (Code Civ. Proc. Sec. 1992). A subpoenaed witness who fails to appear in court may be arrested. (Code Civ. Proc. Sec. 1993).

Witnesses who are prisoners in the county where the action is pending may be required to attend court proceedings. If the witness is confined outside the county, examination, if allowed, must be taken by deposition. (Code Civ. Proc. Sec. 1997).

b. Responding to subpoenas

Any person who is subpoenaed to appear at a court hearing or deposition to produce documents or other evidence may, by agreement of the requesting party, provide them at a different date. (Code Civ. Proc. Sec. 1985.1). Any failure to appear and produce the documents as agreed is punishable as a contempt of the court issuing the subpoena. Proof of the agreement to produce documents or things at a different date and the failure to appear may be made by declaration. (*Id.*)

2. Subpoenas *duces tecum*

a. Special requirements for service of subpoena

The attorney for the requesting party must sign the subpoena *duces tecum* (subpoena for documents). (Code Civ. Proc. Sec. 1985(c)).

The subpoena *duces tecum* must be accompanied by an affidavit by the attorney for the party serving the subpoena,

> showing good cause for the production of the matters and things described in the subpoena, specifying the exact matters or things desired to be produced, setting forth in full detail the materiality thereof to the issues involved in the case, and stating that the witness has the desired matters or things in his or her possession or under his or her control.

(Code Civ. Proc. Sec. 1985(b)). This affidavit is not required if the subpoena is not requesting documents, but just the third party's attendance at a deposition. (*Id.*)

b. Compliance

When a subpoena is served on the custodian of documents of a business or government agency which is not a party nor the site where the cause of action arose, compliance is sufficient if the custodian mails copies of the records to the clerk, or another person described in Code Civ. Proc. Sec. 2026.010(d), and an affidavit under Evid. Code Sec. 1561, within 15 days after receipt of the subpoena. (Evid. Code Sec. 1560(b)).

The custodian of documents shall submit with the records an affidavit stating the custodian or other witness supplying the documents is a qualified witness with the authority to certify records; that the copy is a true copy of all the records designated in the subpoena; that the records were delivered to the attorney, his/her agent, or deposition officer at the custodian's place of business; that "the records were prepared in the ordinary course of business at or near the time of the act, condition or event;" the identity of the records; and "a description of the mode of preparation of the records." (Evid. Code Sec. 1561(a)).

If the business does not have some or all of the records requested, the affidavit must so state, and the custodian must deliver the records that are available. (Evid. Code Sec. 1561(b)).

If the records are produced for inspection and copying at the custodian's place of business, an affidavit must be provided stating the copy is a true copy of all the records delivered to the attorney or court reporter for copying. (Evid. Code Sec. 1561(c)).

If more than one party serves subpoenas *duces tecum* against a witness and the custodian's personal attendance is required, the witness is deemed the witness of the party serving the first subpoena *duces tecum*. (Evid. Code Sec. 1565).

The custodian's personal attendance and the production of the original records is not required unless the requesting party states in the subpoena *duces tecum*:

> The personal attendance of the custodian or other qualified witness and the production of the original records are required by this subpoena. The procedure authorized pursuant to subdivision (b) of Section 1560, and Sections 1561 and 1562, of the Evidence Code will not be deemed sufficient compliance with this subpoena.

(Code Civ. Proc. Sec. 1564).

On motion, the court may quash a subpoena under the procedures of Code Civ. Proc. Sec. 1987.1.

c. Special rules for personal records of a consumer or employee

When the subpoena *duces tecum* demands the production of "personal records of a consumer or employment records of an employee" the consumer or employee must be served with a copy of the deposition notice, a copy of the deposition subpoena, and the notice of privacy rights specified in Code Civ. Proc. Sec. 1985.3(e) or Code Civ. Proc. Sec. 1985.6.

"Personal records" is defined as

> the original, any copy of books, documents, other writings, or electronically stored information pertaining to a consumer and which are maintained by ... a physician, dentist, ophthalmologist, optometrist, chiropractor, physical therapist, acupuncturist, podiatrist, veterinarian, veterinary hospital, veterinary clinic, pharmacist, pharmacy, hospital, medical center, clinic, radiology or MRI center, clinical or diagnostic laboratory, state or national bank, state or federal

> association [defined in Fin. Code Sec 5102], state or federal credit union, trust company, anyone authorized by this state to make or arrange loans that are secured by real property, security brokerage firm, insurance company, title insurance company, underwritten title company, escrow agent licensed pursuant to [Fin. Code Sec. 17000 et seq.] ... or exempt from licensure pursuant to [Fin. Code Sec. 17006], attorney, accountant, institution of the Farm Credit System [12 U.S. Code Sec. 2002], or telephone corporation which is a public utility , as defined in [Pub. Util. Code Sec. 216], or psychotherapist, as defined in [Evid. Code Sec. 1010], or a private or public preschool, elementary school, secondary school, or postsecondary school as described in [Educ. Code Sec. 76244].

(Code Civ. Proc. Sec. 1985.3(a)(1)).

"Consumer" is defined as:

> any individual, partnership of five or fewer persons, association, or trust which has transacted business with, or has used the services of, the witness or for whom the witness has acted as agent or fiduciary.

(Code Civ. Proc. Sec. 1985.3(a)(2)).

The "notice of privacy rights" required by Code Civ. Proc. Sec. 1985.3(e) is a notice in a font designed to call attention to the notice (e.g. bold and/or a larger font) indicating that

> (1) records about the consumer are being sought from the witness named on the subpoena; (2) if the consumer objects to the witness furnishing the records to the party seeking the records, the consumer must file papers with the court or serve a [motion under Code Civ. Proc. Sec. 1987.1 to quash or modify the subpoena *duces tecum*] prior

to the date specified for production on the subpoena; and (3) if the party who is seeking the records will not agree in writing to cancel or limit the subpoena, an attorney should be consulted about the consumer's interest in protecting his or her rights of privacy.

(Code Civ. Proc. Sec. 1985.3(e)). See Code Civ. Proc. Sec. 1987.1 for the requirements and procedures for motions to quash.

d. Responding to a subpoena *duces tecum*

The person responding to a subpoena *duces tecum* directed to a third party witness, must put the records in an envelope, seal it, and write or type, on the outside of the envelope, the title of the case, case number, name of witness, and the date of the subpoena. That sealed envelope must then be placed in another sealed envelope or wrapper and sent to the clerk of the court, if the subpoena directs attendance at court, or, if it compels attendance at a deposition, to the court reporter. (Evid. Code Sec. 1560(c)).

Alternatively, the subpoenaing party may direct the witness to make the records available for inspection and copying by the party's attorney or representative, at the witness' business address during business hours, and under reasonable conditions. When provided at least 5 business days' advance notice the witness shall designate a period of at least 6 continuous hours during which the party may inspect and copy records.

e. Witness fees for subpoenas *duces tecum*

Non-party witnesses who are served subpoenas *duces tecum* are entitled to reasonable costs including 10 cents per page for copying, 20 cents per page for copying documents on microfilm, and the actual cost of copying oversize documents. Clerical costs in locating and making the records are billed at up to $24 per hour per person, billed in 1/4 hours increments ($6 per quarter hour). Actual postage charges are reimbursable, as are actual costs charged by third party entities for the retrieval of records held offsite by that entity. (Evid. Code Sec. 1563(b)(1)).

The witness must submit an itemized statement of the charges due, and if those exceed the costs specified in Evid. Code Sec. 1563(b)(1), the witness must, upon demand, furnish a statement describing the actions justifying the cost. (Evid. Code Sec. 1563(b)(3)).

The requesting party must pay the fees due simultaneously with the delivery of the records, and the witness may withhold the records if the fees are not paid. (Evid. Code Sec. 1563(b)(2)).

The requesting party may petition the court to recover from the witness all or part of the costs paid the witness on the grounds the costs were excessive. If the court finds the costs were excessive and charged in bad faith, or were not authorized by Evid. Code Sec. 1563(b)(1), the court may order that the excess be refunded – or if not paid, excuse the requesting party from paying them. The court may also order the witness to pay the requesting party the attorney's fees and costs incurred in litigating the petition. If the court finds they were not excessive, the court shall order the requesting party to pay the witness's attorney's fees incurred in defending the petition. (Evid. Code Sec. 1563(b)(4)).

If a subpoena for business records is served and then withdrawn or quashed, the witness is entitled to reimbursement of any costs incurred in compliance up to the time he/she is notified that the subpoena is withdrawn or quashed. (Evid. Code Sec. 1563(b)(5)).

If the records are delivered to the attorney at the witness's place of business, the charges are limited to $15 plus the actual charges for retrieval of records held offsite by a third party entity. (Evid. Code Sec. 1563(b)(6)).

If the custodian is compelled to appear in a civil proceeding, the normal witness fees and mileage reimbursements apply. (Evid. Code Sec. 1563(c)).

H. Limiting discovery with a protective order

A party may move for a protective order limiting the extent or frequency of discovery. The motion must be accompanied by a meet and confer declaration under Code Civ. Proc. Sec. 2016.040. (Code Civ. Proc. Sec. 2019.030(b)).

The court may restrict the frequency or extent of discovery if it finds:

> (1) The discovery sought is unreasonably cumulative or duplicative, or is obtainable from some other source that is more convenient, less burdensome, or less expensive.
>
> (2) The selected method of discovery is unduly burdensome or expensive, taking into account the needs of the case, the amount in controversy, and the importance of the issues at stake in the litigation.

(Code Civ. Proc. Sec. 2019.030(a)(1)-(2)). The court shall impose a monetary sanction on any party who unsuccessfully makes or opposes a motion for protective order unless the party was substantially justified or other circumstances make an award unjust. (Code Civ. Proc. Sec. 2019.030(c)).

On motion for a protective order, the court shall limit the scope of discovery if it finds "the burden, expense, or intrusiveness of that discovery clearly outweighs the likelihood that the information sought will lead to the discovery of admissible evidence." (Code Civ. Proc. Sec. 2017.020(a)).

The court must impose a monetary sanction on the unsuccessful party on a motion for protective order unless it finds the party was substantially justified or other circumstances make an award unjust. (Code Civ. Proc. Sec. 2017.020(b)).

> [T]he court shall not impose sanctions on a party that fails to provide electronically stored information that has been lost, damaged, altered or overwritten as the result of a routine, good faith operation of the electronic information system.

(Code Civ. Proc. Sec. 2017.020(c)(1)). This provision does not alter any obligation to preserve discoverable information. (Code Civ. Proc. Sec. 2017.020(c)(2)).

I. Discovery objections

1. Relevance

The scope of permissible discovery is very broad, so a simple claim that the requested material is "not relevant" is not enough to avoid giving discovery of it.

To properly object on relevancy grounds the objection needs to be that the matter requested would not be admissible as evidence nor is it reasonably calculated to lead to the discovery of admissible evidence.

Unless limited by another statute or a court order,

> any party may obtain discovery regarding any matter, not privileged, that is relevant to the subject matter involved in the pending action or to the determination of any motion made in that action, if the matter either is itself admissible in evidence or appears reasonably calculated to lead to the discovery of admissible evidence. Discovery may relate to the claim or defense of the party seeking discovery or of any other party to the action. Discovery may be obtained of the identity and location of persons

having knowledge of any discoverable matter, as well as of the existence, description, nature, custody, condition, and location of any document, electronically stored information, tangible thing, or land or other property.

(Code Civ. Proc. Sec. 2017.010).

2. Exceeding statutory limit on number of requests

One common objection is that a party has exceeded the statutory limits on discovery.

In forfeiture cases where the property is worth less than $25,000, the case is a limited civil case, and the parties are limited to a total of 35 special interrogatories, documents requests and requests for admission combined.

In unlimited cases (worth $25,000 or more) there is a limit of 35 special interrogatories and 35 requests for admission not involving authenticity of documents. (There is no limit for requests for admissions involving authenticity of documents.) Any more than that requires a declaration for additional discovery.

If the propounding party fails to serve a declaration, the responding party should object under Code Civ. Proc. Sec. 2030.030(a)(1), 2030.240(b), 2033.030(a), or 2033.230(b). If the responding party believes that the declaration does not justify additional discovery he/she should object under Code Civ. Proc. Sec. 2030.040(b), 2030.090, 2033.040(b), and/or 2033.080. See Chapter 10 Sections C and E above.

3. Improper discovery requests to non-parties

Some discovery devices used by the parties in civil litigation – such as interrogatories, requests for production of documents, and requests for admission – do not apply to people and entities who are not parties to the lawsuit.

The proper process to compel testimony or production of documents from a person or entity that is not a party in the case is through a deposition subpoena. (Code Civ. Proc. Sec. 2020.010). See Chapter 10 Section G, above.

4. Privileges in general

Unless a statute creates a privilege which is applicable, no person has a privilege to refuse to be a witness, disclose any matter, or produce any document or thing. (Evid. Code Sec. 911).

If a party or witness exercises a privilege, neither the judge nor counsel may comment on it, no presumption may arise from it, and the trier of fact may not draw any unfavorable inference from it as to credibility or any issue in the proceeding. (Evid. Code Sec. 913(a)).

At the request of the party that exercises a privilege, the court

> shall instruct the jury that no presumption arises because of the exercise of the privilege and that the jury may not draw any inference therefrom as to the credibility of the witness or as to any matter at issue in the proceeding.

(Evid. Code Sec. 913(b.))

A person cannot be held in contempt for failing to disclose information claimed to be privileged unless the court has ordered him/her to disclose it. (Evid. Code Sec. 914(b)).

a. Waiver

A privilege is waived

> if any holder of the privilege, without coercion, has disclosed a significant part of the communication or has consented to disclosure made by anyone. Consent to disclosure is manifested by any statement or other conduct of the holder of the privilege indicating consent

> to the disclosure, including failure to claim the privilege in any proceeding in which the holder has legal standing and the opportunity to claim the privilege.

(Evid. Code Sec. 912(a)). However, a disclosure in confidence of a matter protected by a privilege does not waive the privilege when the disclosure is reasonably necessary for the purpose of the consultation with a lawyer, physician, human trafficking caseworker, etc. (Evid. Code Sec. 912(d)).

When two or more people are joint holders of a privilege (e.g. doctor and patient, lawyer and client, etc.) a waiver by one person of the right to claim the privilege does not affect the right of the other to claim it. Likewise, the privilege for confidential marital communications can be waived by one spouse but asserted by the other. (Evid. Code Sec. 912(b)).

A communication between persons in such a relationship does not lose its privileged character merely because it was communicated by electronic means or because persons involved in the delivery or storage of the communication may have had access to the content. (Evid. Code Sec. 917(b)).

"A disclosure that is itself privileged is not a waiver of any privilege." (Evid. Code Sec. 912(c)).

b. Proof of privilege

(i). Presumption a statement is made in confidence

A communication is presumed to have been made in confidence if the allegedly privileged matter is

> a communication made in confidence in the course of the lawyer-client, lawyer referral service-client, physician-patient, psychotherapist-patient, clergy-penitent, marital or domestic partnership, sexual assault counselor-victim,

domestic violence counselor-victim, or human trafficking caseworker-victim relationship.

(Evid. Code Sec. 917(a)). The opponent has the burden of proving it was not confidential. *Id.*

(ii). Process for determining if privilege applies

When ruling on claims of informant or official information privilege, trade secret, or attorney work product, if there is no other way to determine whether it is privileged, the court may require the information disclosed in chambers, out of the presence of all but the person claiming the privilege (and persons they want to have present). If the judge determines the information privileged no one may ever disclose what was discussed in chambers without the consent of the person asserting the privilege. (Evid. Code Sec. 915(b)).

The judge, on his/her own motion or the motion of any party, shall exclude information that is privileged if: the person from whom it is sought is not authorized to claim the privilege and no party in the case has authorization to claim the privilege. (Evid. Code Sec. 916(a)(1)-(2)).

The judge may not exclude information if instructed to release it by a person authorized to permit disclosure or if there is no person authorized to claim the privilege. (Evid. Code Sec. 916(b)(1)-(2)).

If a person claimed a privilege but the hearing officer erroneously required it to be disclosed, or the court did not exclude the privileged information as required by Evid. Code Sec. 916, that evidence is inadmissible against the holder of the privilege. (Evid. Code Sec. 919(a)). When a privilege is claimed, yet disclosure of privileged information is erroneously required by the presiding officer, the disclosure is treated as made under coercion, and the failure to disclose or to seek review of the ruling does not constitute a waiver. (Evid. Code Sec. 919(b)).

c. Appeal

A party may appeal a ruling disallowing a claim of privilege only if he is the holder of the privilege, except that a party may appeal a ruling disallowing a claim of spousal privilege raised by his/her spouse. (Evid. Code Sec. 918).

5. Privilege against self-incrimination

Too often in the past, criminal defense attorneys have advised claimants not to contest the civil forfeiture, incorrectly thinking they would be forced to give discovery that could be used against them in a criminal prosecution.

If a civil forfeiture statute truly forced claimants to choose between forfeiting their property and incriminating themselves, the statute would be unconstitutional under a long line of Supreme Court cases beginning over a century ago with *Boyd v. United States* (1886) 116 U.S. 616. That principle is still alive today.

> [W]hen a State compels testimony by threatening to inflict potent sanctions unless the constitutional privilege is surrendered, that testimony is obtained in violation of the Fifth Amendment and cannot be used against the declarant in a subsequent criminal prosecution.

(*Lefkowitz v. Cunningham* (1977) 431 U.S. 801, 805).

In reality, claimants can safely file a claim and defend the civil forfeiture case – rather than default and lose everything.

Claimants who are criminal defendants in the related criminal case can ask to have the forfeiture case postponed until the criminal case is resolved. See Chapter 9 Section C, above. Otherwise, the forfeiture litigation can go forward with the claimant carefully weighing each discovery question for potential incrimination and "taking the Fifth" where appropriate.

On all Fifth Amendment issues, plotting strategy to avoid potential self-incrimination requires a thorough analysis of the facts, including inquiry into other crimes or regulatory violations the claimant may have committed which have not been charged, but which could be charged based on the claimant's admissions.

If each discovery request is analyzed with care, the claimant can participate in civil discovery, answering one question at a time, and asserting the Fifth Amendment privilege whenever he/she "reasonably believes that his disclosures could be used in a criminal prosecution, or could lead to other evidence that could be used in that manner." (*Doe v. Glanzer* (9th Cir. 2000) 232 F.3d 1258, 1263).

Asserting the Fifth Amendment does have consequences, however. See Chapter 10 Section I-5-h below.

a. Elements of the privilege

By defining the scope of the privilege as applying "to the extent that such privilege exists under the [U.S. or California] Constitution," (Evid. Code Sec. 940), the statute incorporates case law defining the constitutional requirements and boundaries of the Fifth Amendment privilege.

For the Fifth Amendment privilege to apply, the witness must be: (1) compelled, (2) to make a testimonial statement, (3) which is incriminating to the witness.

(i). Compelled

> "The Fifth Amendment privilege is not ordinarily self-executing and must be affirmatively claimed by a person whenever self-incrimination is threatened." *United States v. Jenkins,* 785 F.2d 1387, 1393 (9th Cir.1986) "An individual may lose the benefit of the privilege inadvertently, without a knowing and intelligent waiver." *United States v. Scrivner,* 167 F.3d 525, 531 (9th Cir. 1999),

> quoting *United States v. Jenkins*, 785 F.2d 1387, 1393 (9th Cir.1986). Consequently, a valid Fifth Amendment claim must prove that the defendant was compelled to make self-incriminating statements.

(*Lefkowitz v. Cunningham* (1977) 431 U.S. 801, 805).

> The Supreme Court uses the voluntariness test to determine whether a statement was compelled. *Schneckloth v. Bustamonte*, 412 U.S. 218, 225 (1973). The voluntariness test asks whether "the confession [is] the product of an essentially free and unconstrained choice by its maker." *Culombe v. Connecticut*, 367 U.S. 568, 602 (1961). If the statement is essentially freely given, then it may be used against the defendant. *Id.* The Supreme Court looks at the totality of the circumstances to determine whether a confession was made "freely, voluntarily and without compulsion or inducement of any sort." *Haynes v. Washington*, 373 U.S. 503, 513 (1963), quoting *Wilson v. United States*, 162 U.S. 613, 623 (1896). Where a state "compels testimony by threatening to inflict potent sanctions unless the constitutional privilege is surrendered that testimony is obtained in violation of the Fifth Amendment." *United States v. Anderson*, 79 F.3d 1522, 1526 (9th Cir.1996), quoting *Lefkowitz v. Cunningham*, 431 U.S. 801, 805, 97 S.Ct. 2132, 53 L.Ed.2d 1 (1977). The key test is "whether the accused was deprived of his 'free choice to admit, to deny, or to refuse to answer.'" *Garrity v. New Jersey*, 385 U.S. 493, 496 (1967), quoting *Lisenba v. People of State of California*, 314 U.S. 219, 241 (1941). Coercion is not limited to imprisonment or fine, but includes the "imposition of any sanction which makes assertion of the Fifth Amendment privilege 'costly.'"

(*United States v. Scrivner*, 167 F.3d 525, 531-32 (9th Cir. 1999)).

(ii.) Testimonial

> [I]n order to be testimonial, an accused's communication must itself, explicitly or implicitly, relate a factual assertion or disclose information. Only then is a person compelled to be a 'witness' against himself.

(*Doe v. United States* (1988) 487 U.S. 201, 210).

Because "the Fifth Amendment prohibits 'compelling a person to give *testimony*' that incriminates him," *Braswell v. United States* (1988) 487 U.S. 99, 103, quoting *Fisher v. United States* (1976) 425 U.S. 391, 409 (1976) (emphasis added), the contents of records are usually not protected, although the person having custody of the records may implicitly make a testimonial statement by turning over the records. See Chapter 10 Section I-5-c, below.

(iii). Incriminating

The privilege against self-incrimination applies to any request for discovery where the claimant reasonably believes that his disclosures could be used in a criminal prosecution, or could lead to other evidence that could be used in that manner.

It is not necessary that the privileged matter relate to the charges in the parallel criminal case. It is not even necessary that there be criminal charges pending.

> [T]he 'privilege against self-incrimination does not depend upon the likelihood, but upon the possibility of prosecution' and also covers those circumstances where the disclosures would not be directly incriminating, but could provide an indirect link to incriminating evidence. The only way the privilege can be asserted is on a question-by-question basis, and thus as to each question asked, the party has to decide whether or not to raise his Fifth Amendment right.

(*Doe v. Glanzer* (9th Cir. 2000) 232 F.3d 1258, 1263, quoting *United Liquor Co. v. Gard (In re Seper)* (9th Cir. 1983) 705 F.2d 1499, 1501)).

> The Supreme Court has held that the Fifth Amendment not only protects against forcing persons to testify against themselves at trial but also protects them when the answers may incriminate the person in future trials. *Minnesota v. Murphy,* 465 U.S. 420, 426 (1984). Although civil in nature, Fifth Amendment protections apply to forfeiture proceedings. *United States v. Scrivner,* 167 F.3d 525, 531 (9th Cir. 1999), citing *United States v. United States Coin and Currency,* 401 U.S. 715, 718 (1971); *United States v. $84,740.00 Currency,* 981 F.2d 1110, 1114 (9th Cir.1992); *United States v. One 1985 Mercedes,* 917 F.2d 415, 419 (9th Cir.1990).
>
> In order to invoke Fifth Amendment protection, the claimant must be confronted with the "substantial and real, and not merely trifling or imaginary, hazards of incrimination." *United States v. Apfelbaum* (1980) 445 U.S. 115, 128.

(*United States v. Scrivner* (9th Cir. 1999) 167 F.3d 525, 531).

"[W]hen a witness' response will raise no fear of criminal penalty, there is no protection for testimonial privacy at all." (*United States v. Balsys* (1998) 524 U.S. 666, 692). The statement must be one "that the witness reasonably believes could be used in a criminal prosecution or could lead to other evidence that might be so used." (*Kastigar v. United States* (1972) 406 U.S. 441, 445).

The threat of prosecution is limited to prosecutions by a state or the federal government - the threat of prosecution by a foreign government does not give rise to a Fifth Amendment privilege. (*United States v. Balsys* (1998) 524 U.S. 666, 672 & 698-99).

The possibility of self-incrimination includes the possibility of future prosecution for tax evasion, violation of financial transaction reporting requirements, or other possible violations of federal or state statutes and regulations.

Because deportation is not a criminal proceeding, the threat that the statement could be used in deportation proceedings – standing alone – does not rise to the level of incrimination required to trigger the privilege. (*United States v. Balsys* (1988) 524 U.S. 666, 671). Neither does the threat of a civil penalty, if the statute immunizes the speaker from criminal prosecution. (*United States v. Ward* (1980) 448 U.S. 242, 253-54).

b. Who may assert the privilege

The Fifth Amendment says

> "[n]o person . . . shall be compelled in any criminal case to be a witness against himself." Resident aliens such as Balsys are considered "persons" for purposes of the Fifth Amendment, and are entitled to the same protections under the Clause as citizens.

(*United States v. Balsys* (1998) 524 U.S. 666, 671, quoting *Kwong Hai Chew v. Colding* (1953) 344 U.S. 590, 596).

What about corporations? The U.S. Supreme Court's ruling in *Citizens United v. Federal Election Commission* (2010) 558 U.S. 310 – that corporations are "persons" with First Amendment Rights, and that freedom of speech prohibits the government from restricting the amount of money that corporations can spend on political donations – might suggest that corporations are persons with Fifth Amendment privileges as well. But so far, that is not the case. Some constitutional rights are broader than others, the Supreme Court has explained.

The U.S. Supreme Court held in *Hale v. Henkel* (1906) 201 U.S. 43, that corporations do not have a Fifth Amendment privilege against self-incrimination. The privilege against self-incrimination only applies to individuals – and not to "collective entities" such as labor unions, corporations and partnerships – no matter how small they are.

c. The privilege does not apply to documents

Although language in *Boyd v. United States* (1886) 116 U.S. 616 appeared to suggest that the Fifth Amendment privilege might prohibit compelled production of incriminating documents, later cases reject the privilege's application to documents.

> A subpoena served on a taxpayer requiring him to produce an accountant's workpapers in his possession without doubt involves substantial compulsion. But it does not compel oral testimony; nor would it ordinarily compel the taxpayer to restate, repeat, or affirm the truth of the contents of the documents sought. Therefore, the Fifth Amendment would not be violated by the fact alone that the papers on their face might incriminate the taxpayer, for the privilege protects a person only against being incriminated by his own compelled testimonial communications.

(*Fisher v. United States* (1976) 425 U.S. 391, 409).

"[T]he Fifth Amendment provides absolutely no protection for the contents of private papers of any kind." (*United States v. Doe* (1984) 465 U.S. 605, 618 (O'Connor, J. concurring)).

A separate question arises whether the compelled act of turning over business documents can have "testimonial aspects and an incriminating effect" sufficient to implicate the Fifth Amendment privilege. (*United States v. Doe* (1984) 465 U.S. 605, 612).

> Compliance with the subpoena tacitly concedes the existence of the papers demanded and their possession or control by the taxpayer. It also would indicate the taxpayer's belief that the papers are those described in the subpoena. *Curcio v. United States*, 354 U.S. 118, 125 (1957). The elements of compulsion are clearly present, but the more difficult issues are whether the tacit averments of the taxpayer are both 'testimonial' and 'incriminating' for purposes of applying the Fifth Amendment. These questions perhaps do not lend themselves to categorical answers; their resolution may instead depend on the facts and circumstances of particular cases or classes thereof.

(*Fisher v. United States* (1976) 425 U.S. 391, 410). The *Fisher* Court found that the act of turning over the taxpayer records had only a minimal testimonial value and concluded the privilege did not apply to them.

In *Doe*, which involved a sole proprietor's records, the Supreme Court concluded "[t]he act of producing the documents at issue in this case is privileged and cannot be compelled without a statutory grant of use immunity." (*United States v. Doe* (1984) 465 U.S. 605, 617). The Supreme Court relied heavily on the lower court's finding that the act of turning over the business documents by the sole proprietor was testimonial and incriminating.

That rule does not apply to corporations and collective entities such as partnerships and unincorporated associations. The custodian of records for a collective entity may not resist a subpoena for business records on the ground that the act of turning over those documents might incriminate the custodian.

> [T]he custodian of corporate or entity records holds those documents in a representative rather than a personal capacity. Artificial entities such as corporations may act only through their agents, and a custodian's assumption

> of his representative capacity leads to certain obligations, including the duty to produce corporate records on proper demand by the Government. Under those circumstances, the custodian's act of production is not deemed a personal act, but rather an act of the corporation. Any claim of Fifth Amendment privilege asserted by the agent would be tantamount to a claim of privilege by the corporation – which of course possesses no such privilege.

(*Braswell v. United States* (1988) 487 U.S. 99, 109-110).

d. Expiration or extinguishment of the privilege

(i). Threat of criminal prosecution

The Fifth Amendment privilege only lasts so long as there is a threat of criminal prosecution.

As a general rule, once the statute of limitations for criminally prosecuting for the potential offense has expired, the privilege against self-incrimination expires. When computing the statute of limitations for the potential crime, be sure to check both state and federal statutes for the same or related offenses having the same elements, because the privilege is still alive until the threat of prosecution by any sovereign, for any offense, is extinguished.

If the criminal defendant is convicted of the offense, the privilege is extinguished. If the defendant is acquitted of the offense, the threat of criminal prosecution has evaporated, and the Fifth Amendment privilege is extinguished.

These rules have an exception.

(ii). "Same offense"

Whether a person may be prosecuted for a particular crime after a conviction or acquittal for a related offense depends on whether or not the two offenses "merge" – that is, whether both crimes, though codified in different statutes, are in essence the "same offense."

> [A] person [who] has been tried and convicted for a crime which has various incidents included in it, ... cannot be a second time tried for one of those incidents without being twice put in jeopardy for the same offence.

(*In re Nielsen* (1889) 131 U.S. 176, 188). This principle is double jeopardy. Double jeopardy also applies if the defendant is acquitted of the first offense, so long as both crimes charged are the "same offense."

The Supreme Court currently defines "same offense" using the "same-elements" test. (See *United States v. Dixon* (1993) 509 U.S. 608, which reversed *Grady v. Corbin* (1990) 495 U.S. 508 (1990) and reinstated the test of *Blockburger v. United States* (1932) 284 U.S. 299).

Under the "same-elements" test, unless *each* offense contains an element which is not also contained in the other offense, the two offenses are the "same offense" for purposes of double jeopardy analysis.

On the other hand, if only one of the two offenses contains an element which is not contained in the other, then one crime is a "lesser included offense" of the other. For example, in *Harris v. Oklahoma* (1977) 433 U.S. 682, the Court held that a subsequent prosecution for robbery with a firearm was barred because the defendant had already been tried for felony murder based on the same robbery. The Court stated:

> When as here, conviction of a greater crime, murder, cannot be had without conviction of the lesser crime, robbery with firearms, the Double Jeopardy Clause bars prosecution for the lesser crime after conviction of the greater one.

(*Harris v. Oklahoma* (1977) 433 U.S. 682, 683 (*per curiam*)).

e. Waiver of Fifth Amendment privilege

The Fifth Amendment is not self-executing. In order to enjoy the Fifth Amendment's protections, you have to assert the privilege or "take the Fifth" instead of answering the question.

If, instead of asserting the privilege, you voluntarily answer interrogatories, deposition questions, or answer questions at trial that elicit incriminating testimony, you have waived the privilege.

Only persons subjected to "custodial interrogation" are entitled to warnings that anything they say may be used against them – civil discovery devices do not require *Miranda* warnings. (*Miranda v. Arizona* (1966) 384 U.S. 436).

As the Supreme Court explained, the Fifth Amendment

> does not automatically preclude self-incrimination, whether spontaneous or in response to questions put by government officials. "It does not preclude a witness from testifying voluntarily in matters which may incriminate him," *United States v. Monia*, 317 U.S. 424, 427 (1943).for "those competent and free-willed to do so may give evidence against the whole world, themselves included." *United States v. Kimball*, 117 F. 156, 163 (S.D.N.Y. 1902); *Miranda v. Arizona*, 384 U.S. 436, 478 (1966); *Michigan v. Tucker*, 417 U.S. 433 (1974); and *Hoffa v. United States*, 385 U.S. 293 (1966). Indeed, far from being prohibited by the Constitution, admissions of guilt by wrongdoers, if not

> coerced, are inherently desirable. In addition to guaranteeing the right to remain silent unless immunity is granted, the Fifth Amendment proscribes only self-incrimination obtained by a "genuine compulsion of testimony." *Michigan v. Tucker*, 417 U.S. 433, 440 (1974). Absent some officially coerced self-accusation, the Fifth Amendment privilege is not violated by even the most damning admissions.

(*United States v. Washington* (1977) 431 U.S. 181, 186-87).

A claimant who takes the stand in his civil forfeiture case opens the door for cross-examination, and may have to assert the Fifth Amendment in front of the jury. Although a prosecutor who calls a witness to the stand in a criminal trial and intentionally forces the witness to assert the privilege against self-incrimination in front of the jury commits misconduct which usually results in a mistrial, courts are not required to declare a mistrial when the prosecutor's cross-examination of a defense witness (or forfeiture claimant) results in the invocation of the privilege. (See *United States v. $141,770* (8th Cir. 1998) 157 F.3d 600, 606-07; *United States v. Ornelas-Rodriguez* (5th Cir. 1994) 12 F.3d 1339, 1348).

f. Prosecutors can negate privilege by granting immunity

If a prosecutor really wants to get an answer to a question for which the defendant or claimant is asserting a Fifth Amendment privilege, he/she can negate the privilege by granting immunity from prosecution.

(i). Use immunity vs. transactional immunity

There are two kinds of immunity — "transactional" immunity and "use" immunity.

> [T]ransactional immunity... immunizes... witnesses from prosecution for any transaction about which they testify. The more limited use immunity... would permit the State to prosecute [the witness] for any crime of which he may be guilty..., provided only that his own compelled testimony is not used to convict him. Once proper use immunity is granted, the State may use its contempt powers to compel testimony..., without forfeiting the opportunity to prosecute the witness on the basis of evidence derived from other sources.

(*Lefkowitz v. Cunningham* (1977) 431 U.S. 801, 809).

The federal "use immunity" statutes 18 U.S.C. Sec. 6002 and 6003 allow federal prosecutors to force a witness to answer questions despite assertion of a Fifth Amendment privilege. In exchange, the immunity agreement prohibits the government from using the compelled testimony, and its fruits, in any criminal prosecution of the witness.

> Testimony obtained pursuant to a grant of statutory use immunity may be used neither directly nor derivatively. And "[o]ne raising a claim under [the federal immunity] statute need only show that he testified under a grant of immunity in order to shift to the government the heavy burden of proving that all of the evidence it proposes to use was derived from legitimate independent sources." Even in cases where the Government does not employ the immunized testimony for any purpose – direct or derivative – against the witness, the Government's inability to meet the "heavy burden" it bears may result in the preclusion of crucial evidence that was obtained legitimately.

(*Braswell v. United States* (1988) 487 U.S. 99, 117).

The U.S. Supreme Court has upheld the federal "use and derivative use" immunity statute 18 U.S.C. § 6002 against a challenge that transactional immunity is required to overcome the Fifth Amendment privilege. (*Kastigar v. United States* (1972) 406 U.S. 441, 449-62).

> One raising a claim under this [federal] statute need only show that he testified under a grant of immunity in order to shift to the government the heavy burden of proving that all of the evidence it proposes to use was derived from legitimate independent sources.

(*Kastigar v. United States* (1972) 406 U.S. 441, 461-62).

(ii). California immunity statute

Under California law, the process of granting immunity to compel a person to answer questions despite an assertion of the Fifth Amendment privilege is governed by Pen. Code Sec. 1324. That statute by its terms applies only in felony proceedings or any investigation or proceeding before the grand jury for a felony offense. However, Pen. Code Sec. 1324.1 provides similar process for misdemeanor offenses.

If a person refuses to answer questions or produce evidence, the district attorney or other prosecuting agency must request, in writing, that the court order that person to answer the question or produce the evidence. The court will then set a hearing and order the person to show cause why they should not answer the question.

> [T]he court shall order the question answered or the evidence produced unless it finds that to do so would be clearly contrary to the public interest, or could subject the witness to a criminal prosecution in another jurisdiction.

(Pen. Code Sec. 1324).

> If the court orders the person to answer,
>
> no testimony or other information compelled under the order or any information directly or indirectly derived from the testimony or other information may be used against the witness in any criminal case.

(Pen. Code Sec. 1324).

This statute, however, does not preclude prosecutors from granting immunity in other situations.

> Nothing in this section shall prohibit the district attorney or any other prosecuting agency from requesting an order granting use immunity or transactional immunity to a witness compelled to give testimony or produce evidence.

(Pen. Code Sec. 1324).

Pen. Code Sec. 1324.1 applies the process of Pen. Code Sec. 1324 to misdemeanors.

People v. Superior Court (Perry) (1989) 213 Cal.App.3d 536, 541 addressed the question of whether the prosecutor has the unilateral right to grant immunity and force a witness to answer a question when the witness refuses to accept a grant of use immunity. Without complying with Pen. Code Sec. 1324, the prosecutor had offered use immunity to the witness. The court held that where immunity is ordered by the court it must be accompanied by a grant of transactional immunity.

More recently the California Supreme Court refused to force immunity to a public employee before his agency forced him to rely on the Fifth Amendment to refuse to answer questions about his job performance during an internal disciplinary investigation.

> The state and federal self-incrimination clauses say one cannot be made an involuntary witness against himself, or herself, *in a criminal proceeding*. Thus, they do not prohibit officially compelled admissions of wrongdoing as such. They only forbid the criminal use of such statements against the declarant. Constitutionally based prophylactic rules, such as a prior-immunity requirement in some cases, have arisen to protect the core privilege, but the right against self-incrimination is not itself violated until statements obtained by compulsion are used in criminal proceedings against the person from whom the statements were obtained.
>
> As the high court has made clear, the Constitution affords a public employee no right to refuse to account for his or her job performance, or to avoid dismissal as punishment for such a refusal. It simply forbids use of the compelled statements, or the fruits thereof, in a criminal prosecution against the employee.

(*Spielbauer v. County of Santa Clara* (2009) 45 Cal.4th 704, 727) (internal citations omitted).

(iii). Applicability of a grant of immunity to another sovereign

"The information given in response to a grant of immunity may well be more reliable than information beaten from a helpless defendant, but it is no less compelled." (*New Jersey v. Portash* (1979) 440 U.S. 450, 459). For that reason, a grant of immunity by one sovereign has the same effect another sovereign:

> Once a defendant demonstrates that he has testified, under a state grant of immunity, to matters related to the federal prosecution, the federal authorities have the burden of showing that their evidence is not tainted by

> establishing that they had an independent, legitimate source for the disputed evidence. This burden of proof, which we reaffirm as appropriate, is not limited to a negation of taint; rather, it imposes on the prosecution the affirmative duty to prove that the evidence it proposes to use is derived from a legitimate source wholly independent of the compelled testimony.

(*Kastigar v. United States* (1972) 406 U.S. 441, 460 (citation omitted)).

Only certain high ranking government officials can make the decision of whether to grant a witness immunity – the court cannot force them to do so. As the Supreme Court explained:

> [I]n passing the use immunity statute, "Congress gave certain officials in the Department of Justice exclusive authority to grant immunities." *Pillsbury Co. v. Conboy*, 459 U.S. 248, 253-54 (1983). "Congress foresaw the courts as playing only a minor role in the immunizing process...." *Pillsbury Co. v. Conboy*, 459 U.S. 248, 254 n. 11 (1983). The decision to seek use immunity necessarily involves a balancing of the Government's interest in obtaining information against the risk that immunity will frustrate the Government's attempts to prosecute the subject of the investigation. *United States v. Mandujano*, 425 U.S. 564, 575 (1976) (plurality opinion). Congress expressly left this decision exclusively to the Justice Department.

(*United States v. Doe* (1984), 465 U.S. 605, 616-17).

A grant of immunity coextensive with the Fifth Amendment privilege overcomes the privilege, (*Kastigar v. United States* (1972) 406 U.S. 441, 448), and the immunized witnesses is forced to answer the questions, or be jailed for contempt until they comply.

A proposed immunity letter which reserved the right to use the testimony indirectly, "through 'fruits' evidence derived from it, in a future prosecution," is not coextensive with the Fifth Amendment, and the witness cannot be forced to testify. (*United States v. Yerardi* (1st Cir. 1999) 192 F.3d 14, 20-21).

Immunized testimony cannot be used to impeach a defendant's testimony at trial. (*New Jersey v. Portash* (1979) 440 U.S. 450, 458-59).

g. When filing a claim would be incriminating

A related issue arises when a forfeiture claimant is forced to incriminate himself in order to litigate the forfeiture case at all, such as when some of the seized property was contraband. It the claimant wants to file a claim for the non-contraband, the fact that it was seized from the same place as the contraband makes filing a claim incriminating.

An example of this dilemma arose in *United States v. Scrivner* (9th Cir. 1999) 167 F.3d 525, 531. There, numerous items, including a machine gun and silencer (both contraband), were seized from the forfeiture claimant, who was forced to file a verified claim (implicitly admitting ownership of all the items) or lose his right to contest civil forfeiture of all of the seized property. Noting that "Scrivner could not have protected his property by refusing to submit a claim... [and] could not have asserted his Fifth Amendment right and asked the court to stay the forfeiture proceedings" without forcibly incriminating himself by filing the claim, the Ninth Circuit ruled the civil forfeiture claim must be suppressed as evidence. Any incriminating statement Scrivner implicitly made by claiming his non-contraband property could not be used against Scrivner in a later-filed criminal prosecution for possession of the machine gun and silencer. The proper remedy, the Ninth Circuit held, was to bar the government from introducing the verified claim against the claimant in the subsequent criminal case.

When a forfeiture claimant is compelled to waive his Fifth Amendment privilege or automatically suffer a "potent sanction" - "that testimony is obtained in violation of the Fifth Amendment and cannot be used against the declarant in a subsequent criminal prosecution." (*Lefkowitz v. Cunningham* (1977) 431 U.S. 801, 805).

(i). Between a rock and a whirlpool

This dilemma is called "between a rock and a whirlpool."

Under this principle, the Supreme Court has suppressed incriminating statements made under statutes requiring a person to waive the privilege or lose his/her job, or the ability to contract with the state, or the right to run for public office, or require him/her to surrender a bar license. (See *Gardner v. Broderick* (1968) 392 U.S. 273; *Garrity v. New Jersey* (1967) 385 U.S. 493, 496-97; *Slochower v. Board of Higher Educ. of City of New York* (1956) 350 U.S. 551, 557-58; *Lefkowitz v. Turley* (1983) 414 U.S. 70).

> Where the choice is "between the rock and the whirlpool," duress is inherent in deciding to "waive" one or the other. "It always is for the interest of a party under duress to choose the lesser of two evils. But the fact that a choice was made according to interest does not exclude duress. It is the characteristic of duress properly so called."

(*Garrity v. New Jersey* (1967) 385 U.S. 493, 498, quoting *Union Pacific R.R. Co. v. Public Service Commission* (1918) 248 U.S. 67, 70).

California forfeiture law solved the problem of claims that could be incriminating by providing that a verified claim is not admissible in a criminal case. (Health & Saf. Code Sec. 11488.5(c)(1)).

(ii). Sanction must be automatic

For the "between a rock and a whirlpool" rule to apply, the "potent sanction" must be automatic.

If invoking the privilege against self-incrimination merely makes it more difficult to win the civil forfeiture case, that does not force the claimant to give up one constitutional right to preserve the other.

It would have been a different issue entirely if the incriminating statements Scrivner were made arose in answering interrogatories, instead of the verified claim. A verified claim *must* be filed in order for the claimant to have standing to defend the forfeiture.

> Scrivner could not have protected his property by refusing to submit a claim.... Moreover, Scrivner could not have asserted his Fifth Amendment right and asked the court to stay the forfeiture proceedings.

(*United States v. Scrivner* (9th Cir. 1999) 167 F.3d 525, 534).

In contrast, a claimant is not compelled to answer interrogatories that would incriminate him – he can assert the privilege in objections instead of answering the incriminating questions. In *United States v. Kordel* (1970) 397 U.S. 1, 3-4, the U.S. Supreme Court noted that the FDA forfeiture claimants were on notice that they might be indicted when they voluntarily answered the interrogatories, thereby waiving their Fifth Amendment rights when they voluntarily answered.

h. Consequences of asserting the Fifth Amendment

(i). The privilege is a shield, not a sword

The Supreme Court has held that the Fifth Amendment can be used as a shield, but not as a sword:

> [W]hile the assertion of the Fifth Amendment privilege against compulsory self-incrimination may be a valid ground upon which a witness ... declines to answer

> questions, it has never been thought to be in itself a substitute for evidence that would assist in meeting a burden of production. We think the view of the Court of Appeals [that asserting the privilege against self-incrimination satisfies the claimant's burden of proof] would convert the privilege from the shield against compulsory self-incrimination which it was intended to be into a sword whereby a claimant asserting the privilege would be freed from adducing proof in support of a burden which would otherwise have been his. None of our cases support this view.

(*United States v. Rylander* (1983) 460 U.S. 752, 758).

"A party who asserts the privilege against self-incrimination must bear the consequence of lack of evidence." (*United States v. Taylor* (7th Cir. 1992) 975 F.2d 402, 404). "The burden was on [the claimant] to prove that he had standing, and he could not avoid meeting this burden by claiming a Fifth Amendment privilege." (*Mercado v. U.S. Customs* (2nd Cir. 1989) 873 F.2d 641, 644, citing *Baker v. United States* (9th Cir. 1983) 722 F.2d 517, 518-19).

Claimants may assert the privilege on issues relating to any of the elements of the forfeiture statute, and the government will have to prove its case with other evidence – beyond a reasonable doubt under some forfeiture statutes (e.g. Health & Saf. Code Sec. 11488.4 (drug statute), Fin. Code Sec. 5322 (banking offenses), Pen. Code Sec. 186.5 (criminal profiteering)). Because of the government's stiff burden of proof, claimants have a chance of defeating the forfeiture on the merits even while asserting the Fifth Amendment privilege.

For affirmative defenses, the burden of proof remains on the claimant, and the claimant is faced with a difficult choice - forego the defense or risk self-incrimination.

(ii). Adverse inferences from assertion of the privilege

In criminal cases, the "Fifth Amendment... forbids either comment by the prosecution on the accused's silence or instructions by the court that such silence is evidence of guilt." (*Griffin v. California* (1965) 380 U.S. 609, 615).

In *Baxter v. Palmigiano* (1976) 425 U.S. 308, 317-18, the Supreme Court held that, in prison disciplinary hearings, the trier of fact (the prison disciplinary board) is entitled to make a negative inference from the assertion of the Fifth Amendment privilege. This does not violate the "rock and whirlpool" principle because the penalty is not automatically imposed – the adverse inference from the person's silence is but one factor considered by the trier of fact along with other incriminating evidence. (*United States v. Stein* (1st Cir. 2000) 233 F.3d 6, 14-16).

An invocation of the Fifth Amendment "is not a substitute for relevant evidence," and the litigant who seeks to raise an inference from the assertion of the privilege is not "freed from adducing proof in support of a burden which would otherwise have been his." (*United States v. Rylander* (1983) 460 U.S. 752, 758, 761).

Case law has extended this adverse inference rule to garden variety civil cases, with some exceptions. The Ninth Circuit explained in *Doe v. Glanzer*:

> The *Baxter* holding is not a blanket rule that allows adverse inferences to be drawn from invocations of the privilege against self-incrimination under all circumstances in the civil context. Rather, lower courts interpreting *Baxter* have been uniform in suggesting that the key to the *Baxter* holding is that such adverse inference can only be drawn when independent evidence exists of the fact to which the party refuses to answer.

LaSalle Bank Lake View v. Seguban, 54 F.3d 387, 391 (7th Cir. 1995); *Peiffer v. Lebanon Sch. Dist.*, 848 F.2d 44, 46 (3d Cir. 1988). Thus, an adverse inference can be drawn when silence is countered by independent evidence of the fact being questioned, but that same inference cannot be drawn when, for example, silence is the answer to an allegation contained in a complaint. *Nat'l Acceptance Co. v. Bathalter*, 705 F.2d 924, 930 (7th Cir. 1983). In such instances, when there is no corroborating evidence to support the fact under inquiry, the proponent of the fact must come forward with evidence to support the allegation, otherwise no negative inference will be permitted.

The tension between when to allow the adverse inference, and when not to allow it, stems from the consideration that because, in a civil proceeding, "the parties are on a somewhat equal footing, one party's assertion of his constitutional right should not obliterate another party's right to a fair proceeding." *Serafino v. Hasbro, Inc.*, 82 F.3d 515, 518 (1st Cir. 1996). Thus, not allowing the negative inference to be drawn "poses substantial problems for an adverse party who is deprived of a source of information that might conceivably be determinative in a search for the truth." *Doe v. Glanzer*, 232 F.3d 1258, 1264 (9th Cir. 2000) quoting *SEC v. Graystone Nash, Inc.*, 25 F.3d 187, 190 (3d Cir.1994).

... The tension between one party's Fifth Amendment rights and the other party's right to a fair proceeding is resolved by analyzing each instance where the adverse inference was drawn, or not drawn, on a case-by-case basis under the microscope of the circumstances of that particular civil litigation. This approach allows the courts the flexibility to fashion and develop rules pertaining to

> the privilege, and leaves the door open to change. *Trammel v. United States*, 445 U.S. 40, 47 (1980). In each particular circumstance, the competing interests of the party asserting the privilege, and the party against whom the privilege is invoked must be carefully balanced. "Because the privilege is constitutionally based, the detriment to the party asserting it should be no more than is necessary to prevent unfair and unnecessary prejudice to the other side." *SEC v. Graystone Nash, Inc.*, 25 F.3d 187, 192 (3rd Cir. 1994). In that light, no negative inference can be drawn against a civil litigant's assertion of his privilege against self-incrimination unless there is a substantial need for the information and there is not another less burdensome way of obtaining that information.

(*Doe v. Glanzer* (9th Cir. 2000) 232 F.3d 1258, 1264-65).

Unlike garden variety civil litigation, in civil forfeiture cases the parties are not on an equal footing. The plaintiff in a forfeiture case is represented by the county or state prosecutor, who has the exclusive prerogative to prosecute for crimes, and can grant immunity and thereby compel testimony over an assertion of the Fifth Amendment. For that reason the Ninth Circuit has held that adverse inferences may not be drawn from exercise of the Fifth Amendment privilege in civil forfeiture cases. (*United States v. Scrivner* (1999) 167 F.3d 525, 534-35).

i. Withdrawing claim of privilege

A claimant who has invoked the Fifth Amendment privilege in response to a discovery demand is not necessarily stuck with that decision forever.

There may be a very good reason for a claimant's decision to withdraw his previously invoked privilege and take the stand in the forfeiture case. The Fifth Amendment privilege may evaporate while the civil forfeiture action is pending – such as after an acquittal or conviction or after expiration of the statute of limitations for the crime. Or the claimant may simply decide that he/she would rather take the chance of being prosecuted for the testimony rather than lose the forfeiture case by remaining silent.

Any decision to withdraw the assertion of the privilege should be made without undue delay. The court may weigh the harm to the opposing party in denying the request to waive the privilege.

> [B]ecause all parties – those who invoke the Fifth Amendment and those who oppose them – should be afforded every reasonable opportunity to litigate a civil case fully and because exercise of Fifth Amendment rights should not be made unnecessarily costly, courts, upon an appropriate motion, should seek out those ways that further the goal of permitting as much testimony as possible to be presented in the civil litigation, despite the assertion of the privilege. Thus, if there is a timely request made to the court, the court should explore all possible measures in order to "select that means which 'strikes a fair balance... and... accommodates both parties.'" *United States v. U.S. Currency*, 626 F.2d 11, 16 (6th Cir.), cert. denied 449 U.S. 993 (1980), quoting *Shaffer v. United States*, 528 F.2d 920, 922 (4th Cir. 1975). In doing this, it should give due consideration to the nature of the proceeding, how and when the privilege was invoked, and the potential for harm or prejudice to opposing parties. *Wehling v. Columbia Broadcasting System*, 608 F.2d 1084, 1088 (5th Cir.1979) (a court should "measure[ ] the relative weights of the parties' competing interests with a view toward accommodating those interests, if possible").
>
> In some instances, however, a litigant in a civil proceeding who has invoked the Fifth Amendment may not seek any accommodation from the district court, and

may instead simply ask to withdraw the privilege and testify. In other cases, a litigant may ask to give up the privilege rather than accept the accommodation that the court has offered. The district court should, in general, take a liberal view towards such applications, for withdrawal of the privilege allows adjudication based on consideration of all the material facts to occur. The court should be especially inclined to permit withdrawal of the privilege if there are no grounds for believing that opposing parties suffered undue prejudice from a litigant's later-regretted decision to invoke the Fifth Amendment. *SEC v. Graystone Nash, Inc.*, 25 F.3d 187, 190-94 (3rd Cir. 1994), *FTC v. Sharp*, 782 F.Supp. 1445, 1452-53 (D.Nev.1991) (admitting testimony when opposing party was not prejudiced by prior assertion of the privilege); *FTC v. Kitco of Nevada, Inc.*, 612 F.Supp. 1282, 1291 (D.Minn.1985) (same).

This does not mean that withdrawal of the claim of privilege should be permitted carelessly. Courts need to pay particular attention to how and when the privilege was originally invoked. Since an assertion of the Fifth Amendment is an effective way to hinder discovery and provides a convenient method for obstructing a proceeding, trial courts must be especially alert to the danger that the litigant might have invoked the privilege primarily to abuse, manipulate or gain an unfair strategic advantage over opposing parties. *SEC v. Graystone Nash, Inc.*, 25 F.3d 187, 190 (3rd Cir. 1994) (discussing "the potential for exploitation" through abusive assertions of the Fifth Amendment in civil actions). If it appears that a litigant has sought to use the Fifth Amendment to abuse or obstruct the discovery process, trial courts, to prevent prejudice to opposing parties, may adopt remedial procedures or impose sanctions. See *id*. at 190-94; see also

> *Wehling*, 608 F.2d at 1089 (stressing that courts must be "free to fashion whatever remedy is required to prevent unfairness"). In such circumstances, particularly if the litigant's request to waive comes only at the "eleventh hour" and appears to be part of a manipulative, "cat-and-mouse approach" to the litigation, a trial court may be fully entitled, for example, to bar a litigant from testifying later about matters previously hidden from discovery through an invocation of the privilege.

(*United States v. 4003-4005 5th Ave., Brooklyn* (2nd Cir. 1995) 55 F.3d 78, 83-85).

6. Attorney-client privilege

"[T]he client, whether or not a party, has a privilege to refuse to disclose, and to prevent another from disclosing, a confidential communication between client and lawyer" if the privilege is claimed by the holder of the privilege, or person authorized by the holder, or by the lawyer, unless there is no holder of the privilege in existence or if he/she has been instructed by an authorized person to permit the disclosure. A legal corporation has the same privilege as a lawyer when performing legal services with clients. (Evid. Code Sec. 954).

a. Definitions

The statute defines "confidential communication between client and lawyer" as:

> information transmitted between a client and his or her lawyer in the course of that relationship and in confidence by a means which, so far as the client is aware, discloses the information to no third persons other than those who are present to further the interest of the client in the consultation or those to whom disclosure is reasonably

> necessary for the transmission of the information or the accomplishment of the purpose for which the lawyer is consulted, and includes a legal opinion formed and the advice given by the lawyer in the course of that relationship.

(Evid. Code Sec. 952).

Lawyer is defined as "a person authorized, or reasonably believed by the client to be authorized, to practice law in any state or nation." (Evid. Code Sec. 950).

"'[C]lient' means a person who, directly or through an authorized representative, consults a lawyer for the purpose of retaining the lawyer or securing legal service or advice from him in his professional capacity, and includes an incompetent (a) who himself so consults the lawyer or (b) whose guardian or conservator so consults the lawyer in behalf of the incompetent." (Evid. Code Sec. 951).

The holder of the privilege is the client, if the client has no conservator or guardian; the conservator or guardian if the client is incompetent or an infant; the personal representative of a dead client; or the successor or other representative of a corporation, association, trust, public entity or other association that is no longer in existence. (Evid. Code Sec. 953).

b. Lawyer's duties

The lawyer who received or made the privileged communication shall claim the lawyer client privilege whenever he/she is present when disclosure is requested, so long as he/she is authorized to claim the privilege under Evid. Code Sec. 954. (Evid. Code Sec. 955).

c. Exceptions

There is no privilege if the attorney's services were sought "to enable or aid anyone to commit or plan to commit a crime or fraud," (Evid. Code Sec. 956); or when the lawyer reasonably believes the disclosure is "necessary to prevent a criminal act that the lawyer reasonably believes is likely to result in the death of, or substantial bodily harm to, an individual." (Evid. Code Sec. 956.5).

The privilege does not exist with regard to

> a communication relevant to an issue between parties all of whom claim through a deceased client, regardless of whether the claims are by testate or intestate succession, nonprobate transfer, or *inter vivos* transaction.

(Evid. Code Sec. 957).

Also not privileged are communications "relevant to an issue concerning the validity of a deed of conveyance, will, or other writing, executed by a client, now deceased, purporting to affect an interest in property." (Evid. Code Sec. 961).

No privilege exists with regard to a communication about

> the intention or competence of a client executing an attested document of which the lawyer is an attesting witness, or concerning the execution or attestation of such a document.

(Evid. Code Sec. 959).

When two or more clients consult an attorney on a matter of common interest, none of them or their successors in interest may claim a privilege to attorney client communications when they are offered in a civil proceeding between the clients and/or their successors. (Evid. Code Sec. 962).

Nor does the privilege exist "as to a communication relevant to an issue of breach, by the lawyer or by the client, of a duty arising out of the lawyer-client relationship." (Evid. Code Sec. 958).

If the client is dead, there is no attorney client privilege as to communications relevant to the client's intentions "with respect to a deed of conveyance, will, or other writing, executed by the client, purporting to affect an interest in property." (Evid. Code Sec. 960).

7. Lawyer referral service-client privilege

A client, whether or not a party, has the right to refuse to disclose confidential communications made between himself/herself and a lawyer referral service or its staff. (Evid. Code Sec. 966(a)). The privilege must be claimed by the holder of the privilege, a person authorized by him/her, or an employee of the lawyer referral service, unless they were instructed to permit disclosure. (Evid. Code Sec. 966(a)(1)-(3)).

a. Definitions

For purposes of this privilege, "client" is defined as someone who consults a lawyer referral service "for the purpose of retaining, or securing legal services or advice from, a lawyer" including an incompetent person or his/her guardian, or the conservator who consults the lawyer referral service on behalf of the incompetent person. (Evid. Code Sec. 965(a)).

"Confidential communication" means a communication by the person to the referral service outside the presence of third persons who are there to serve the client's interests, or who are reasonably necessary for the transmission of the information. (Evid. Code Sec. 965(b)).

The "holder of the privilege" means the client unless they have a guardian or conservator; the guardian or conservator; a deceased client's personal representative; or a successor or similar representative of a corporation, organization or public entity that is no longer in existence. (Evid. Code Sec. 965(c)(1)-(4)).

"Lawyer referral service" means an organization certified and operating in compliance with Bus. & Prof. Code Sec. 6155, or reasonably believed by the client to be such an entity. (Evid. Code Sec. 965(d)).

The lawyer referral service shall claim the privilege whenever communications are sought to be disclosed unless the client consents to disclosure. (Evid. Code Sec. 967).

b. Exceptions

There is no privilege if the services were sought to aid anyone in committing or planning a crime or fraud, (Evid. Code Sec. 968(a)); or if the staff person of the lawyer referral service reasonably believes that disclosure is necessary to prevent a crime that is likely to result in death or substantial bodily harm to another person. (Evid. Code Sec. 968(b)).

8. Attorney work product privilege

The work product privilege protects documents created by an attorney in the investigation and preparation of the case.

> (a) A writing that reflects an attorney's impressions, conclusions, opinions, or legal research or theories is not discoverable under any circumstances.
>
> (b) The work product of an attorney, other than a writing described in subdivision (a), is not discoverable unless the court determines that denial of discovery will unfairly prejudice the party seeking discovery in preparing that party's claim or defense or will result in an injustice.

(Code Civ. Proc. Sec. 2018.030(a)-(b)).

> The purpose of the attorney work product doctrine is to:
>
> (a) Preserve the rights of attorneys to prepare cases for trial with that degree of privacy necessary to encourage them to prepare their cases thoroughly and to investigate not only the favorable but the unfavorable aspects of those cases.
>
> (b) Prevent attorneys from taking undue advantage of their adversary's industry and efforts.

(Code Civ. Proc. Sec. 2018.020(a)-(b)).

In some circumstances the attorney's work product loses protection from discovery. Under the crime fraud exception,

> when a lawyer is suspected of knowingly participating in a crime or fraud, there is no protection of work product under this chapter in any official investigation by a law enforcement agency or proceeding or action brought by a public prosecutor in the name of the people of the State of California if the services of the lawyer were sought or obtained to enable or aid anyone to commit or plan to commit a crime or fraud.

(Code Civ. Proc. Sec. 2018.050).

The attorney may request an in camera hearing to determine if matter is privileged under the work product doctrine. (*People v. Superior Court (Laff)* (2001) 25 Cal.4th 703).

The court may not require disclosure of information for which attorney work product privilege is asserted in order to rule on the claim of privilege. (Evid. Code Sec. 915(a)).

Evid. Code Sec. 915(a) provides that if there is no other feasible means to rule on the validity of the work product claim, the court may require the information disclosed in chambers, out of the presence of everyone but the person claiming the privilege (and persons they want to have present). If the judge determines the information privileged no one may ever disclose what was discussed in chambers without the consent of the person asserting the privilege. (Evid. Code Sec. 915(b)).

9. Informant privilege and confidential official information

a. Identity of informant

A government agency has a privilege to refuse to disclose the identity of an informant who furnished evidence in confidence to a law enforcement officer if disclosing the informant's identity "is against the public interest because the necessity for preserving the confidentiality of his or her identity outweighs the necessity for disclosure in the interest of justice." (Evid. Code Sec. 1041(a)(2) and 1041(b)(1)). If the informer consented to disclosure, the privilege does not apply.

> In determining whether disclosure of the identity of the informer is against the public interest, the interest of the public entity as a party in the outcome of the proceeding shall not be considered.

(Evid. Code Sec. 1041(a)(2)). Thus, in forfeiture cases, the government's interest in forfeiting the property at stake cannot be considered in determining whether disclosing the identity of the informer is against the public interest.

The United States Supreme Court described the policy behind protecting the identity of persons providing information about crimes:

> Communications of this kind ought to receive encouragement. They are discouraged if the informer's identity is disclosed. Whether an informer is motivated

> by good citizenship, promise of leniency or prospect of pecuniary award, he will usually condition his cooperation on an assurance of anonymity—to protect himself and his family from harm, to preclude adverse social reactions and to avoid the risk of defamation or malicious prosecution actions against him. The government also has an interest in nondisclosure of the identity of its informers. Law enforcement officers often depend upon professional informers to furnish them with a flow of information about criminal activities. Revelation of the dual role played by such persons ends their usefulness to the government and discourages others from entering into a like relationship.

(*McCray v. Illinois* (1967) 386 U.S. 300, 308-309).

> It is clear that the public interest would suffer if the disclosure were compelled of the names of those citizens who inform public officers of violations of law and who assist such officers in the performance of their duty to apprehend law violators. A citizen who knows that the fact would be made public that he had disclosed such information to public officers may be loath to cooperate in the administration of justice by exercising his right and duty to make such disclosures because he would justifiably believe himself to be in danger of physical violence from those upon whom he had informed, as well as in danger of actions of slander and malicious prosecution.

(*People v. Gonzales* (1955) 136 Cal.App.2d 437, 441.)

The United States Supreme Court outlined the scope of the common law privilege to refuse disclosure of the identity of a confidential informant:

> The scope of the privilege is limited by its underlying purpose. Thus, where the disclosure of the contents of a communication will not tend to reveal the identity of an informer, the contents are not privileged. Likewise, once the identity of the informer has been disclosed ... the privilege is no longer applicable. A further limitation on the applicability of the privilege arises from the fundamental requirements of fairness. Where the disclosure of an informer's identity, or of the contents of his communication, is relevant and helpful to the defense of an accused, or is essential to a fair determination of a cause, the privilege must give way. In these situations the trial court may require disclosure and, if the Government withholds the information, dismiss the action.

(*Roviaro v. United States* (1956) 353 U.S. 53, 60-61 (footnotes omitted)).

> Whether disclosure of an informant's identity or the contents of his communication are "relevant and helpful to the defense of an accused" or "essential to a fair determination of a cause" will depend in large part on whether the informant is a potential material witness on the issue of guilt. As we explained in *People v. McShann, supra,* 50 Cal.2d at page 808: "Disclosure is frequently a problem in such cases as the present one involving violations of the narcotics laws, when the so-called informer is also a material witness on the issue of guilt. A mere informer has a limited role. 'When such a person is truly an informant he simply points the finger of suspicion toward a person who has violated the law. He puts the wheels in motion which cause the defendant to be suspected and perhaps arrested, but he plays no part in the criminal act with which the defendant is later charged.' ... His identity is ordinarily not necessary to the

defendant's case, and the privilege against disclosure properly applies. When it appears from the evidence, however, that the informer is also a material witness on the issue of guilt, his identity is relevant and may be helpful to the defendant. Nondisclosure would deprive him of a fair trial. Thus, when it appears from the evidence that the informer is a material witness on the issue of guilt and the accused seeks disclosure on cross-examination, the People must either disclose his identity or incur a dismissal. *See Roviaro v. United States, supra,* 353 U.S. at 61.

In contrast to the situation where the defendant is seeking to discover whether a confidential informant is a material witness on the issue of guilt or innocence, where the defendant merely seeks to discover the informant's identity in connection with a challenge to the legality of a search based on information furnished by the informant, a critical distinction is drawn in the case law between searches conducted pursuant to warrant and warrantless searches. It has long been the rule in California that the identity of an informant who has supplied probable cause for the issuance of a search warrant need not be disclosed where such disclosure is sought merely to aid in attacking probable cause. (*People v. Borunda* (1974) 11 Cal.3d 523, 527 [113 Cal.Rptr. 825, 522 P.2d 1]; *People v. Keener* (1961) 55 Cal.2d 714, 723 [12 Cal.Rptr. 859, 361 P.2d 587]; *Seibel,* supra, 219 Cal.App.3d at p. 1288; *People v. Greenstreet* (1990) 218 Cal.App.3d 1516, 1518 [267 Cal.Rptr. 377]; *People v. Flannery* (1985) 164 Cal.App.3d 1112, 1116-1117 [210 Cal.Rptr. 899]; *Cooper v. Superior Court* (1981) 118 Cal.App.3d 499, 508-509 [173 Cal.Rptr. 520]; 2 Witkin, Cal. Evidence (3d ed. 1986) Witnesses, § 1281, pp. 1223-1224; see also *McCray v. Illinois,* supra, 386 U.S. 300; *United*

States v. Ventresca (1965) 380 U.S. 102, 108 [13 L.Ed.2d 684, 688, 85 S.Ct. 741].)

(*People v. Hobbs* (Cal. Sup. Ct. 1994) 7 Cal.App.4th 948, 959 – 960).

b. Official information obtained in confidence

A government agency has a privilege to refuse to disclose "official information" and to prevent others from disclosing it under certain circumstances. (Evid. Code Sec. 1040(b)). "Official information" is defined as "information acquired in confidence by a public employee in the course of his or her duty and not open, or officially disclosed, to the public prior to the time the claim of privilege is made." (Evid. Code Sec. 1040(a)).

One of the circumstances giving rise to a privilege to refuse disclosure of public information is when disclosure is against the public interest "because there is a necessity for preserving the confidentiality of the information that outweighs the necessity for disclosure in the interest of justice." (Evid. Code Sec. 1040(b)(2)). In weighing whether disclosure is against the public interest, the court may not consider "the interest of the public entity as a party in the outcome of the proceeding." (Evid. Code Sec. 1040(b)(2)).

No privilege exists if the informant consented to the disclosure.

c. Police personnel records and citizen complaints

When a criminal defendant and/or forfeiture claimant alleges police misconduct or dishonesty as a part of a defense, he/she may move for discovery of prior complaints against the officer for similar misconduct. This motion is commonly called a "*Pitchess* motion" – named after the criminal case establishing the process. (*Pitchess v. Superior Court* (1974) 11 Cal.3d 531.) This process is now codified in the Evidence Code.

The party seeking discovery of police personnel records must file a written motion, and give written notice to the agency which has the records. The agency then notifies the employee. (Evid. Code Sec. 1043(a)).

The motion must identify the proceeding in which discovery is sought, the party seeking discovery, the officer whose records are sought, the agency which has custody of the records, and the time and place at which the motion will be heard, (Evid. Code Sec. 1043(b)(1)), and must describe the records or information sought. (Evid. Code Sec. 1043(b)(2)). The must be accompanied by an affidavit showing good cause for the discovery, describing the materiality of the information to the issues in the case, and stating upon reasonable belief that the agency has the records. (Evid. Code Sec. 1043(b)(3)).

If showing good cause for the discovery would reveal a claimant's strategy, the attorney may file that portion of the motion under seal, and only the judge will review it. (*Alford v. Superior Court* (2003) 29 Cal.4th 1033.) Even when filing under seal, the claimant must give the agency notice of the motion.

If the court finds the information relevant to the subject matter of the pending litigation the judge may grant access to records of complaints, investigation of complaints, or discipline imposed because of those investigations, concerning an event or transaction in which the officer participated. (Evid. Code Sec. 1045(a)).

In determining relevance the judge must examine the records in chambers and exclude from disclosure conduct occurring more than 5 years before the event that is the subject matter of the litigation. (Evid. Code Sec. 1045(b)(1)). The court must deny disclosure of the conclusions of the officer(s) investigating a complaint against an officer (Evid. Code Sec. 1045(b)(2)), and facts "that are so remote as to make disclosure of little or no practical benefit." (Evid. Code Sec. 1045(b)(3)). If the evidence sought concerns the policies or pattern of conduct of police agencies, the court must consider whether the information could be obtained from sources other than individual police personnel records. (Evid. Code Sec. 1045(c)).

Personnel records of officers who were not present during the arrest, had no contact with the party seeking disclosure, or were not present at the time the alleged misconduct occurred are not subject to disclosure. (Evid. Code Sec. 1047).

On motion by the agency which has control of the records, the court, on good cause, "may make any order which justice requires to protect the officer or agency from unnecessary annoyance, embarrassment or oppression." (Evid. Code Sec. 1045(d)). If the court permits disclosure, it must order that the records disclosed "may not be used for any purpose other than a court proceeding pursuant to applicable law."

10. Spousal privilege

a. Privilege not to testify against spouse

Unless provided otherwise by statute, a married person has a privilege not to testify against his/her spouse in any proceeding. (Evid. Code Sec. 970).

An adverse party may not call one spouse to testify against the other without the prior express consent of the spouse having the spousal privilege, unless the adverse party calling the witness does so in good faith without knowledge the parties are married. (Evid. Code Sec. 971).

The spousal privilege does not apply in criminal proceedings: (1) against spouse A involving a crime against spouse B or one of their children or relatives or cohabitants, (Evid. Code Sec. 972(e)(1)); (2) against a third party when the crime was committed during the course of a crime against spouse B, (Evid. Code Sec. 972(e)(2)); or (3) resulting from a crime committed before they were married if spouse B knew about the arrest or charges before they were married, (Evid. Code Sec. 972(f)).

b. Confidential marital communications

This privilege applies to domestic partners as well. A spouse or domestic partner

> has a privilege during the marital or domestic partnership relationship and afterwards to refuse to disclose, and to prevent another from disclosing, a communication if he or she claims the privilege and the communication was made in confidence between him or her and the other spouse while they were spouses.

(Evid. Code Sec. 980).

There is no privilege for confidential marital communications if the communication was made "to enable or aid anyone to commit or plan to commit a crime or a fraud." (Evid. Code Sec. 981). Nor does it apply "in a criminal proceeding in which the communication is offered in evidence by a defendant who is one of the spouses between whom the communication was made." (Evid. Code Sec. 987).

11. Physician patient privilege

The physician patient privilege protects "information obtained by an examination of the patient, transmitted between a patient and his physician" in confidence, in the presence of only the doctor and medical staff "or those to whom disclosure is reasonably necessary for the transmission of the information or the accomplishment of the purpose for which the physician is consulted," including any diagnosis or advice given by the physician. (Evid. Code Sec. 992).

The holder of the privilege is the patient, unless he/she has a guardian or conservator, in which the guardian or conservator is the holder of the privilege. If the patient is dead, the personal representative is the holder. (Evid. Code Sec. 993(a)-(c)).

A patient, whether or not a party, has a privilege to avoid disclosing and prevent others from disclosing confidential communications with his/her doctor. The privilege can be claimed by the holder of the privilege, the person authorized to assert the privilege by the holder, or the doctor unless the doctor is instructed otherwise by a person authorized to permit the disclosure, or there is no holder of the privilege in existence. (Evid. Code Sec. 994). The doctor who received confidential patient communications must assert the privilege if he/she is present when the communication is sought to be disclosed. (Evid. Code Sec. 995).

There is no privilege "to an issue concerning the condition of the patient" if the issue is tendered by the patient, or any party claiming through, or as a beneficiary of, the patient. (Evid. Code Sec. 996).

There is no privilege if the services of the physician were used to aid anyone to commit a crime or tort, or to escape detection after the commission of a crime or tort. (Evid. Code Sec. 997).

There is no physician patient privilege in a criminal proceeding. (Evid. Code Sec. 997).

There are other exceptions to the privilege as well, but they are unlikely to arise in a forfeiture case.

12. Psychotherapist-patient privilege

Confidential communications between a psychotherapist and his/her patient are protected by the psychotherapist-patient privilege.

The holder of the privilege (or other person authorized to claim the privilege) has the right to refuse to disclose and prevent others from disclosing confidential communications between patient and psychotherapist. (Evid. Code Sec. 1014(a)-(b)). The psychotherapist also has the right to claim the privilege unless instructed to disclose by a person authorized to permit disclosure. (Evid. Code Sec. 1014(c)).

"Holder of the privilege" means the patient, if he/she has no guardian or conservator; the guardian or conservator if the patient has one; and the personal representative if the patient is dead. (Evid. Code Sec. 1013).

"Confidential communication" is defined as:

> information, including information obtained by an examination of the patient, transmitted between a patient and his psychotherapist in the course of that relationship and in confidence by a means which, so far as the patient is aware, discloses the information to no third persons other than those who are present to further the interest of the patient in the consultation, or those to whom disclosure is reasonably necessary for the transmission of the information or the accomplishment of the purpose for which the psychotherapist is consulted, and includes a diagnosis made and the advice given by the psychotherapist in the course of that relationship.

(Evid. Code Sec. 1012).

For purposes of this privilege "patient" is defined as "a person who consults a psychotherapist or submits to an examination by a psychotherapist for the purpose of securing a diagnosis or preventive, palliative, or curative treatment of his mental or emotional condition or who submits to an examination of his mental or emotional condition for the purpose of scientific research on mental or emotional problems." (Evid. Code Sec. 1011).

Psychotherapist is defined as a person who is, or who the patient reasonably believes is, authorized to practice medicine and devotes a substantial portion of his/her time practicing psychiatry; a licensed psychologist, a licensed clinical social worker engaged in non-medical psychotherapy; a credentialed school psychologist; a licensed marriage and family therapist; a registered psychological assistance under the supervision of a licensed or board certified psychiatrist; a registered marriage and family therapist intern under supervision of a licensed marriage and family therapist; a licensed clinical social worker, or licensed physician and surgeon certified in psychiatry; a registered associate clinical social worker under supervision of one of the professionals listed in Bus. & Prof. Code Sec. 4996.23; a registered psychologist under supervision of a licensed psychologist or board certified psychiatrist; a psychological intern under supervision of a licensed psychologist or board certified psychiatrist; a trainee undergoing his/her supervised practicum; a licensed registered nurse with a master's degree in psychiatric-mental health nursing who is listed as a psychiatric-mental health nurse by the Board of Registered Nursing; an advanced practice registered nurse certified as a clinical nurse specialist and who participates in expert clinical practice in psychiatric-mental health nursing; a person rendering mental health counseling pursuant to FAM Sec. 6924; a licensed professional clinical counselor; a registered clinical counselor intern under supervision of licensed professional clinical counselor, marriage and family therapist, clinical social worker, psychologist, or physician and surgeon certified in psychiatry; or a clinical counselor trainee fulfilling his/her supervised practicum under supervision of a licensed psychologist, clinical social worker, marriage and family therapist, professional clinical counselor, or board certified psychiatrist. (Evid. Code Sec. 1010).

A communication between a patient and a licensed educational psychologist is also privileged under the psychotherapist-patient privilege. (Evid. Code Sec. 1010.5).

For purposes of this privilege "patient" is defined as

> a person who consults a psychotherapist or submits to an examination by a psychotherapist for the purpose of securing a diagnosis or preventive, palliative, or curative treatment of his mental or emotional condition or who submits to an examination of his mental or emotional condition for the purpose of scientific research on mental or emotional problems.

(Evid. Code Sec. 1011).

There is no privilege when the psychotherapist is appointed by the court to examine the patient, except when the court appointment was at the request of a defense lawyer in a criminal proceeding against the patient. (Evid. Code Sec. 1017(a)). There is no privilege when the psychotherapist is appointed by the Board of Prison Terms under Pen. Code Sec. 2960 *et seq.* (Evid. Code Sec. 1017(b)). Nor is there a privilege if the psychotherapist services were obtained to aid anyone to commit a crime or evade detection of a crime. (Evid. Code Sec. 1018).

There are many other exceptions to the psychotherapist-patient privilege but they appear unlikely to arise in forfeiture cases. (See Evid. Code Sec. 1019 – 1027).

13. Clergy-penitent privilege

"[A] penitent, whether or not a party, has a privilege to refuse to disclose, and to prevent another from disclosing, a penitential communication." (Evid. Code Sec. 1033). A member of the clergy also has a privilege to refuse to disclose penitential communications. (Evid. Code Sec. 1034).

A "penitential communication" is:

> a communication made in confidence, in the presence of no third person so far as the penitent is aware, to a

> member of the clergy who, in the course of the discipline or practice of the clergy member's church, denomination, or organization, is authorized or accustomed to hear those communications and, under the discipline or tenets of his or her church, denomination, or organization, has a duty to keep those communications secret.

(Evid. Code Sec. 1032).

14. Sexual assault counselor-victim privilege

> A victim of a sexual assault, whether or not a party, has a privilege to refuse to disclose, and to prevent another from disclosing, a confidential communication between the victim and a sexual assault counselor.

(Evid. Code Sec. 1035.8).

"Victim" is defined as "a person who consults a sexual assault counselor for the purpose of securing advice or assistance concerning a mental, physical, or emotional condition caused by a sexual assault." (Evid. Code Sec. 1035).

"Sexual assault counselor" is any person who works in an office, hospital, institution, or rape crisis center, and who has a certificate evidencing training in counseling sexual assault victims, and who meets the training qualifications outlined in Evid. Code Sec. 1035.2.

See Evid. Code Sec. 1035.6, 1035.8 and 1036 for the persons who can claim the privilege. For the definition of "sexual assault" see Evid. Code Sec. 1036.2.

This privilege is probably rare in forfeiture cases, but could arise in cases brought under the human trafficking forfeiture statute, Pen. Code Sec. 236 – 237.

15. Domestic violence counselor-victim privilege

The Domestic Violence Counselor-Victim privilege is very similar to the sexual assault counselor-victim privilege. It is unlikely to arise in forfeiture cases, so it will not be covered here. See Evid. Code Sec. 1037 – 1037.8 for the requirements of the privilege.

16. Human trafficking caseworker-victim privilege

The human trafficking caseworker-victim privilege has many of the features of the domestic violence counselor-victim privilege, but the protection of the victim's confidential communications is not as thorough.

If criminal charges are pending against the alleged perpetrator of the offense against the human trafficking victim and the court determines the probative value of the information outweighs the effect of disclosure on the victim, the counseling relationship or counseling services, the court may compel disclosure. The court may also compel disclosure if the victim is dead or not the complaining witness in the criminal action. (Evid. Code Sec. 1038.1(a)).

In ruling on the claim the court may compel the person from whom disclosure is sought to appear for a hearing in chambers, outside the hearing of all persons except the person who claims the privilege and other persons that he/she chooses to have present. (Evid. Code Sec. 1038.1(b)).

If the court determines the information is privileged neither the judge nor any other person may disclose any information revealed during the hearing without the consent of the person authorized to permit disclosure. If the court determines the information shall be disclosed it will be ordered disclosed and shared with the criminal defendant. (Evid. Code Sec. 1038.1(c)).

"Human trafficking caseworker" is defined in detail in Evid. Code Sec. 1038.2(b). "Victim" is defined in Pen. Code Sec. 236.1.

17. Tax return privilege

California recognizes a "privilege against forced disclosure of tax returns" in "civil discovery proceedings." *Schnabel v. Superior Court* (1993) 5 Cal.4th 704, 719, 720.

> The law was collected in *Weingarten v. Superior Court* (2002) 102 Cal.App.4th 268, 274 [125 Cal. Rptr. 2d 371] (*Weingarten*): "There is no recognized federal or state constitutional right to maintain the privacy of tax returns." (*See Couch v. United States* (1973) 409 U.S. 322, 336-337 [34 L. Ed. 2d 548, 93 S. Ct. 611]; *Deary v. Superior Court* (2001) 87 Cal.App.4th 1072, 1075, fn. 2, 1077-1078 [105 Cal. Rptr. 2d 132].) California courts, however, have interpreted state taxation statutes as creating a statutory privilege against disclosing tax returns. (*Schnabel v. Superior Court* (1993) 5 Cal.4th 704, 718-721 [21 Cal. Rptr. 2d 200, 854 P.2d 1117]; *Webb v. Standard Oil Co.* (1957) 49 Cal.2d 509, 513 [319 P.2d 621].) The purpose of the privilege is to encourage voluntary filing of tax returns and truthful reporting of income, and thus to facilitate tax collection. (*Webb v. Standard Oil Co., supra,* 49 Cal.2d at p. 513.)"
>
> However, as *Schnabel* held, and *Weingarten* confirmed, the "privilege is not absolute." (*Schnabel v. Superior Court, supra,* 5 Cal.4th at p. 721.) Rather, the privilege "will not be upheld" in three situations: when (1) the circumstances indicate an intentional waiver of the privilege; (2) the gravamen of the lawsuit is inconsistent with the privilege; or (3) a public policy greater than that of the confidentiality of tax returns is involved. (*Weingarten, supra,* 102 Cal.App.4th at p. 274.) This last exception is

> narrow and "applies only 'when warranted by a legislatively declared public policy.'"(*Ibid.*)

(*Li v. Yan* (2016) 247 Cal.App.4th 56, 66-67).

Li v. Yan involved judgment debtor collection proceedings against Yan, an attorney who had acted as an unlicensed attorney for the plaintiff while still a law student, and committed breaches of conflicts of interest rules, among other misconduct. After the plaintiff won a judgment, which was affirmed on appeal, Yan made various fraudulent conveyances to hide assets, and was uncooperative in providing credible financial information during judgment debtor examinations. The court found that Yan's tax return privilege was overridden by public policy, quoting *Weingarten*:

> In reaching our conclusion the trial court did not abuse its discretion, we caution against compelled disclosure of personal tax returns except in those rare instances where the public policy underlying the tax privilege is outweighed by other compelling public policies or where waiver principles apply. The fact that financial records are difficult to obtain or that a tax return would be helpful, enlightening or the most efficient way to establish financial worth is not enough. Likewise, standing alone, a finding of liability for punitive damages is insufficient. But disclosure may be ordered where a defendant has been found liable for punitive damages and the party requesting disclosure establishes (1) the defendant has refused to produce relevant nonprivileged financial records or has produced only meaningless and unreliable financial information in response to punitive damage discovery; (2) the defendant has engaged in a pattern of improperly obstructing efforts to obtain financial records through means that do not implicate the privilege and it is reasonable to assume this pattern of conduct will continue; and (3) less intrusive methods to

> obtain the financial records have been unsuccessful. Although the trial court did not specifically articulate these factors, upon reviewing the entire record before us, we are satisfied the trial court found each of these factors existed before ordering production of the tax returns.

(*Weingarten, supra,* 102 Cal.App.4th at pp. 276–277).

J. Motions to compel discovery

1. Interrogatories

Failure to respond timely to interrogatories waives all objections, including objections based on privilege or work product, but the court may relieve a party from his/her waiver it they serve a timely response and show the delay was the result of mistake, inadvertence, or excusable neglect. (Code Civ. Proc. Sec. 2030.290(a)).

If a party fails to file a timely response to interrogatories the propounding party may file a motion to compel a response. (Code Civ. Proc. Sec. 2030.290(b)).

The proponent may also move to compel if an interrogatory answer is evasive or incomplete, if an objection is too general or meritless, or if the respondent's production of documents instead of answering is unwarranted or inadequate. (Code Civ. Proc. Sec. 2030.300(a)).

The motion must be accompanied by a meet and confer declaration, showing the parties conferred in the attempt to voluntarily resolve the dispute. (Code Civ. Proc. Sec. 2016.040, 2030.300(b)).

The court shall impose a monetary sanction under Code Civ. Proc. Sec. 2023.010 et seq., on a party or attorney who unsuccessfully makes or opposes a motion to compel, unless the court finds that person was substantially justified or other circumstances make imposing sanctions unjust. (Code Civ. Proc. Sec. 2030.290(c)).

If a party fails to obey an order compelling answers, the court may impose a monetary sanction, an issue sanction, an evidence sanction, or a terminating sanction under Code Civ. Proc. Sec. 2023.010 et seq. (Code Civ. Proc. Sec. 2030.290(c)).

2. Demands for production of documents or things

Failure to file a timely response to a demand for production of documents waives all objections, including objections based on privilege or work product, but the court may relieve a party from his/her waiver it they serve a timely response and show the delay was the result of mistake, inadvertence, or excusable neglect. (Code Civ. Proc. Sec. 2031.300(a)(1)-(2)).

If a party fails to timely respond to a demand for production of documents or things, the proponent may move to compel. (Code Civ. Proc. Sec. 2031.300(b)). The propounding party may also move for an order compelling further response if the responding party serves an incomplete or evasive statement of compliance, or if a representation of inability to comply is inadequate, incomplete, or evasive; or if an objection is too general or meritless. (Code Civ. Proc. Sec. 2031.310(a)).

The court may impose monetary sanctions on any party that unsuccessfully makes or opposes a motion to compel, unless it finds the party acted with substantial justification or other circumstances make a monetary sanction unjust. If a party fails to obey an order compelling a response the court may impose an issue sanction, an evidence sanction, or a terminating sanction, and/or a monetary sanction. (Code Civ. Proc. Sec. 2031.300(c)).

The motion must set forth specific facts showing good cause justifying the discovery sought. (Code Civ. Proc. Sec. 2031.310(b)(1)).

It must be accompanied by a meet and confer declaration under Code Civ. Proc. Sec. 2016.040. (Code Civ. Proc. Sec. 2031.310(b)(2)).

The motion must be filed and served within 45 days of service of the response (or the date to which the parties have agreed in writing) or the right to compel a further response is waived. (Code Civ. Proc. Sec. 2031.310(c)).

The party opposing the motion to compel further response may object "that the information is from a source that is not reasonably accessible because of the undue burden or expense" but they have the burden of proving it. (Code Civ. Proc. Sec. 2031.310(d)). The court may nonetheless order discovery of the information if the demanding party shows good cause, subject to the limitations of Code Civ. Proc. Sec. 2031.310(g). (Code Civ. Proc. Sec. 2031.310(e)). In such cases the court may set conditions for discovery including allocating expenses of discovery. (Code Civ. Proc. Sec. 2031.310(f)).

The court shall impose a monetary sanction against a party who unsuccessfully makes or opposes a motion to compel further response unless it finds the party acted with substantial justification or other circumstances make sanctions unjust. (Code Civ. Proc. Sec. 2031.310(h)). If a party fails to obey an order compelling discovery the court may impose an issue sanction, an evidence sanction, a terminating sanction, and/or a monetary sanction. (Code Civ. Proc. Sec. 2031.310(i)).

Unless there are exceptional circumstances, a court shall not impose sanctions for failing to provide electronically stored information that has been lost, damaged, altered or overwritten as a result of a routine, good faith operation of an electronic information system. (Code Civ. Proc. Sec. 2031.300(d)(1)). This provision does not alter the obligation to preserve discoverable information. (Code Civ. Proc. Sec. 2031.300(d)(2)).

11. Motions and pretrial conference

A. General requirements for all motions

1. Deadlines

Unless court orders or specific statutes provide otherwise, all motions and supporting documents must be filed at least 16 court days before the hearing date. The method of service used may trigger a longer period. If notice is mailed to parties within California, 5 calendar days are added; if either place of mailing or address of recipient is outside California but within the U.S., add 10 calendar days; if one party is outside the U.S., add 20 calendar days; if notice is sent by fax, express mail or other overnight delivery, add 2 calendar days. (Code Civ. Proc. Sec. 1005(b)).

When computing time under the California Rules of Court, exclude the first day and include the last day unless it is a Saturday, Sunday or legal holiday. (Cal. Rule of Court Sec. 1.10(a)). When the last day is excluded, the period is extended to the next day that is not a weekend or holiday. (Cal. Rule of Court Sec. 1.10(b)). The court may extend or shorten time unless otherwise provided by law. (Cal. Rule of Court Sec. 1.10(c)).

All oppositions to motions must be filed and served at least 9 court days before the hearing. All replies must be filed and served at least 5 court days before the hearing. (Code Civ. Proc. Sec. 1005(b)).

Notice that some of these statutory provisions measure deadlines by court days and some by calendar days. Computing deadlines can be very tricky when there are intervening court holidays, so compute the deadline carefully.

2. Proof of service

When a rule requires that a document be filed and served, that means it must be served on each party's attorney, or the party himself/herself if the party is in pro per (representing himself/herself), and that it be filed with a proof of service attached. (Cal. Rule of Court Sec. 1.21(b)).

A proof of service is a declaration stating that service has been provided upon the each of the parties, and must state which party each of the attorneys is representing. (Cal. Rule of Court Sec. 1.21(c)).

A document is deemed filed on the date it is received by the clerk. (Cal. Rule of Court Sec. 1.20). When the statute provides for service by mail, service is complete when the document is mailed, but the party being served may have more time for responding to it. (Cal. Code Civil Proc. Sec. 1013).

3. Declarations

Motions that rely on assertions of fact must be supported by declarations, affidavits, and/or documentary evidence establishing each fact alleged. (See e.g. Code Civ. Proc. Sec. 437c(b)(1), 2015.5).

"The caption of a declaration must state the name of the declarant and must specifically identify the motion or other proceeding that it supports or opposes." (Cal. Rules of Court 3.1115).

Declarations made within California must either state the date and place of execution, or must state the date of execution and that it is declared under the laws of the State of California. (*People v. Superior Court* (*Plascencia)* (2002) 103 Cal.App.4th 409).

4. Meet and confer declarations

The rules require that many types of motions be accompanied by meet and confer declarations, showing the parties tried to resolve the dispute informally before resorting to the filing of a motion.

The requirements are the same for all of them. "A meet and confer declaration in support of a motion shall state facts showing a reasonable and good faith attempt at an informal resolution of each issue presented by the motion." (Code Civ. Proc. Sec. 2016.040).

5. Judicial Council forms

For many types of motions and pleadings there is a Judicial Council form that can or must be used for the motion itself. Judicial Council forms can be obtained from clerk's offices or downloaded from http://www.courts.ca.gov/forms.

Whenever a form number on the Judicial Council website is marked with an asterisk, that means the form is mandatory and must be used instead of a custom made form. (Cal. Rules of Court 1.31(a)-(b)). If the Judicial Council form is not mandatory the party may at their own option use the Judicial Council form for the motion or create their own custom motion.

6. Memorandum of points and authorities

Each motion must be accompanied by a memorandum of points and authorities setting out the legal arguments why the motion should be granted along with citations to statutes, rules or case law supporting the arguments.

a. Applicability of authorities

California provides free online access to the current California statutes at http://leginfo.legislature.ca.gov/faces/codes.xhtml.

In addition to the California statutes authorizing forfeiture for the particular triggering offense, statutes codified in the Code of Civil Procedure, Evidence Code, Government Code, and California Rules of Court may apply to any given issue. If the issue involves a person's interest in property, the statute will probably be in the Civil

Code. If the issue involves a corporate claimant, the statute will be in the Corporations Code.

If you have trouble finding what you are looking for, click the Text Search tab and run a text search using key words and phrases. Click the "select all" box to search every code.

In state court, unlike federal courts, you don't have to worry about local rules of the court and standing orders of the particular judge overriding the statute or court rule.

> The Judicial Council has preempted all local rules relating to pleadings, demurrers, ex parte applications, motions, discovery, provisional remedies, and the form and format of papers. No trial court, or any division or branch of a trial court, may enact or enforce any local rule concerning these fields. All local rules concerning these fields are null and void unless otherwise permitted or required by a statute or a rule in the California Rules of Court.

(Cal. Rules of Court Sec. 3.20). However, local rules apply too as long as they do not fall into one those categories which the Judicial Council preempted.

b. Citations to authorities

If you've ever compared the styles for citations used in state court with those used in federal court you probably noticed the elements of a citation appear in a different order.

Federal courts require the citation style used in the Bluebook: A Uniform System of Citation.

For many years California courts required the citation rules of the California Style Manual but today California courts permit citations in compliance with either the California Style Manual or the Bluebook: A Uniform System of Citation. It doesn't matter which one you use, but the same style must be used throughout the document. (Cal. Rules of Court 1.200). Many California judges still use the California Style Manual, as do all of the official reporters of state court opinions.

Download the California Style manual from http://www.sdap.org/downloads/Style-Manual.pdf. The Blue Book is copyrighted. It can be purchased on line, but beware of websites pretending to offer free downloads, some sites have malware.

To compare California Style Manual and Blue Book styles, see https://community.pepperdine.edu/law/writing-center/content/bluebook-v-california-style.pdf.

For the convenience of state court litigators, this book uses the case citation style of the California Style Manual, except that, within quotations from federal cases, the quoted matter remains in the style in which it was published.

7. Proposed order

Sometimes the rules require the moving party to submit a proposed order along with the motion, but whether or not it is required, it is wise to submit a proposed order, stating exactly what you want the judge to order. This makes it easy for the judge to just sign it, rather than have to draft an order from scratch, and the judge is more likely to grant it immediately.

Only the moving party needs to submit a proposed order.

The Sacramento County Public Law Library website has a sample order which can be found starting at page 16 of its Motions in Civil Cases guide. See http://saclaw.org/sbs-motions-in-civil-cases-2/.

8. Filing fees

All motions requiring a hearing require a $60 filing fee. (Gov. Code Sec. 70617(a)). In addition there is a fee for the court reporter of $30 for hearings lasting less than an hour, $431 for 1/2 day, and $862 for a full day. (Gov. Code Sec. 68086(a)(1)-(2)).

A $60 filing fee also applies to the following motions: motions for an order to attend a deposition more than 150 miles from deponent's residence under Code Civ. Proc. Sec. 2025.260; motions to set aside default or default judgment under Code Civ. Proc. Sec. 473.5; motions to set aside default and for leave to amend under Code Civ. Proc. Sec. 585.5; discovery motions under Code Civ. Proc. Sec. 2016.010; motions to continue the trial date; and motions for new trial. (Gov. Code Sec. 70617(a)).

Motions to continue hearings or case management conferences have a $20 filing fee. (Gov. Code Sec. 70617(c)(1)).

Motions for summary judgment or for summary adjudication require $500 filing fees. (Gov. Code Sec. 70617(d)).

Motions for change of venue require a $50 processing fee, payable to the court from which the transfer is requested (for the cost of making up the record and sending it) — plus a separate check for the uniform first paper filing fee payable to the court to which the case is to be transferred. (Gov. Code Sec. 70618).

The Uniform fee for the first paper varies from $0 to $355, depending on the value of the property being forfeited. (Health & Saf. Code Sec. 11488.5, incorporating the fees set in Gov. Code Sec. 70612). See Chapter 6 Section B-1-c above.

B. Motion to consolidate

A claimant who has several items or parcels of property seized may end up fighting separate forfeiture cases for each one. This will quickly become unmanageable as deadlines overlap, duplicate motions must be answered separately, and filing fees pile up. It is a good idea to file a motion to consolidate them as soon as possible.

The motion to consolidate must:

(A) List all named parties in each case, the names of those who have appeared, and the names of their respective attorneys of record;

(B) Contain the captions of all the cases sought to be consolidated, with the lowest numbered case shown first; and

(C) Be filed in each case sought to be consolidated.

(Cal. Rules of Court 3.350(a)(1)). Even though the motion is filed in every case to be consolidated, the motion to consolidate requires only one filing fee. (Cal. Rules of Court 3.350(a)(2)(A)). Supporting memoranda, declarations and other supporting documents are filed only in the lowest numbered case. (Cal. Rules of Court 3.350(a)(2)(A)). It must be served on all parties or their attorneys if they are represented, (Cal. Rules of Court 3.350(a)(2)(B)), and must have a proof of service. (Cal. Rules of Court 3.350(a)(2)(C)).

The lowest numbered case is the lead case. (Cal. Rules of Court 3.350(b)). Once consolidation is granted, any subsequent document must be served only in the lead case. (Cal. Rules of Court 3.350(c)).

Once they are consolidated, all subsequent filings must include the caption and case number of the lead case, followed by the case numbers of the other consolidated cases. (Cal. Rules of Court 3.350(d)).

C. Motion to suppress evidence

The Fourth Amendment exclusionary rule applies in forfeitures cases as well as criminal cases. (*Plymouth Sedan v. Pennsylvania* (1965) 380 U.S. 693).

The grounds for motions to suppress are set out in Pen. Code Sec. 1538.5(a)(1) – the same statute that governs motions for the return of property. These grounds are:

(A) the warrantless search was unreasonable;

(B) the search with a warrant was unreasonable because: (i) "the warrant was insufficient on its face," (ii) the evidence seized was not that described in the warrant, (iii) probable cause did not exist for issuance of the warrant, (iv) the method of execution of the warrant violated the federal or state constitution, or (v) any other violation of the federal or state constitution. (Pen. Code Sec. 1538.5(a)(1)(A)-(B)).

The suppression motion must be made in writing, supported by a memorandum of law, and must list the specific evidence sought to be suppressed and the factual basis and legal authorities that demonstrate why the motion should be granted. (Pen. Code Sec. 1538.5(a)(2)).

The standards for illegal search and seizure in forfeiture cases are the same standards used in criminal cases. Search and seizure law is too complex and detailed to cover in this book. Consult a treatise on search and seizure law.

The court must hold an evidentiary hearing on the suppression motion. (Pen. Code Sec. 1538.5(c)(1)). On request, witnesses may be excluded from the court until after they have testified, (Pen. Code Sec. 1538.5(c)(2)) – but the investigating officer, defense investigator, and officers having custody of a person brought to court may not be excluded. (Pen. Code Sec. 1538.5(c)(4)).

> If the motion is granted, the suppressed evidence
>
> shall not be admissible against the movant at any trial or other hearing unless further proceedings authorized by this section, Section 871.5, 1238, or 1466 are utilized by the people.

(Pen. Code Sec. 1538.5(d)).

The defendant may move to suppress at the preliminary examination in the criminal case, if he/she files and serves the motion at least 5 court days before the preliminary examination. (Pen. Code Sec. 1538.5(f)(2)). The court may grant a continuance of the preliminary examination in order to allow the defendant to file a motion to suppress if the defendant can show he/she was not aware of the evidence or the grounds for suppression before the preliminary examination. (Pen. Code Sec. 1538.5(f)(2)).

The defendant/claimant must state in his/her motion to suppress why the warrantless search was illegal.

> [W]hen the basis of a motion to suppress is a warrantless search or seizure, the requisite specificity is generally satisfied, in the first instance, if defendants simply assert the absence of a warrant and make a prima facie showing to support that assertion. Of course, if defendants have a specific, argument other than the lack of a warrant as to why a warrantless search or seizure was unreasonable, they must specify that argument as part of their motion to suppress and give the prosecution an opportunity to offer evidence on the point.

(*People v. Williams* (Cal. Sup. Ct. 1999) 20 Cal.4th 119, 83 Cal.Rptr2d 275, 282).

When a seizure is made after a warrantless entry of premises, the prosecution bears the burden of proof at the suppression hearing.

> Such an entry, of course, presumptively violates the Fourth Amendment and taints the evidence seized as a result. The presumption of unlawfulness, to be sure, can be rebutted – but the burden rests squarely on the prosecution.

(*People v. Ledesma* (Cal. Sup. Ct. 1987) 43 Cal.3d 171, 227 (internal citations omitted)).

When searches are conducted pursuant to a warrant, the defendant has the burden of proving the warrant is deficient.

> In *Franks v. Delaware* (1978) 438 U.S. 154, the United States Supreme Court held that a defendant may challenge the veracity of statements contained in an affidavit of probable cause made in support of the issuance of a search warrant. When presented with such a challenge, the lower courts must conduct an evidentiary hearing if a defendant makes a substantial showing that: (1) the affidavit contains statements that are deliberately false or were made in reckless disregard of the truth and (2) the affidavit's remaining contents, after the false statements are excised, are insufficient to justify a finding of probable cause. At the evidentiary hearing, if the statements are proved by a preponderance of the evidence to be false or reckless, they must be considered excised. If the remaining contents of the affidavit are insufficient to establish probable cause, the warrant must be voided and any evidence seized pursuant to that warrant must be suppressed. (*Id.* at pp. 155-156.)
>
> A defendant who challenges a search warrant based upon an affidavit containing omissions bears the burden of showing that the omissions were material to the determination of probable cause. (See *People v. Luttenberger* (1990) 50 Cal.3d 1, 14-15 & fn. 4 [265 Cal. Rptr.

> 690, 784 P.2d 633].) "Pursuant to [California Constitution, article I,] section 28[, subdivision] (d), materiality is evaluated by the test of *Illinois v. Gates* (1983) 462 U.S. 213 ..., which looks to the totality of the circumstances in determining whether a warrant affidavit establishes good cause for a search. [Citation.]" (*People v. Luttenberger*, supra, 50 Cal.3d 1, 23.)

(*People v. Bradford* (1997) 15 Cal.4th 1229, 1297).

Winning the suppression motion is often enough to prevent the government from meeting its burden of proof. Any drugs or other indicia of a crime found during an illegal search cannot be used to prove the property is forfeitable. "[F]orfeitability may not be proved with unconstitutionally obtained evidence." (*People v. $497,590* (1997) 58 Cal.App.4th 145, quoting *People v. Superior Court* (*Moraza)* (1989) 210 Cal.App.3d 592, 598-599).

Illegal seizure of the res (the property that is being forfeited) does not immunize the res from forfeiture. (*People v. $497,590* (1997) 58 Cal.App.4th 145. However, when the res itself was illegally seized, a successful suppression motion means the prosecution cannot rely on any evidence or inferences arising from the appearance, quantity, or other qualities of the illegally seized res. For example, if the illegally seized res is a large amount of cash, in small denominations, wrapped in bundles secured by rubber bands, with a strong odor, the prosecution can't rely on any inferences arising from the large amount of cash, small denominations, rubber bands, or the odor, to prove circumstantially that the cash was "furnished or intended to be furnished" in exchange for a controlled substance.

If the initial stop which led to the forfeiture case is declared an illegal search and seizure, any later arising "fruits" of that initial illegality – such as admissions obtained during civil discovery – may also be suppressed under the "fruit of the poisonous tree" doctrine. See Chapter 11 Section D-2, below.

D. Motion to suppress statements

1. *Miranda v. Arizona* and voluntariness

In criminal cases, when the defendant is detained and questioned in violation of *Miranda v. Arizona* (1966) 384 U.S. 436, and makes statements damaging to his/her criminal case, the statements can be suppressed as evidence. However, the *Miranda* rule does not apply to civil forfeiture cases. (*People v. $48,715* (1997) 58 Cal.App.4th 1507).

> Violation of the prophylactic rule of *Miranda v. Arizona* (1966) 384 U.S. 436 is not a violation of the Fifth Amendment; evidence resulting from a *Miranda* violation should be suppressed only with great caution. (*See Oregon v. Elstad* (1985) 470 U.S. 298, 309.) In the absence of a very persuasive reason to do so, ..., we can see no reason to expand *Miranda* into the area of civil forfeitures, where the defendant's right to counsel (*People v. $ 30,000 United States Currency* (1995) 35 Cal.App.4th 936, 943-944) and possibly other constitutional rights (*see United States v. Ursery* (1996) 518 U.S. 267 [double jeopardy]) differ markedly from those applicable in a criminal prosecution.

(*People v. $48,715* (1997) 58 Cal.App.4th 1507, 1518 fn. 10).

On the other hand, even in forfeiture cases the statements may be suppressed if they were not voluntary.

An involuntary statement is inherently untrustworthy. (*Spano v. New York* (1959) 360 U.S. 315, 320). A third party who did not make the involuntary statement may also have standing to move to suppress it. (*United States ex rel. Cunningham v. DeRobertis* (7th Cir. 1983) 719 F.2d 892, 896).

Voluntariness of a statement is determined by analysis of the totality of the circumstances. These factors are relevant: the length of time between the arrest and statement, whether the defendant knew the nature of the crime he/she was suspected of at the time of the statement, whether he/she had been advised of the right to remain silent and the right to an attorney (which would mitigate the coercion), the age and mental state of the suspect. The essential factor is coercive police conduct. No statement would be suppressed as involuntary unless it was coerced by the conduct of the police. (*Colorado v. Connelly* (1986) 479 U.S. 157).

Statements obtained through physical coercion such as a beating or similar physical violence are *per se* inadmissible. (*United States v. Jenkins* (9th Cir. 1991) 938 F.2d 934, 938).

Psychological coercion, such as a threat that a person's spouse would be arrested or their children would be taken away, may be sufficient grounds to prove a statement in response to the threat was involuntary. (*Lynumm v. Illinois* (1963) 372 U.S. 528; *Rogers v. Richmond* (1961) 365 U.S. 534).

Intense, prolonged questioning can be sufficiently coercive to render a statement involuntary, especially if the person is deprived of food or sleep. (*David v. North Carolina* (1966) 384 U.S. 737; *Reck v. Pate* (1961) 367 U.S. 433; *Ashcraft v. Tennessee* (1944) 322 U.S. 143).

2. Fruit of the poisonous tree

Statements may also be suppressed on Fourth Amendment grounds as the fruit of an illegal search and seizure, otherwise known as the "fruit of the poisonous tree."

For example, the police may not use information obtained during an illegal search to subpoena the same documents they had seen during the illegal search, or to obtain that same evidence during discovery. (*Silverthorne Lumber Co. v. United States* (1920) 251 U.S. 385).

The fruit of the poisonous tree doctrine also authorizes suppression of statements made during an illegal search and seizure.

> The exclusionary rule has traditionally barred from trial physical, tangible materials obtained either during or as a direct result of an unlawful invasion. It follows from our holding in *Silverman v. United States*, 365 U.S. 505, that the Fourth Amendment may protect against the overhearing of verbal statements as well as against the more traditional seizure of "papers and effects." Similarly, testimony as to matters observed during an unlawful invasion has been excluded in order to enforce the basic constitutional policies. *McGinnis v. United States*, 227 F.2d 598. Thus, verbal evidence which derives so immediately from an unlawful entry and an unauthorized arrest as the officers' action in the present case is no less the "fruit" of official illegality than the more common tangible fruits of the unwarranted intrusion. See *Nueslein v. District of Columbia*, 115 F.2d 690. Nor do the policies underlying the exclusionary rule invite any logical distinction between physical and verbal evidence.

(*Wong Sun v. United States* (1963) 371 U.S. 471, 485-486).

In addition to statements made during the illegal seizure, derivative evidence – that is statements or evidence discovered later, as a result of information learned during the illegal arrest or an illegal search – can be suppressed as a fruit of the poisonous tree, but there are limitations and exceptions to that doctrine.

The person moving to suppress it must have standing to challenge the initial illegal search. (*Arizona v. Hicks* (1987) 480 U.S. 321; *Segura v. United States* (1984) 468 U.S. 796; *United States v. Karo* (1984) 468 U.S. 705).

> There are three exceptions to this doctrine:
>
> Three of these exceptions involve the causal relationship between the unconstitutional act and the discovery of evidence. First, the independent source doctrine allows trial courts to admit evidence obtained in an unlawful search if officers independently acquired it from a separate, independent source. See *Murray v. United States,* 487 U. S. 533, 537, 108 S. Ct. 2529, 101 L. Ed. 2d 472 (1988). Second, the inevitable discovery doctrine allows for the admission of evidence that would have been discovered even without the unconstitutional source. See *Nix v. Williams,* 467 U. S. 431, 443-444, 104 S. Ct. 2501, 81 L. Ed. 2d 377 (1984). Third, and at issue here, is the attenuation doctrine: Evidence is admissible when the connection between unconstitutional police conduct and the evidence is remote or has been interrupted by some intervening circumstance, so that "the interest protected by the constitutional guarantee that has been violated would not be served by suppression of the evidence obtained." *Hudson* [*v. Michigan,* 547 U.S. 586, 593 (2006)].

(*Utah v. Strieff* (2016) 136 S. Ct. 2056, 2061).

An example of "attenuation" arose in *Wong Sun*. When a number of days passed between the illegal arrest and the statement the defendant made to investigators, the statement had "become so attenuated as to dissipate the taint." (*Wong Sun v. United States* (1963) 371 U.S. 471, 491).

Another exception arises when untainted evidence is obtained through an independent source, instead of merely through the illegal search and seizure. An example of this is when a person is stopped without probable cause but police immediately discover the person has an outstanding arrest warrant. (*Utah v. Strieff* (2016) 579 U.S. __, 136 S. Ct. 2056).

Inevitable discovery requires a reasonably strong possibility that the evidence would have been discovered even without the illegal seizure. (*People v. Superior Court* (*Tunch*) (1978) 80 Cal.App.3d 665, 680-681).

E. Summary judgment and summary adjudication

When a party contends that the plaintiff cannot prove a necessary element of its case, or that the defendant/claimant cannot prove a valid defense, the quickest way to resolve it is to file a motion for summary judgment.

> A party may move for summary judgment in an action or proceeding if it is contended that the action has no merit or that there is no defense to the action or proceeding.

(Code Civ. Proc. Sec. 437c(a)(1)).

> The purpose of the law of summary judgment is to provide courts with a mechanism to cut through the parties' pleadings in order to determine whether, despite their allegations, trial is in fact necessary to resolve their dispute.

(*Aguilar v. Atlantic Richfield Co.* (2001) 25 Cal.4th 826, 843).

If the court grants summary judgment, the case is over without a trial.

Motions for summary adjudication are very similar to summary judgment motions, except they resolve only some of the claims or defenses in the case, with the remainder of the issues to be resolved at trial. (Code Civ. Proc. Sec. 437c(n)(1)). They follow the same rules as summary judgment motions.

Even when summary adjudication does not obviate the need for a trial, if the court grants summary adjudication on some issues, those issues will be excluded from the trial, saving time and the expense of putting on witnesses and introducing evidence to prove those issues.

Summary adjudication of some issues often resolves the whole case without a trial. Even when it does not, once the case is cut down to size by the elimination of certain claims and defenses, the parties find they are close enough to agreement to settle the case.

1. Requirements for motions for summary judgment

Summary judgment is not a mini trial before the real trial. There are no evidentiary hearings and no ability to put on witnesses to testify about facts. The parties submit affidavits and documents establishing the facts they claim are not in dispute.

Parties moving for summary judgment must present enough evidence – through affidavits and documents – to establish a prima facie case on every element of each claim or defense for which they seek summary judgment. Parties opposing summary judgment must present evidence – through affidavits and documents – sufficient to create a factual dispute on one or more material elements of the opponent's claim or defense.

In deciding motions for summary judgment, the judge may not weigh evidence or make findings of fact, but merely determines whether there is a factual dispute on one or more material elements of a claim or defense. If there are no facts in dispute the court must apply the law and grant summary judgment.

a. Deadlines and timing

> A motion for summary judgment may be filed
>
> at any time after 60 days have elapsed since the general appearance in the action or proceeding of each party against whom the motion is directed or at any earlier time

> after the general appearance that the court, with or without notice and upon good cause shown, may direct.

(Code Civ. Proc. Sec. 437c(a)(1)).

The motion for summary judgment must be served on all parties at least 75 days before the hearing date. If it is served by mail, add 5 additional days for addresses inside California, 10 additional days for areas inside the U.S. but outside California, and 20 days if outside the U.S.

If served by fax or overnight mail, add 2 court days to the time period. (Code Civ. Proc. Sec. 437c(a)(2)).

The motion must be heard no later than 30 days before trial unless the court rules otherwise. Filing a motion for summary judgment does not extend the time for filing a responsive pleading (e.g. an answer or demurrer). (Code Civ. Proc. Sec. 437c(a)(3)).

b. Supporting papers for motions for summary judgment

Summary judgment involves a lot more paperwork than most motions. Under the 2017 California Rules of Court, Rule 3.1350(c) the motion must be include the following documents:

> (1) Notice of motion by [moving party] for summary judgment or summary adjudication or both;
>
> (2) Separate statement of undisputed material facts in support of [moving party's] motion for summary judgment or summary adjudication or both;
>
> (3) Memorandum in support of [moving party's] motion for summary judgment or summary adjudication or both;

> (4) Evidence in support of [moving party's] motion for summary judgment or summary adjudication or both; and
>
> (5) Request for judicial notice in support of [moving party's] motion for summary judgment or summary adjudication or both (if appropriate).

(Cal. Rules Ct. Rule 3.1350(c)).

Each of these component documents must be produced and organized in compliance with the local rules of the superior court where the case is brought. Links to the local rules of various courts are listed at http://www.courts.ca.gov/3027.htm.

The notice of motion and the memorandum of points and authorities use the same format used in other civil motions. If you need help with the formatting of the notice of motion or memorandum, look at the step-by-step guide for "Motions in Civil Cases" on the Sacramento County Public Law Library website (available at http://www.saclaw.org/motions-general) – but beware of differences between Sacramento County's local rules and the local rules of your court. If you are going to use that guide as a template, read your local rules again and make sure your motion conforms to your court's requirements.

(i). Supporting evidence

> The motion shall be supported by affidavits, declarations, admissions, answers to interrogatories, depositions, and matters of which judicial notice shall or may be taken.

(Code Civ. Proc. Sec. 437c(b)(1)).

The "matters for which judicial notice may be taken" are explained in Chapter 8 Section B-1-a, above.

> Supporting and opposing affidavits or declarations shall be made by a person on personal knowledge, shall set forth admissible evidence, and shall show affirmatively that the affiant is competent to testify to the matters stated in the affidavits or declarations.

(Code Civ. Proc. Sec. 437c(d)). An affidavit must be "taken before any officer authorized to administer oaths" e.g. court reporter or notary public. Code Civ. Proc. Sec. 2012.

In lieu of taking an oath before a court reporter or notary public, a declaration may be proved by an unsworn statement under penalty of perjury. The verification should recite that the witness declares it to be true under penalty of perjury. It must be signed by the witness and state the date and place in which the witness executed the declaration.

If executed in California the verification should state:

"I certify (or declare) under penalty of perjury that the foregoing is true and correct":

________________ ______________

(Date and Place) (Signature)

(Code Civ. Proc. Sec 2015.5(a)).

If executed outside California it should state:

"I certify (or declare) under penalty of perjury under the laws of the State of California that the foregoing is true and correct":

________________ ______________

(Date) (Signature)

(Code Civ. Proc. Sec 2015.5(b)).

> [A] declaration made within the State of California must either state the date and place of execution or must state the date of execution and that it is declared under the laws of the State of California.

(*Johnson v. Superior Court* (2006) 143 Cal.App.4th 297, 302 fn.3, citing Code Civ. Proc. Sec. 2015.5).

Any objections to the failure of a declaration to show it was made by a person with personal knowledge who would be competent to testify – and any objections to the admissibility of evidence submitted in support of summary judgment – must be made at the hearing or they are waived. *Id.*

(ii). Request for judicial notice

To request judicial notice of a fact you have to file a separate "request for judicial notice" as a supporting document to your motion for summary judgment.

For the substantive law on matters which may be judicial noticed, see Chapter 8 Sec. B-1-a, above.

A request for judicial notice is a separate document listing, in separate numbered paragraphs, and describing, the matters or documents for which you are requesting judicial notice. The documents must be attached as exhibits. For the format and examples see the sample on the Sacramento County Public Law Library website at http://saclaw.org/legal-forms/request-for-judicial-notice/form-request-for-judicial-notice-instructions/. To download a template in Word, see: https://saclaw.org/wp-content/uploads/2015/03/form-request-for-judicial-notice.rtf.

(iii). Statement of undisputed material facts

A motion for summary judgment or summary adjudication must also include a separate document that is not required for other motions – a statement of material facts that are not in dispute.

> The supporting papers shall include a separate statement setting forth plainly and concisely all material facts that the moving party contends are undisputed. Each of the material facts stated shall be followed by a reference to the supporting evidence. The failure to comply with this requirement of a separate statement may in the court's discretion constitute a sufficient ground for denying the motion.

(Code Civ. Proc. Sec. 437c(b)(1)).

> (1) The Separate Statement of Undisputed Material Facts in support of a motion must separately identify:
>
> (A) Each cause of action, claim for damages, issue of duty, or affirmative defense that is the subject of the motion; and
>
> (B) Each supporting material fact claimed to be without dispute with respect to the cause of action, claim for damages, issue of duty, or affirmative defense that is the subject of the motion.
>
> (2) The separate statement should include only material facts and not any facts that are not pertinent to the disposition of the motion.
>
> (3) The separate statement must be in the two-column format specified in (h). The statement must state in numerical sequence the undisputed material facts in the first column followed by the evidence that establishes those undisputed facts in that same column. Citation to

> the evidence in support of each material fact must include reference to the exhibit, title, page, and line numbers.

(Cal. Rules Ct. Rule 3.1350(d)).

The statement of material facts for a motion for summary judgment will have two columns on the page, the left one captioned "Moving Party's Undisputed Material Facts and Supporting Evidence" and the right one captioned "Opposing Party's Response and Supporting Evidence." In the first column each undisputed fact is set out in a separate paragraph, numbered consecutively. Each contention of undisputed fact is set out in a brief sentence. After each sentence list the references to all the supporting evidence. The second column would be left blank for the moving party's statement.

If you are confused by the "two column format" see http://www.courts.ca.gov/cms/rules/index.cfm?title=three&linkid=rule3_1350

The opposing party's statement in opposition will leave the left column exactly the way it was in the movant's statement and add the opposing party's response in the right column beside it. If the matter is undisputed, the right column beside that item will simply say "undisputed." If the matter in the left column is disputed, the right column will say "disputed" and briefly state in a simple sentence the facts showing the issue is disputed, followed by the references to the supporting evidence.

The "references to the supporting evidence" means the exhibit and page numbers in your supporting exhibits which establish each of the material facts. They should be written in this format [Title of Exhibit] [Exhibit #] : [page number(s)]. For example "Smith declaration, 3:7-21" means the Smith declaration, exhibit 3, pages 7 through 21.

c. Collateral estoppel effect of rulings in the criminal case

In summary judgment motions, parties may use the doctrine of collateral estoppel to avoid relitigating issues that were necessarily decided in an earlier proceeding, such as the parallel criminal prosecution.

> Collateral estoppel precludes relitigation of issues argued and decided in prior proceedings. Traditionally, we have applied the doctrine only if several threshold requirements are fulfilled. First, the issue sought to be precluded from relitigation must be identical to that decided in a former proceeding. Second, this issue must have been actually litigated in the former proceeding. Third, it must have been necessarily decided in the former proceeding. Fourth, the decision in the former proceeding must be final and on the merits. Finally, the party against whom preclusion is sought must be the same as, or in privity with, the party to the former proceeding. The party asserting collateral estoppel bears the burden of establishing these requirements.

(*Lucido v. Superior Court* (1990) 51 Cal.3d 335, 341 (internal citations omitted)).

If the court rules in the criminal case that the search and seizure was illegal, the government can't use the suppressed evidence against the defendant-claimant in the forfeiture case. But that does not settle the question of whether the illegally seized evidence can be used against a forfeiture claimant who was not charged in the criminal case. The fifth prong of the *Lucido* test might prevent collateral estoppel from being used by the third party because the third party lacked standing to challenge the search and seizure (e.g., because the search did not violate his or her "expectation of privacy.")

d. Moving for summary judgment against the government

Forfeiture claimants may move for summary judgment against the government, on the grounds that the government cannot prove its forfeiture case because one or more of the elements of its cause of action cannot be established. This is fertile ground for a defense motion for summary judgment – particularly in forfeiture cases where the government's burden of proof is "clear and convincing evidence" or "beyond a reasonable doubt." See Chapter 11 Section E-6-a below.

The claimant may also move for summary judgment on one of its defenses, such as statute of limitations, on the grounds that the government cannot disprove the defense. (Code Civ. Proc. Sec. 437c(o)(1)-(2)).

> A defendant ... has met his or her burden of showing that a cause of action has no merit if the party has shown that one or more elements of the cause of action, even if not separately pleaded, cannot be established, or that there is a complete defense to the cause of action. Once the defendant or cross-defendant has met that burden, the burden shifts to the plaintiff or cross-complainant to show that a triable issue of one or more material facts exists as to the cause of action or a defense thereto. The plaintiff or cross-complainant shall not rely upon the allegations or denials of its pleadings to show that a triable issue of material fact exists but, instead, shall set forth the specific facts showing that a triable issue of material fact exists as to the cause of action or a defense thereto.

(Code Civ. Proc. Sec. 437c(p)(2)).

If the claimant cannot make the initial showing that the plaintiff's (government's) complaint has no merit because one or more elements cannot be established, "it is unnecessary to examine the plaintiff's opposing evidence, and the motion must be denied." (*Powell v. Kleinman* (2007) 151 Cal.App.4th 112, 121).

> To satisfy its burden in seeking summary judgment, a moving defendant [claimant] is not required to "conclusively negate an element of the [government's] cause of action. ...All that the [claimant] need do is to 'show[] that one or more elements of the cause of action... cannot be established' by the plaintiff." (*Aguilar*, supra, 25 Cal.4th 826, 853, fn. omitted.) Once this defendant's burden is met, the "burden shifts to the [government] ... to show that a triable issue of one or more material facts exists...." (§ 437c, subd. (p)(2).) As the opposing party, the [government] must direct any opposition evidence toward the issues raised by the pleadings. (*Distefano,* supra, 85 Cal.App.4th 1249, 1264-1265.)

(*Howard v. Omni Hotels Management* (2012) 203 Cal.App.4th 403).

Statute of limitations defects are often resolved by summary judgment, if not earlier by a motion for judgment on the pleadings. The difference between those two is that motions for judgment on the pleadings must be resolved from the allegations in the complaint, sometimes aided by facts on which the court may take judicial notice, such as the filing dates of related cases.

Claimants should examine the government's allegations in the complaint in light of the elements of the criminal act which triggered the forfeiture and the requirements of the applicable forfeiture statute. Some California forfeiture statutes require that the underlying offense be a felony, for instance. If the criminal case is charged as a misdemeanor that would be a fertile ground for summary judgment. Also, where there is a criminal conviction requirement, if the criminal case ends in acquittal and the government does not automatically dismiss the forfeiture, summary judgment would be the proper way to dispose of the forfeiture case.

2. Requirements for summary adjudication

> A party may move for summary adjudication as to one or more causes of action within an action, one or more affirmative defenses, one or more claims for damages, or one or more issues of duty, if the party contends that the cause of action has no merit, that there is no affirmative defense to the cause of action, that there is no merit to an affirmative defense as to any cause of action.... A motion for summary adjudication shall be granted only if it completely disposes of a cause of action, an affirmative defense, a claim for damages, or an issue of duty.

(Code Civ. Proc. Sec. 437c(f)(1)).

Additionally, "a party may move for summary adjudication of a legal issue... that does not completely dispose of a cause of action, [or] affirmative defense...." (Code Civ. Proc. Sec. 437c(t)).

A motion may ask in the alternative for summary judgment or for summary adjudication.

> If made in the alternative, a motion for summary adjudication may make reference to and depend on the same evidence submitted in support of the summary judgment motion. If summary adjudication is sought, whether separately or as an alternative to the motion for summary judgment, the specific cause of action, affirmative defense, claims for damages, or issues of duty must be stated specifically in the notice of motion and be

> repeated, verbatim, in the separate statement of undisputed material facts.

(Cal. Rules Ct. 3.1350(b)).

Before filing a motion for summary adjudication, "the parties whose claims or defenses are put at issue by the motion" must file a joint stipulation outlining the issues to be adjudicated, and "a declaration from each stipulating party that the motion will further the interest of judicial economy by decreasing trial time or significantly increasing the likelihood of settlement." (Code Civ. Proc. Sec. 437c(t)(1)(A)(i)-(ii)). The stipulation must be served on all parties, but not filed. (Code Civ. Proc. Sec. 437c(t)(1)(B)) until the court gives permission to file a motion for summary adjudication.

The other parties may file objections to the joint stipulation within 10 days after the stipulation was received. (Code Civ. Proc. Sec. 437c(t)(1)(B)(2)).

Within 15 days after receipt, unless extended, the judge will notify the stipulating parties whether the motion may be filed. (Code Civ. Proc. Sec. 437c(t)(1)(B)(2)).

If the court does not allow the stipulation and declarations to be filed, the stipulating parties may request an informal hearing, but may not file additional papers. (Code Civ. Proc. Sec. 437c(t)(1)(B)(3)).

If the court allows it to be filed, the motion for summary adjudication must include a notice indicating the motion was made pursuant to Code Civ. Proc. Sec. 437c(t), and contain essentially the following language:

> This motion is made pursuant to subdivision (t) of Section 437c of the Code of Civil Procedure. The parties to this motion stipulate that the court shall hear this motion and that the resolution of this motion will further the interest

of judicial economy by decreasing trial time or significantly increasing the likelihood of settlement.

(Code Civ. Proc. Sec. 437c(t)(1)(B)(4)(A)).

The motion must be signed by all parties to the motion, or their counsel. (Code Civ. Proc. Sec. 437c(t)(1)(B)(4)(B)). All the other requirements of summary judgment apply.

Motions for summary adjudication follow the same rules as summary judgment motions except for these additional requirements noted above.

A party may not move for summary judgment on issues raised in a prior summary adjudication motion unless there is newly discovered evidence or a change of law. (Code Civ. Proc. Sec. 437c(f)(2)).

At trial the parties, witnesses, and the judge are prohibited from commenting to the jury about the grant or denial of summary adjudication. (Code Civ. Proc. Sec. 437c(n)(3)).

3. Opposing summary judgment

If any party fails to oppose summary judgment the court will grant summary judgment to the moving party. Likewise the court will grant summary adjudication on any issue which the opposing party fails to oppose, or on which they fail to demonstrate any triable issues of fact.

a. Timing

Oppositions must be filed no more than 14 days before the hearing date unless the court rules otherwise. (Code Civ. Proc. Sec. 437c(b)(2)).

b. Contents

Oppositions must include:

> a separate statement that responds to each of the material facts contended by the moving party to be undisputed, indicating if the opposing party agrees or disagrees that those facts are undisputed. The statement also shall set forth plainly and concisely any other material facts the opposing party contends are disputed. Each material fact contended by the opposing party to be disputed shall be followed by a reference to the supporting evidence. Failure to comply with this requirement of a separate statement may constitute a sufficient ground, in the court's discretion, for granting the motion.

(Code Civ. Proc. Sec. 437c(b)(3)).

Factual contentions in the opposition must be supported by "affidavits, declarations, admissions, answers to interrogatories, depositions, and matters of which judicial notice shall or may be taken." (Code Civ. Proc. Sec. 437c(b)(2)).

The party opposing summary judgment may not "rely upon the allegations or denials of its pleadings to show that a triable issue of material fact exists but, instead, shall set forth the specific facts showing that a triable issue of material fact exists as to the cause of action or a defense thereto." (Code Civ. Proc. Sec. 437c(p)(1)).

c. Delaying summary judgment to obtain additional discovery

If responding to summary judgment requires you to prove facts that you do not currently have evidence to support, and discovery is still open, you may move to delay filing an opposition until after additional discovery is produced.

> If it appears from the affidavits submitted in opposition to a motion for summary judgment or summary adjudication, or both, that facts essential to justify opposition may exist but cannot, for reasons stated, be presented, the court shall deny the motion, order a continuance to permit affidavits to be obtained or discovery to be had, or make any other order as may be just. The application to continue the motion to obtain necessary discovery may also be made by ex parte motion at any time on or before the date the opposition response to the motion is due.

(Code Civ. Proc. Sec. 437c(h)).

> If, after granting a continuance to allow specified additional discovery, the court determines that the party seeking summary judgment has unreasonably failed to allow the discovery to be conducted, the court shall grant a continuance to permit the discovery to go forward or deny the motion for summary judgment or summary adjudication.

(Code Civ. Proc. Sec. 437c(i)).

d. Fugitive disentitlement

Under the fugitive disentitlement doctrine, a claimant who is a fugitive from justice in a related criminal case is not allowed to defend against summary judgment. In *People v. $4,503* (1996) 49 Cal.App.4th 1743, the claimant's motion for summary judgment was denied because he was a fugitive from justice and did not comply with discovery. The court of appeals, citing Code Civ. Proc. Sec. 437c(h), affirmed the granting of summary judgment, saying facts essential to the government's defense against summary judgment may exist, but since the claimant was a fugitive, and unable to give discovery relative to the issue, the claimant's summary judgment motion is denied.

4. Replies

The party moving for summary judgment may file a reply to the opposition motion, but it must be filed no less than 5 days before the hearing unless the court orders otherwise. (Code Civ. Proc. Sec. 437c(b)(4)).

5. Hearing on summary judgment

Evidentiary objections not made at the hearing are waived. (Code Civ. Proc. Sec. 437c(b)(5)).

> The party moving for summary judgment bears "the burden of persuasion" that there are no triable issues of material fact and that the moving party is entitled to judgment as a matter of law. (*Aguilar* [*v. Atlantic Richfield Co.* (2001) 25 Cal.4th 826], 850.) The moving party also "bears an initial burden of production to make a prima facie showing of the nonexistence of any triable issue of material fact; if he carries his burden of production, he causes a shift, and the opposing party is then subjected to a burden of production of his own to make a prima facie showing of the existence of a triable issue of material fact." (*Id.* at p. 850.) "A prima facie showing is one that is sufficient to support the position of the party in question." (*Aguilar*, at p. 851.)

(*Weinstein v. Dept. of Transportation* (2006) 139 Cal.App.4th 52, 57).

> There is a triable issue of material fact if the evidence on the motion would allow a reasonable trier of fact to find the underlying fact in favor of the party opposing the motion given the applicable standard of proof.

(*Bushling v. Fremont Medical Center* (2004) 117 Cal.App.4th 493, 506).

The court may not make factual determinations or weigh evidence at the hearing on the motion for summary judgment.

> The trial court's sole function on a motion for summary judgment is issue finding, not issue determination. (*Black v. Sullivan* (1975) 48 Cal.App.3d 557, 567.) The summary judgment procedure should be used with caution and any doubt as to the propriety of granting summary judgment should be resolved in favor of the party opposing the motion. (*Mann v. Cracchiolo* (1985) 38 Cal.3d 18, 35-36.)
>
> When a defendant moves for summary judgment, "its declarations and evidence must either establish a complete defense to plaintiff's action or demonstrate the absence of an essential element of plaintiff's case. If plaintiff does not counter with opposing declarations showing there are triable issues of fact with respect to that defense or an essential element of its case, the summary judgment must be granted." (*Gray v. America West Airlines, Inc.* (1989) 209 Cal.App.3d 76, 81).

(*Saldana v. Glove-Weis Systems Co.* (1991) 233 Cal.App.3d 1505).

The court must consider all of the evidence and reasonable inferences arising from it. "[S]ummary judgment may not be granted by the court based on inferences reasonably deducible from the papers submitted if such inferences are contradicted by other inferences raising a triable issue of fact." (*Saldana v. Glove-Weis Systems Co.* (1991) 233 Cal.App.3d 1505, citing *Hepp v. Lockheed-California Co.* (1978) 86 Cal.App.3d 714, 717-718).

> Any doubts about the propriety of granting a summary judgment motion must be resolved in favor of the party opposing the motion. (*Kolodge v. Boyd* (2001) 88 Cal.App.4th 349, 355.) Courts must abide by the strong public policy favoring disposition on the merits over judicial efficiency. (*Bahl v. Bank of America* (2001) 89

Cal.App.4th 389, 398.) The purpose of summary judgment is to provide a means to determine whether issues which appear to be raised by the pleadings are real, or merely the product of adept pleading. (*College Hospital Inc. v. Superior Court* (1994) 8 Cal.4th 704, 720, fn. 7.) The summary judgment provisions were never intended to deprive a party of a right to a trial. (*Richter v. United Calif. Theatres, Inc.* (1960) 177 Cal.App.2d 126, 131.)

Section 437c provides in pertinent part that the trial court shall grant a summary judgment motion if all the papers submitted show there is no triable issue of material fact and the moving party is entitled to a judgment as a matter of law. (§437c, subd. (c).)

(*Johnson v. Superior Court* (2006) 143 Cal.App.4th 297, __, 49 Cal.Rptr.3d 52, 57).

6. Rulings on summary judgment

The motion for summary judgment shall be granted if all the papers submitted show that there is no triable issue as to any material fact and that the moving party is entitled to a judgment as a matter of law. In determining if the papers show that there is no triable issue as to any material fact, the court shall consider all of the evidence set forth in the papers, except the evidence to which objections have been made and sustained by the court, and all inferences reasonably deducible from the evidence, except summary judgment shall not be granted by the court based on inferences reasonably deducible from the evidence if contradicted by other inferences or evidence that raise a triable issue as to any material fact.

(Code Civ. Proc. Sec. 437c(c)).

a. Relevance of burden of proof

> In determining whether the parties have met their respective burdens, the court must "consider all of the evidence" and "all of the inferences reasonably drawn therefrom," and "must view such evidence [citations] and such inferences [citations] … in the light most favorable to the opposing party." (*Aguilar* [*v. Atlantic Richfield Co.* (2001) 25 Cal.4th 826], 844–845.) "There is a triable issue of material fact if, and only if, the evidence would allow a reasonable trier of fact to find the underlying fact in favor of the party opposing the motion in accordance with the applicable standard of proof." (*Id.* at p. 850, fn. omitted.)"

(*Powell v. Kleinman* (2007) 151 Cal.App.4th 112).

It takes some mental gymnastics to determine whether a reasonable trier of fact could find the underlying fact in favor of the plaintiff when the burden of proof is preponderance of the evidence as in *Kleinman.* But mental gymnastics or not, where the government's burden of proof is "clear and convincing evidence" or "beyond a reasonable doubt" – as it is under many forfeiture statutes – claimants have a good chance of winning on summary judgment.

If a party is otherwise entitled to summary judgment under these standards, the court may not deny summary judgment on grounds of credibility or because the opponent did not get a chance to cross-examine witnesses who furnished declarations. However, the court has discretion to deny summary judgment

> if the only proof of a material fact offered in support of the summary judgment is an affidavit or declaration made by an individual who was the sole witness to that fact; or if a material fact is an individual's state of mind,

> or lack thereof, and that fact is sought to be established solely by the individual's [declaration or affidavit].

(Code Civ. Proc. Sec. 437c(e)).

If the court denies summary judgment or adjudication on the ground that there are triable issues of material fact, it must state in an oral or written order the material facts on which there is a factual dispute, and must refer to the specific evidence in the moving and opposition papers that show the legitimate dispute. (Code Civ. Proc. Sec. 437c(g)).

If the court grants summary judgment on the grounds that there is no triable issue of material fact, the court must issue a written or oral order stating the reasons for its ruling, and must specifically refer to the evidence submitted in support of (and if applicable, in opposition to) the motion that indicate no triable issue exists. (Code Civ. Proc. Sec. 437c(g)).

b. Affidavits submitted in bad faith

If a court finds any affidavits submitted with a motion for summary judgment were made in bad faith, the court shall order the offending party to pay the opponent's reasonable expenses caused thereby. (Code Civ. Proc. Sec. 437c(j)).

Sanctions may not be imposed unless requested in the injured party's moving papers or, if the court imposes sanctions on its own motion, it must give advance notice and the opportunity to be heard before imposing sanctions. (Code Civ. Proc. Sec. 437c(j)).

> In granting or denying a motion for summary judgment or summary adjudication, the court need rule only on those objections to evidence that it deems material to its disposition of the motion. Objections to evidence that are

> not ruled on for purposes of the motion shall be preserved for appellate review.

(Code Civ. Proc. Sec. 437c(q)).

7. Appeals

If the court grants summary judgment, that is an appealable judgment. Any other order is not final and appealable, but a party may petition for a peremptory writ, in which appellate review is discretionary. The deadline for filing such a petition is 20 days after service of the order. Add 5 days to the date of service if served by mail inside California; 10 days if served outside California but in the U.S.; and 20 days if served outside the U.S. Add 2 days if served by fax. For good cause the court may extend the deadline by no more than 10 days. (Code Civ. Proc. Sec. 437c(m)(1)).

> Before a reviewing court affirms an order granting summary judgment or summary adjudication on a ground not relied upon by the trial court, the reviewing court shall afford the parties an opportunity to present their views on the issue by submitting supplemental briefs. The supplemental briefs may include an argument that additional evidence relating to that ground exists, but the party has not had an adequate opportunity to present the evidence or to conduct discovery on the issue. The court may reverse or remand based upon the supplemental briefs to allow the parties to present additional evidence or to conduct discovery on the issue. If the court fails to allow supplemental briefs, a rehearing shall be ordered upon timely petition of a party.

(Code Civ. Proc. Sec. 437c(m)(2)).

F. Motions in limine

A motion in limine (Latin for "at the outset") is a pretrial motion that seeks an advance ruling on whether certain evidence will be admissible at trial. The motion most frequently seeks to exclude evidence the opposing party is likely to introduce, but it can also be used to allow the moving party to admit evidence that the opposing party may challenge as objectionable.

Getting an advance ruling on a motion in limine shapes the trial in advance, saving time and money bringing in witnesses whose testimony may or may not be allowed. Resolving the issue before trial saves the jury from sitting idle while the parties argue the evidentiary issue, disrupting the trial's momentum. An advance ruling also allows parties to know whether they will be able to talk about the evidence in opening statement.

> The usual purpose of motions in limine is to preclude the presentation of evidence deemed inadmissible and prejudicial by the moving party. A typical order in limine excludes the challenged evidence and directs counsel, parties, and witnesses not to refer to the excluded matters during trial. (3 Witkin, Cal. Evidence, supra, § 2011 at p. 1969.) "The advantage of such motions is to avoid the obviously futile attempt to 'unring the bell' in the event a motion to strike is granted in the proceedings before the jury." (*Hyatt v. Sierra Boat Co.* (1978) 79 Cal. App.3d 325, 337 [145 Cal. Rptr. 47].)
>
> Motions in limine serve other purposes as well. They permit more careful consideration of evidentiary issues than would take place in the heat of battle during trial. They minimize side-bar conferences and disruptions during trial, allowing for an uninterrupted flow of evidence. Finally, by resolving potentially critical issues

> at the outset, they enhance the efficiency of trials and promote settlements.

(*People v. Morris* (1991) 53 Cal.3d 152, 188).

Once a court rules on an issue in a motion in limine, the party against whom the court ruled does not have to make any further objections or motions at trial to preserve the issue for appeal, unless an event occurs at trial "after the in limine ruling and before the evidence was offered that so changed the context as to constitute a basis for reconsideration of the ruling." If objecting at trial would be a mere repetition of the same objection decided in the motion in limine, objecting would serve no purpose and the issue is preserved for appeal. (*People v. Morris,* supra, 53 Cal.3d at 189).

> In summary, we hold that a motion in limine to exclude evidence is a sufficient manifestation of objection to protect the record on appeal when it satisfies the basic requirements of Evidence Code section 353, i.e.: (1) a specific legal ground for exclusion is advanced and subsequently raised on appeal; (2) the motion is directed to a particular, identifiable body of evidence; and (3) the motion is made at a time before or during trial when the trial judge can determine the evidentiary question in its appropriate context. When such a motion is made and denied, the issue is preserved for appeal. On the other hand, if a motion in limine does not satisfy each of these requirements, a proper objection satisfying Evidence Code section 353 must be made to preserve the evidentiary issue for appeal.

(*Id.* at 190).

A motion in limine may be made during trial too. In *Hyatt v. Sierra Boat Co.* (1978) 79 Cal.App.3d 325, 337, the plaintiff made a motion in limine after resting his case, during the defense case in chief. Plaintiff's motion sought to keep the expert from rendering an opinion on the speed of the vehicle, since there was no evidence which could form a factual basis for the expert's opinion. That ruling was upheld on appeal, the court noting that the defendant did not introduce evidence laying a factual basis for the opinion.

1. Uses of motions in limine

In *People v. Morris* the defendant moved in limine to preclude questioning about an allegedly coercive plea bargain and immunity agreement given to the accomplice-turned-informant. The plea bargain conditioned the grant of immunity on the fact that the accomplice did not personally injure the victim. The defendant contended this impermissibly coerced the witness to testify that the defendant, not the witness, was the one who injured the victim. The motion in limine was unsuccessful and the court of appeals upheld the ruling, saying the witness's testimony on that issue was limited and was corroborated by other evidence.

Motions in limine are frequently used to keep out evidence that is more prejudicial than probative. In *People v. Williams* (1997) 16 Cal.4th 153, 194, the defendant sought to exclude any evidence of his membership in a gang. Admissibility was upheld because the defendant was charged with a gang-related crime and the court held the evidence was relevant to motive or identity. Similar issues that a party may want a pretrial ruling precluding as more prejudicial than probative are: a party's status as an illegal alien, membership in a cult or radical organization, etc.

Sometimes a motion in limine is used to prevent the opposing party from eliciting expert testimony from a witness whose credentials as an expert are weak or suspect. For example, a regular accountant who ordinarily does tax returns may not be sufficiently qualified to testify as an expert forensic accountant on the issue of tracing proceeds. A drug dog handler's testimony about a drug dog alert might be challenged if discovery shows the dog had a record of false positives in performance testing.

Motions in limine may not be used to keep a witness from testifying differently at trial than in a pretrial deposition. "It is a misuse of a motion in limine to attempt to compel a witness or a party to conform his or her trial testimony to a preconceived factual scenario based on testimony given during pretrial discovery." (*Kelly v. New West Federal Savings* (1996) 49 Cal.App.4th 659, 672).

2. The ruling may change during trial

The court's ruling on a motion in limine may be "preliminary" – leaving the issue open but requiring the opponent to obtain the court's permission out of the presence of the jury before introducing the challenged evidence.

A court may revisit its ruling on a motion in limine at any time during trial, as evidence is produced that undermines the factual basis on which the court relied in its pretrial ruling.

A party may open the door for the excluded evidence by raising questions that make the excluded evidence more relevant and/or probative.

If the excluded evidence becomes relevant to a new issue that has arisen, but the prior objectionable use is still valid, the court may allow the evidence and give a limiting instruction, telling the jury the evidence is relevant to show X but not Y.

A party who, having succeeded in excluding certain evidence, offers that evidence during a witness's testimony, may not claim on appeal that the admission of the evidence was erroneous. (*Ohler v. United States* (2000) 529 U.S. 753).

3. Remedy for violations of order limiting testimony

A party who violates the court's motion in limine order may be adjudged in contempt and punished with a fine of up to $1,000. (Code Civ. Proc. Sec. 1218(a)).

The court will admonish the jury to disregard the offending testimony. "[A] jury must be deemed capable, if so instructed, of ignoring references to a litigant's personal or corporate virtues and confining itself to the merits of the case." (*Sabella v. Southern Pacific Co.* (1969) 70 Cal.2d 311, 320). Once the jury is so instructed, it is presumed that the jury will follow the instructions and disregard the inadmissible matter. (*Grimshaw v. Ford Motor Co.* (1981) 119 Cal.App.3d 757, 794-95).

G. Case management conference statement

At some point the court will set a date for a case management conference in the forfeiture case.

The parties must meet and confer 30 calendar days before the initial case management conference to consider the issues set out in Cal. Rule of Court 3.727, and try to resolve any outstanding discovery disputes; identify any anticipated motions; identify the facts and issues that are uncontested and in dispute; determine whether the issues can be narrowed by motions; identify dates when parties, attorneys, and witnesses are unavailable for trial and their reasons; and try to settle the case. (Cal. Rule of Court 3.724).

The issues set out in Cal. Rule of Court 3.727 are: whether there are related cases; whether all parties have been served; whether additional parties may be added; whether other matters may affect the jurisdiction of the case; whether alternative dispute resolution should be explored; whether the parties want an early settlement conference; whether discovery is completed; and if not the date for completion; any anticipated discovery issues; whether the case should be bifurcated; whether the case is entitled to a statutory preference; whether a jury trial is demanded; the date the case will probably be ready for trial and available trial dates; estimated trial length; and any other matters that should be considered in the case management conference to facilitate progress in the case.

A case management conference statement must be filed at least 15 calendar days before the date of the conference. (Cal. Rules of Court Sec. 3.725(a)). Two or more parties may file a joint CMC statement. (Cal. Rules of Court Sec. 3.725(b)). Parties must use the Case Management Statement form created for this purpose by the Judicial Council form CM-110. Download the form from http://www.courts.ca.gov/documents/cm010.pdf.

All applicable items on the form must be completed. (Cal. Rules of Court Sec. 3.725(c)).

There is no filing fee for civil case management statements. (Gov. Code Sec. GC 70617(b)(3)).

12. Trials

A. Right to jury trial

> If there is an underlying or related criminal action, and a criminal conviction is required before a judgment of forfeiture may be entered, the issue of forfeiture shall be tried in conjunction therewith. In such a case, the issue of forfeiture shall be bifurcated from the criminal trial and tried after conviction unless waived by the parties. Trial shall be by jury unless waived by all parties. If there is no underlying or related criminal action, the presiding judge of the superior court shall assign the action brought pursuant to this chapter for trial.

(Health & Saf. Code Sec. 11488.4(i)(5)).

> A person facing civil forfeiture of her property has a constitutional and statutory right to a jury trial. "Trial by jury is an inviolate right" under the California Constitution. (Cal. Const., art. I, § 16.) Section 11488.4, subdivision (i)(5) echoes this right, providing that "[t]rial shall be by jury unless waived by all parties." (§ 11488.4, subd. (i)(5).) But civil forfeiture proceedings are "civil in nature," despite their connection to an ongoing criminal proceeding. (*[People v.] $17,522.08* (2006) 142 Cal.App.4th 1076, 1083.)
>
> The right to a jury trial in civil proceedings is different from the right to a jury trial in criminal proceedings. In civil cases, the right may be forfeited through nonassertion or by conduct (Code Civ. Proc., § 631, subds. (a), (f)); in criminal cases, the right must be knowingly and intelligently waived (*People v. Weaver* (2012) 53 Cal.4th 1056, 1071-1072). More to the point, in civil cases the right to jury trial does not ripen "unless there is a

> genuine issue of material fact suitable for a jury to resolve." (*Etalook v. Exxon Pipeline Co.* (9th Cir. 1987) 831 F.2d 1440, 1447.) This is why courts may grant summary judgment in civil cases without offending the losing party's right to a jury trial (*Kurokawa v. Blum* (1988) 199 Cal.App.3d 976, 991 [summary judgment "does not improperly take away [the] constitutional right to a jury trial"]), and why courts demand strict compliance with summary judgment procedures to avoid infringing that right. (*Bahl v. Bank of America* (2001) 89 Cal.App.4th 389, 395.

(*People v. $2,709* (2014) 231 Cal.App.4th 1278, 1285).

What happens to the requirement that "forfeiture shall be tried in conjunction" with the related criminal case when a defendant pleads guilty?

In *People v. $2,709* (2014) 231 Cal.App.4th 1278, the court held that the simultaneous trial requirement was designed to conserve judicial resources. "When a defendant enters a plea, there will be at most one trial; the policy behind subsections (i)(3) and (i)(5) of section 11488.4 is simply not implicated."

> A person facing civil forfeiture of her property has a constitutional and statutory right to a jury trial. "Trial by jury is an inviolate right" under the California Constitution. (Cal. Const., art. I, § 16.) Section 11488.4, subdivision (i)(5) echoes this right, providing that "[t]rial shall be by jury unless waived by all parties." (§ 11488.4, subd. (i)(5).) But civil forfeiture proceedings are "civil in nature," despite their connection to an ongoing criminal proceeding. (*$17,522.08,* supra, 142 Cal.App.4th at p. 1083.)
>
> The right to a jury trial in civil proceedings is different from the right to a jury trial in criminal proceedings. In

> civil cases, the right may be forfeited through nonassertion or by conduct (Code Civ. Proc., § 631, subds. (a), (f)); in criminal cases, the right must be knowingly and intelligently waived (*People v. Weaver* (2012) 53 Cal.4th 1056, 1071-1072). More to the point, in civil cases the right to jury trial does not ripen "unless there is a genuine issue of material fact suitable for a jury to resolve." (*Etalook v. Exxon Pipeline Co.* (9th Cir. 1987) 831 F.2d 1440, 1447.) This is why courts may grant summary judgment in civil cases without offending the losing party's right to a jury trial (*Kurokawa v. Blum* (1988) 199 Cal.App.3d 976, 991 [summary judgment "does not improperly take away [the] constitutional right to a jury trial"]), and why courts demand strict compliance with summary judgment procedures to avoid infringing that right. (*Bahl v. Bank of America* (2001) 89 Cal.App.4th 389, 395.)

(*People v. $2,709* (2014) 231 Cal.App.4th 1278, 1285).

B. Evidentiary issues

1. Presumption from possession of property

> A presumption is an assumption of fact that the law requires to be made from another fact or group of facts found or otherwise established in the action. A presumption is not evidence.

(Evid. Code Sec. 600(a)). Presumptions are either conclusive or rebuttable.

Under the California law, there is a rebuttable presumption that the person from whom property is seized is the owner of it. "The things which a person possesses are presumed to be owned by him." (Evid. Code Sec. 637). "A person who exercises acts of ownership over property is presumed to be the owner of it." (Evid. Code Sec. 638).

Health & Safety Code § 11488(a) authorizes police to seize evidence and any item subject to forfeiture under the drug laws, but the statute requires the police to give a receipt to the person from whom it was taken.

> Receipts for property seized pursuant to this section shall be delivered to any person out of whose possession such property was seized, in accordance with Section 1412 of the Penal Code. In the event property seized was not seized out of anyone's possession, receipt for the property shall be delivered to the individual in possession of the premises at which the property was seized.

(Health & Saf. Code Sec. 11488(b)). "[G]iving a receipt creates a presumption that the person to whom a receipt was issued is the owner of the property." (Health & Saf. Code Sec. 11488(c).

The Penal Code has a similar provision, applicable to property seizures for all offenses:

> When the officer takes property under the warrant, he must give a receipt for the property taken (specifying it in detail) to the person from whom it was taken by him, or in whose possession it was found; or, in the absence of any person, he must leave it in the place where he found the property.

(Pen. Code Sec. 1535).

The receipt also tells the agency where to return the money if the property is no longer needed as evidence and no forfeiture has been commenced – "the officer shall return the property to the individual designated in the receipt therefor." (Health & Saf. Code Sec. 11488.2).

If a petition for forfeiture is filed it "shall be served on every individual designated in a receipt issued for the property seized." (Health & Saf. Code Sec. 11488.4(c)).

> There shall be a presumption affecting the burden of proof that the person to whom a receipt for property was issued is the owner thereof. This presumption may, however, be rebutted at the forfeiture hearing specified in Section 11488.5.

(Health & Saf. Code Sec. 11488(c)).

"The effect of a presumption affecting the burden of proof is to impose upon the party against whom it operates the burden of proof as to the nonexistence of the presumed fact." (Evid. Code Sec. 606).

In other words, when the police take property from someone it is presumed to be theirs, and at the forfeiture hearing, the government has the burden of rebutting that presumption. The person does not have to prove that the money taken from them in fact was theirs. Accordingly, when the government challenges a claimant's standing to defend against the forfeiture of money seized from them, simple possession of the property is enough to show standing.

2. Expert witnesses

Forfeiture cases – particularly those brought under the drug statutes – often involve expert testimony.

"Expert" police officer witnesses may be called to testify about their expert opinion about whether a particular method of packaging cash is indicative of drug trafficking. Expert testimony may be introduced, through a drug dog's handler, that a particular reaction by a "K-9" drug dog during a search of a vehicle or item is a "drug dog alert," probative of a connection between that item and recent contact with controlled substances or bombs, etc. An expert chemist may testify that a seized substance is a particular controlled substance.

In financial crimes and cases involving alleged proceeds of crime, forensic accountants may be called to give their expert opinions about whether money in a bank account is traceable proceeds of a particular transaction, or whether a person's net worth analysis shows unreported income, indicative of ill-gotten gains.

Grounds for attacking testimony by these specific experts is beyond the scope of this book, but a few basic rules apply to all expert testimony.

a. Threshold requirements

(i). Will it assist the jury?

> [T]he decisive consideration in determining the admissibility of expert opinion evidence is whether the subject of inquiry is one of such common knowledge that men of ordinary education could reach a conclusion as intelligently as the witness or whether, on the other hand, the matter is sufficiently beyond common experience that the opinion of an expert would assist the trier of fact.

(*People v. Cole* (1956) 47 Cal.2d 99, 103).

(ii). Qualifications as an expert

The witness offering expert testimony must be shown to have "special knowledge, skill, experience, training, or education sufficient to qualify him as an expert on the subject to which his testimony relates." If a party objects to an expert, the witness's "special knowledge, skill, experience, training, or education must be shown before the witness may testify as an expert." (Evid. Code Sec. 720(a)). The qualifications can be shown by any admissible evidence including the witness's own testimony. (Evid. Code Sec. 720(b)).

(iii). Foundation

There has to be an adequate foundation for the expert's opinion. An expert witness's opinion must be

> [b]ased on matter (including his special knowledge, skill, experience, training, and education) perceived by or personally known to the witness or made known to him at or before the hearing, whether or not admissible, that is of a type that reasonably may be relied upon by an expert in forming an opinion upon the subject to which his testimony relates...."

(Evid. Code Sec. 801(b); *Kotla v. Regents of University of California* (2004) 115 Cal.App.4th 283, 292.

A proper foundation is established through testimony and documentary evidence put into the record during the hearing, before the expert's testimony. An expert may also rely upon hearsay in forming his/her opinion.

> Although an expert "may rely on inadmissible hearsay in forming his or her opinion [citation], and may state on direct examination the matters on which he or she relied, the expert may not testify as to the details of those matters if they are otherwise inadmissible."

(*Korsak v. Atlas Hotels, Inc.* (1992) 2 Cal.App.4th 1516, 1523, quoting *Continental Airlines, Inc. v. McDonnell Douglas Corp.* (1989) 216 Cal. App.3d 388, 415).

(iv). Opinion on "ultimate issue"

An "ultimate issue of fact" is an issue which the jury is charged with deciding. An expert may give his/her opinion as to an ultimate issue if the expert has expertise that would assist the trier of fact.

Juries may give the expert testimony however much weight they think it deserves.

In *People v. Douglas* the prosecutor asked a police officer a hypothetical question about whether certain conduct of a purported seller and of a purported buyer, plus the weight and packaging of 14 bindles of marijuana, and 44 dollar bills found in the purported seller's possession indicated the marijuana was possessed for sale or for personal use. The defense contended this was not a proper subject of expert opinion. On appeal the court affirmed, concluding that the interpretation of such evidence of drug activity was "sufficiently beyond common experience that the opinion of an expert would assist the trier of fact" and that "expert opinion is [not] inadmissible merely because it coincides with an ultimate issue of fact." (*People v. Douglas* (1987) 193 Cal.App.3d 1691, 1694).

C. Burden of proof

1. Motions to suppress and for return of property

With regard to motions to suppress evidence or for return of property, the burden of proof varies depending on whether or not there was a warrant. Warrantless seizures are presumed unreasonable, so the prosecution has the burden of proof, by a preponderance of the evidence. (See *People v. James* (1977) 19 Cal.3d 99, 106 ("Inasmuch as the search herein was conducted without a warrant, the burden was on the People to establish justification under a recognized exception to the warrant requirement..."); *People v. Williams* (1999) 20 Cal.4th 119, 127 ("Here, of course, the search was without a warrant. Defendant notes that the prosecution has the burden of proving, if it can, some justification for a warrantless search or seizure, and therefore a warrantless search is presumptively unreasonable."))

If there was a warrant, the search is presumed reasonable, so the person challenging the seizure or seeking return of property must prove that the seizure was illegal by a preponderance of the evidence. (See *People v. Murray* (1978) 77 Cal.App.3d 305, 310).

2. Vehicle code and computer crimes forfeiture cases

In Vehicle Code cases for vehicles seized for driving without a license, the burden of proof in the forfeiture trial is on the prosecuting agency, by a preponderance of the evidence. (Veh. Code Sec. 14607.6(e)(5)).

Preponderance of the evidence is also the government's burden of proof in cases based on computer hacking, or computer equipment related crimes. (Pen. Code Sec. 502.01(a)(1)).

The justification for these lower burdens of proof may be the quasi-remedial nature of these forfeiture statutes – taking away the means of committing the offense again.

The Vehicle Code forfeiture statute targets only repeat offender DUI and driving without a license or on an expired license offenses, and the only property forfeited under that statute is the vehicle used in the offense.

In the forfeiture statute for computer hacking and telecommunications or computer equipment related crimes, the property being forfeited is the computer equipment or telecommunications equipment owned and used by the defendant in the crime.

3. Drug cases

For cash and negotiable instruments of $40,000 or more, the prosecutor's burden of proof in the forfeiture case is clear and convincing evidence. (Health & Saf. Code Sec. 11488.4(i)(4)).

For all property other than contraband, including real estate, vehicles, things of value and cash or negotiable instruments totaling less than $40,000, the prosecutor's burden of proof in the forfeiture case is beyond a reasonable doubt. (Health & Saf. Code Sec. 11488.4(i)(1)-(2)).

4. Other forfeiture statutes

Under the forfeiture statute relating to banking, the prosecution has the burden of proving beyond a reasonable doubt that the property is forfeitable. (Fin. Code Sec. 5322(d)).

In forfeiture based on criminal profiteering activity the government must prove beyond a reasonable doubt that the defendant engaged in a pattern of criminal profiteering and that the property is forfeitable under Pen. Code Sec. 186.3(b) or (c). (Pen. Code Sec. 196.5).

In forfeitures for dog fighting and cock fighting, etc., the prosecution has the burden of proving beyond a reasonable doubt that the defendant was engaged in one of the crimes listed in Pen. Code Sec. 597.5 or 597b(b), and that the property comes within the provisions of Pen. Code Sec. 597b(b). (Pen. Code Sec. 598.1(g)).

In human trafficking forfeiture cases the prosecution's burden of proof in the forfeiture hearing is also beyond a reasonable doubt. (Pen. Code Sec. 236.9(d)).

13. Post-trial matters

A. Proportionality motion

Even if the jury of judge finds property forfeitable, there is a separate question whether forfeiting the property would be grossly disproportionate punishment for the property owner's offense.

In federal cases the proportionality issue is decided after the forfeiture trial by a judge, without a jury. The courts reason that proportioning the forfeiture as punishment is akin to sentencing the criminal defendant, a matter that it traditionally decided by the judge, not the jury.

There are apparently no state forfeiture cases on this issue. California courts are much more protective of the right to jury trial than federal courts, so there may be an argument that the proportioning of the forfeiture should be decided by the jury, since, in garden variety civil cases juries traditionally assess damages as well as liability.

For the substantive law on the Eighth Amendment Excessive Fines clause see Chapter 4 Section E, above.

B. Obtaining an award for costs

Attorneys' fees of prevailing claimants are not reimbursable under California forfeiture law as they are under federal law, but costs are recoverable by the prevailing party.

1. Requirements

A prevailing party in a forfeiture case is "entitled as a matter of right to recover costs." (Code Civ. Proc. Sec. 1032(b)). For purposes of this statute,

> "[p]revailing party" includes the party with a net monetary recovery, a defendant in whose favor a dismissal is entered, a defendant where neither plaintiff nor defendant obtains any relief, and a defendant as against those plaintiffs who do not recover any relief against that defendant. When any party recovers other than monetary relief and in situations other than as specified, the "prevailing party" shall be as determined by the court, and under those circumstances, the court, in its discretion, may allow costs or not and, if allowed may apportion costs between the parties on the same or adverse sides pursuant to rules adopted under Section 1034.

(Code Civ. Prod. 1032(a)(4)).

> A prevailing party who claims costs must serve and file a memorandum of costs within 15 days after the date of service of the notice of entry of judgment or dismissal by the clerk under Code of Civil Procedure section 664.5 or the date of service of written notice of entry of judgment or dismissal, or within 180 days after entry of judgment, whichever is first. The memorandum of costs must be verified by a statement of the party, attorney, or agent that to the best of his or her knowledge the items of cost are correct and were necessarily incurred in the case.

(Cal. Rules Ct. Rule 3.1700(a)(1)).

The party requesting costs and the party contesting them can agree to extend the deadline for filing the cost memorandum. The agreement must be in writing, specify the new deadline, and be filed with the clerk. If the opposing side does not agree, on motion the court may extend the deadline for no more than 30 days. (Cal. Rules Ct. Rule 3.1700(b)(3)).

2. Recoverable costs

Costs that can be recovered in a forfeiture case include:

(1) Filing, motion, and jury fees.

(2) Juror food and lodging while they are kept together during trial and after the jury retires for deliberation.

(3) (A) Taking, video recording, and transcribing necessary depositions, including an original and one copy of those taken by the claimant and one copy of depositions taken by the party against whom costs are allowed. (B) Fees of a certified or registered interpreter for the deposition of a party or witness who does not proficiently speak or understand the English language. (C) Travel expenses to attend depositions.

(4) Service of process by a public officer, registered process server, or other means, as follows: (A) When service is by a public officer,...the fee authorized by law at the time of service. (B) If service is by a process server..., the amount actually incurred in effecting service, including, but not limited to, a stakeout or other means employed in locating the person to be served, unless those charges are successfully challenged by a party to the action. (C) When service is by publication,... the sum actually incurred in effecting service. (D) When service is by a means other than that set forth in subparagraph (A), (B), or (C), the recoverable cost is the lesser of the sum actually incurred, or the amount allowed to a public officer in this state for that service,

> except that the court may allow the sum actually incurred in effecting service upon application pursuant to paragraph (4) of subdivision (c).
>
> (7) Ordinary witness fees pursuant to Section 68093 of the Government Code....
>
> (9) Transcripts of court proceedings ordered by the court....
>
> (11) Court reporter fees....
>
> (13) Models and enlargements of exhibits and photocopies of exhibits may be allowed if they were reasonably helpful to aid the trier of fact.

(Code Civ. Proc. Sec. 1033.5(a)).

> The following are not recoverable costs:
>
> (1) Fees of experts not ordered by the court.
>
> (2) Investigation expenses in preparing the case for trial.
>
> (3) Postage, telephone, and photocopying charges, except for exhibits.
>
> (4) Costs in investigation of jurors or in preparation for voir dire.
>
> (5) Transcripts of court proceedings not ordered by the court.

(Code Civ. Proc. Sec. 1033.5(b)).

Allowable costs must be reasonable in amount and "reasonably necessary to the conduct of the litigation rather than merely convenient or beneficial to its preparation." (Code Civ. Proc. Sec. 1033.5(c)(2)-(3)). "Items not mentioned in this section ... may be allowed or denied at the court's discretion." (Code Civ. Proc. Sec. 1033.5(c)(4)).

3. Objecting to costs

Any motion opposing the claim for costs must be served within 15 days after service of the cost memorandum.

If the cost memorandum was served by mail, the deadline is extended by Code Civ. Proc. 1013, as follows: if the address of the sender and the recipient are both inside California add 5 calendar days; if either is outside California but within the U.S. add 10 days; if either is outside the U.S. add 20 calendar days.

If served electronically, the deadline is extended by two court days pursuant to Code Civ. Proc. 1010.6(a)(4). (Cal. Rules Ct. Rule 3.1700(b)(1)).

> Unless objection is made to the entire cost memorandum, the motion to strike or tax costs must refer to each item objected to by the same number and appear in the same order as the corresponding cost item claimed on the memorandum of costs and must state why the item is objectionable.

(Cal. Rules Ct. Rule 3.1700(b)(2)).

C. Government claims for storage and towing fees

After seizing claimants' cars and holding them hostage for a year or more pending trial, the government racks up hundreds if not thousands of dollars per vehicle in storage fees. Claimants who settle or win their forfeiture cases often are presented with a bill for storage fees that the agency demands they pay before getting their cars back. However, successful claimants cannot be made to pay storage costs.

> A determination that the property is not subject to forfeiture is tantamount to a finding that the government

has failed in its attempt to establish a nexus between the property seized and drug trafficking. (*People v. $ 497,590 United States Currency, supra,* 58 Cal.App.4th at p. 154.) When the court or jury determines the seized property is not subject to forfeiture, no justification remains for withholding it from the claimant, and the court must order the property returned. (§ 11488.5, subd. (g).) If the claimant holds only a partial interest in an item of property, or if less than all of an item of property is declared forfeited, the court shall order the claimant's interest in the property returned to him. (§ 11488.5, subd. (h).)

Storage costs are not mentioned in section 11488.5, and nothing contained in that section suggests the Legislature intended that claimants be required to satisfy storage costs on their seized property before it may be returned, in whole or in part. To the contrary, these subdivisions indicate an intent by the Legislature that property determined not to be subject to forfeiture be released to the claimant without payment of storage costs. In addition, logic and equity compel the conclusion that a person who has successfully overcome efforts to associate his property with unlawful activity should not be obliged thereafter to underwrite those efforts.

(*People v. 6344 Skyway* (1999) 71 Cal.App.4th 1026, 1033-34).

A similar result is expressly compelled by Vehicle Code sections governing the imposition of towing charges. The owner of an impounded car must pay towing and storage charges for the release of his vehicle or suffer its loss (Veh. Code, § 22851), unless he can prove that probable cause for towing and impounding his car did not exist, in which event the towing and storage costs are generally borne by the law enforcement entity responsible for the towing

> (Veh. Code, § 22852; *People v. Martinez* (1981) 118 Cal.App.3d 624, 633-634, fn. 5 [173 Cal. Rptr. 554]; 68 Cal. Ops. Atty. Gen. 94 (1985); see 69 Cal. Ops. Atty. Gen. 36 (1986)).

(*People v. 6344 Skyway* (1999) 71 Cal.App.4th 1026, 1029 n. 6).

14. Collateral remedies

A. Motion for return of property

There are a number of statutory provisions for getting back property which has been seized by police.

Property detained as evidence in a criminal case and introduced at a hearing, can be recovered pursuant to Pen. Code Sec. 1417.5. That statute directs the clerk to return or dispose of exhibits (including documents and tangible objects) within 60 days after final determination of the case. The clerk sends notice to the persons from whom it was seized, telling them they have 15 days to file an application for the release of the property. The property is to be returned to the person from whom it was seized, so long as that person had lawful possession of it. (Pen. Code Sec. 1417.5(b)(1)). A person other than the person from whom it was taken may obtain release by establishing title or the right of possession. (Pen. Code Sec. 1417.5(b)(2)). If no one files an application, the property is destroyed or taken into government use. (Pen. Code Sec. 1417.5(c)).

Pen. Code Sec. 1538.5 is the general provision for return of property, applicable to all types of cases. This is the same statutory provision that governs motions to suppress evidence. A defendant moving to suppress evidence can simultaneously move for both suppression and return of the property. See Chapter 14 Section A-1-b, below.

The Health and Safety Code has its own return of property process for drug cases. The criminal defendant may file the motion in his/her criminal case. (Health & Saf. Code Sec. 11488.4(h)(1)).

Those not charged have to file it as a separate civil action. See Chapter 14 Section A-1-a, below.

> There is also a common law remedy.
>
> A defendant may also bring a nonstatutory motion for return of property seized by warrant or incident to arrest which was not introduced into evidence but remained in possession of the seizing officer.

(*People v. Lamonte* (1997) 53 Cal. App. 4th 544, 549, citing *Gershenhorn v. Superior Court* (1964) 227 Cal. App.2d 361, 364-365.) See Chapter 14 Section A-1-c, below.

1. Grounds for return of property

a. Drug cases

(i). Motions by defendants

> If there is an underlying or related criminal action, a defendant may move for the return of the property on the grounds that there is not probable cause to believe that the property is forfeitable pursuant to [Health & Saf. Code Sec. 11470(a)-(g)]... and is not automatically made forfeitable or subject to court order of forfeiture or destruction by another provision of [Health & Saf. Code Sec. 11469-11495].

(Health & Saf. Code Sec. 11488.4(h)(1)).

The property rendered forfeitable by Health & Saf. Code Sec. 11470(a)-(g) are:

(a) controlled substances manufactured or distributed, etc., in violation of the Controlled Substances Act;

(b) raw materials used or intended for use in manufacturing, etc., controlled substances;

(c) property used or intended for use as a container, except real property, boats, airplanes and vehicles;

(d) books, records, research, materials, formulas;

(e) boats, airplanes, vehicles used to facilitate manufacture, sale or possession for sale of certain minimum quantities of controlled substances (e.g. 10 pounds or more of cannabis);

(f) money, negotiable instruments and things of value furnished or intended to be furnished in exchange for a controlled substance; all proceeds traceable to such an exchange; and money, negotiable instruments and securities used to facilitate a violation of Health & Saf. Code Sec. 11351, 11351.5, 11352, 11355, 11359, 11360, 11378, 11378.5, 11379, 11379.5, 11379.6, 11380, 11382, or 11383, or a felony violation or 11366.8 or Pen. Code Sec. 182 – "insofar as the offense involves the manufacture, sale, possession for sale, offer for sale, offer to manufacture, or conspiracy;"

(g) real property, if any property owner is convicted of violating Health & Saf. Code Sec. 11366, 11366.5, or 11366.6 involving the property. However, if the property is used as a family residence or other lawful purposes, and a co-owner had no knowledge of its unlawful use, it is not forfeitable.

A return of property motion "may be made prior to, during, or subsequent to the preliminary examination." If made after the preliminary examination, the government may submit the preliminary hearing transcript as evidence that probable cause exists to believe the criminal violations have occurred. (Health & Saf. Code Sec. 11488.4(h)(1)).

When alleged medical marijuana is seized and the person is not prosecuted or charges are dismissed, the owner may file a motion for return of property seeking the return of the marijuana, even though marijuana remains illegal under federal law. (*City of Garden Grove v. Superior Court* (2007) 157 Cal.App.4th 355, 379 ("California courts do not enforce the federal marijuana possession laws when defendants prosecuted for marijuana possession have a qualified immunity under [the CUA].").)

When an otherwise qualified patient is convicted of possessing an amount of medical marijuana in excess of the amount permitted under the statute, he/she cannot get back the amount he/she was legally allowed to possess under the laws. (*Chavez v. Superior Court* (2004) 123 Cal.App.4th 104, ___, 20 Cal. Rptr. 3d 21, 25).

(ii). Property owners not charged in the criminal case

A person, other than the defendant, who claims an interest in the seized property may move for return of property under Sec. 11488.4(g) – apparently even if a forfeiture case is pending against the property.

> *Nothing contained in this chapter* [Health & Saf. Code Sec. 11469-11495, the forfeiture provisions governing drug crimes] shall preclude a person, other than a defendant, claiming an interest in property actually seized from moving for a return of property if that person can show standing by proving an interest in the property not assigned subsequent to the seizure or filing of the forfeiture petition.

(Health & Saf. Code Sec. 11488.4(g)). This passage is somewhat cryptic, but, since it refers to the filing of the forfeiture petition, apparently it means a motion for return of property can be filed even if there is a forfeiture complaint pending.

The court ordered money returned while a forfeiture action was pending in *People v. Property Subject to Disposition, $260,353.25*, Super. Ct. for the County of San Francisco No. CPF-15-514568. Viola Liu, the person from whom the money was seized, filed a motion for return of property. The charges had been dropped against her but a forfeiture petition had been filed against the property. Despite the pending forfeiture case the court granted the motion and ordered the money paid to her lawyer's trust account. Unfortunately the court did not give its reasoning – it merely signed the proposed order.

To show standing the movant must prove "an interest in the property not assigned subsequent to the seizure or filing of the forfeiture petition." (Health & Saf. Code Sec. 11488.4(g)). The government then has the burden of showing probable cause to believe the property is forfeitable, or that it is needed as evidence in a criminal case, or some other legal basis for continued detention.

If the Franchise Tax Board issued a notice to withhold against the property for tax debts, a portion of the property sufficient to pay that tax debt will be detained. If nothing else holds the property, the portion needed to satisfy the tax debt is forwarded to the Franchise Tax Board and the rest returned to the claimant. (Health & Saf. Code Sec. 11488.2).

b. Penal Code Section 1538.5

Penal Code Section 1538.5 contains the procedures for motions for return of property as well as suppression motions. Using this statute, the criminal defendant may simultaneously move for suppression and return of the property.

Pen. Code Sec. 1538.5(a)(1) says it applies to both types of motions, but the standards it sets out in Sec. 1538.5(a)(1)(A) through (B)(v) sound exactly like the standards for suppression of evidence for violation of the Fourth Amendment.

> If a search or seizure motion is granted at a trial, the property shall be returned upon order of the court unless it is otherwise subject to lawful detention. If the motion is granted at a special hearing, the property shall be returned upon order of the court only if, after the conclusion of any further proceedings authorized by this section, Section 1238 or 1466, the property is not subject

> to lawful detention or if the time for initiating the proceedings has expired, whichever occurs last. If the motion is granted at a preliminary hearing, the property shall be returned upon order of the court after 10 days unless the property is otherwise subject to lawful detention or unless, within that time, further proceedings authorized by this section, Section 871.5 or 1238 are utilized; if they are utilized, the property shall be returned only if, after the conclusion of the proceedings, the property is no longer subject to lawful detention.

(Pen. Code Sec. 1538.5(e)).

However, the illegal seizure of the res does not automatically immunize it from forfeiture. Even though evidence is suppressed for Fourth Amendment violations, the government can still prove its forfeiture case through independently obtained, untainted evidence. (*People v. Superior Court* (*Brent*) (1992) 2 Cal. App. 4th 675.)

When the allegedly independent evidence is obtained during civil discovery in the forfeiture case, that evidence may be tainted too, as "fruit of the poisonous tree," if the forfeiture case was a product of the initial illegal search and seizure. That interesting issue was raised and discussed in *Brent*, but the court did not reach it, because the appeals court lacked jurisdiction over the appeal, the government having filed the notice of appeal too late.

Under Pen. Code Sec. 1539-1540,

> a nondefendant may move for return of property on grounds that the property taken was not the same as that described in the warrant, or that there was no probable cause to believe the existence of the grounds on which the warrant was issued. *People v. Superior Court* (*Chico etc. Health Center*) (1986) 187 Cal.App.3d 648, 650, 232 Cal.Rptr. 165.

> However, only legal property may be returned to the person from whom it was taken. "[T]he People have the right to detain any property which it is unlawful to possess, and such right exists whether the property was lawfully seized or not." (*People v. Superior Court* (*McGraw*) (1979) 100 Cal.App.3d 154, 157, 160 Cal.Rptr. 663....) It is unlawful to possess property which is stolen. (*Ibid.*)

(*Ensoniq Corp. v. Superior Court* (1998) 77 Cal. Rptr. 2d 507, 512).

If a third party who did not have possession of the property when it was seized files a motion for return of property alleging the property was stolen from him/her by the person from whom it was seized, and no charges are ever filed, the government must prove the property is stolen by a preponderance of the evidence. Otherwise, the property must be returned to the person from whom it was seized, not the third party. (*Ensoniq, supra,* 77 Cal. Rptr. 2d 507).

> [T]he subject property is presumed to be owned by the real parties in interest until the state has presented evidence which would support a finding that real parties did not in fact own the property. The People would be required to prove the property was stolen by a preponderance of the evidence, as in all determinations of ownership.... In the event the People fail in their burden of proving the property to be stolen, then the property must be returned to real parties.

(*People v. Superior Court* (*McGraw*) (1979) 100 Cal.App.3d 154, 159-160).

c. Non-statutory motions for return of property

A defendant may also bring a nonstatutory motion for return of property seized by warrant or incident to arrest which was not introduced into evidence but remained in possession of the seizing officer.

(*People v. Lamonte* (1997) 53 Cal. App. 4th 544, 549, citing *Gershenhorn v. Superior Court* (1964) 227 Cal. App.2d 361, 364-365.)

Even though there are statutory procedures available for return of property, the non-statutory remedy is still cited in recent cases. (See *People v. Hopkins*, 171 Cal. App. 4th 305, 308 (2009) ("A criminal defendant may bring a nonstatutory motion for return of property seized by warrant or incident to arrest, which was not introduced into evidence but remained in possession of the seizing officer")).

Non-statutory motions for return of property can be used to retrieve property that was seized as evidence but not stolen, embezzled, contraband, subject to forfeiture, or needed as evidence in a future proceeding. Once the statute of limitations has passed on any forfeiture action without a forfeiture complaint being filed against it, property can no longer be detained as "subject to forfeiture."

Property cannot be permanently detained merely because it was used in a crime if there is no forfeiture statute that authorizes its forfeiture. "The court may not refuse to return legal property to a convicted person to deter possible future crime." (*People v. Lamonte* (1997) 53 Cal. App. 4th 544, 553.)

There is no right to appeal from denial of non-statutory motions for return of property. The proper way to seek review is through a petition for writ of mandate. (*People v. Hopkins* (2009) 171 Cal.App.4th 305, 308).

2. Statute of limitations

The statute of limitations for bringing motions for return of property is 3 years from the property's seizure. (Code Civ. Proc. Sec. 338(c)(1)). This is the statute of limitations applicable to "an action for taking, detaining, or injuring goods or chattels, including actions for the specific recovery of personal property."

> We are convinced that section 338, subdivision (c), was applicable here because the gravamen of plaintiffs' actions filed in the trial court was plainly (Code Civ. Proc., § 338, subd. (c)(1).) Moreover, the conclusion we reach on this issue is supported by the conclusion reached by the Supreme Court on similar facts in *Minsky* [*v. City of Los Angeles*] ([1974]) 11 Cal.3d [113], 119.

(*Ramirez v. Tulare County Dist. Atty.* (2017) 9 Cal.App. 5th 911).

The government's statute of limitations for filing a petition to forfeit property is one year from the date of seizure of the property. (Health & Saf. Code Sec. 11488.4(a)(2)).

3. Format and content of motion

The motion for return of property must be in writing and filed along with a memorandum of points and authorities, proposed order, and a proof of service. (Pen. Code Sec. 1538.5(a)(2)).

When there is no related criminal case pending, the motion is filed as an original "special proceeding."

> If no criminal action is pending, an owner's motion for return of seized property is classified as a special proceeding. (*Avelar v. Superior Court* (1992) 7 Cal.App.4th 1270, 1276, 9 Cal.Rptr.2d 536 [motion under §§ 1539-1540 is a special proceeding].) A "special proceeding" is one which is distinct from any underlying litigation. (Id. at p. 1275, 9 Cal. Rptr.2d 536.)

(*Ensoniq Corp. v. Superior Court* (1998) 77 Cal. Rptr. 2d 507, 511).

a. Caption and parties

The caption of motions for return of property is usually "[Claimant's name] v. [Superior Court of ____ County]." Sometimes the motion is captioned "People v. [description of the property]" or "In the matter of [description of the property].

The criminal prosecutor is a real party in interest in the motion for return of property and must be allowed to participate in the proceedings. (*People v. Superior Court of San Francisco (Aquino)* (1998) 201 Cal.App.3d 1346). A real party in interest is "any person or entity whose interest will be directly affected by the proceeding." (*Sonoma County Nuclear Free Zone '86 v. Superior Court* (1987) 189 Cal.App.3d 167, 173). The motion must be served on the prosecutor's office.

b. Required contents

The motion and memorandum must list the specific items of property sought to be returned, the factual basis for relief, and the legal authorities showing why the motion should be granted. (Pen. Code Sec. 1538.5(a)(2)).

Be sure to state facts showing standing – i.e. "an interest in the property not assigned subsequent to the seizure or filing of the forfeiture petition." (Health & Saf. Code Sec. 11488.4(g)). State that you own the property – or an interest in the property (e.g. co-ownership with spouse as community property, or a lien) and state when you acquired your interest.

To have standing the interest must be a legal interest – ownership, possession, or a lienholder interest.

In *People v. $28,500 (Aguilar)* (1996) the court looked to federal law to define the contours of standing in forfeiture cases.

> Because the California forfeiture statute is patterned after the federal statute (21 U.S.C. § 881), federal case law is instructive. The federal courts have held that although an unsecured creditor has a broad interest in the entire estate of a criminal defendant, an unsecured creditor has no interest in any particular asset. Thus, the interest of an

> unsecured creditor in seized currency is not cognizable in forfeiture proceedings. (E.g. *United States v. Campos* (6th Cir.1988) 859 F.2d 1233, 1238-1239 [creditors owed money wages and money for goods sold were not interested parties entitled to challenge forfeiture]; see *United States v. Reckmeyer* [(4th Cir. 1987)] 836 F.2d [200,] 206, fn. 3; cf. *United States v. $41,305 in Currency* (11th Cir. 1986) 802 F.2d 1339, 1346 [creditor proving perfected security interest in money may intervene in forfeiture proceeding].) It has also been held that even when the debtor criminal defendant had earmarked the funds for the benefit of another, the intended recipient has no legally cognizable interest in the assets. (*United States v. Four Million, Two Hundred Fifty-Five Thous.* (11th Cir.1985) 762 F.2d 895, 907, *cert. den.* 474 U.S. 1056 [88 L.Ed.2d 772, 106 S.Ct. 795] [holder of check drawn on seized bank account has neither legal nor equitable interest in deposited funds]; *United States v. $47,875.00 in U.S. Currency* (5th Cir.1984) 746 F.2d 291, 293-294 [parents who gave son money to finance oil venture had no legally cognizable interest in seized currency].)" (218 Cal. App.3d at pp. 724-725.)

(*People v. $28,500 (Aguilar)* (1996) 51 Cal.App.4th 447, 478-69).

The fact that money or other property was seized from someone's possession creates a rebuttable presumption of ownership. "The things which a person possesses are presumed to be owned by him." (Evid. Code Sec. 637). "A person who exercises acts of ownership over property is presumed to be the owner of it." (Evid. Code Sec. 638). See Chapter 12 Sec. B-1. The presumption can be overcome by evidence to the contrary.

For more detail on the law of standing see Chapter 2 Section D-6, Chapter 8 Section B-1-d, and Chapter 12 Section B-1.

4. Discovery

A defendant filing a motion for return of property may request discovery of any prior application for a search warrant which was denied by a magistrate for lack of probable cause. (Pen. Code Sec. 1539(c)).

5. Hearing

The motion for return of property is generally heard by the magistrate who issued the warrant (Pen. Code Sec. 1538.5(b)), unless the judge is disqualified pursuant to Code Civ. Proc. Sec. 170 through 170.6.

a. Grounds for disqualification of the judge

Grounds for disqualification of a judge include the judge having first-hand knowledge of the disputed facts, a blood relationship between the judge or judge's spouse and a material witness in the proceedings, the judge's prior service as a lawyer for a party, the judge's prior employment within the past two years in the same agency or firm as a lawyer in the case, and the judge or a family member's financial interest in the subject matter of the proceedings. Those are just a few of the grounds for disqualifying a judge. (See Code Civ. Proc. Sec. 170.1 for other grounds).

Code Civ. Proc. Sec. 170.6 provides a procedure for disqualifying a judge for prejudice against an attorney or party. A judge may disqualify himself/herself under Code Civ. Proc. Sec. 170.3, but the parties may waive the grounds for disqualification in some circumstances.

b. Conduct of hearing

In a felony case "...if the grounds on which the warrant was issued are controverted and a motion to return property is made (i) by a defendant on grounds not covered by Section 1538.5, (ii) by a defendant whose property has not been offered or will not be offered as evidence against the defendant, or (iii) by a person who is not a defendant in a criminal action at the time the hearing is held, the judge or magistrate shall proceed to take testimony in relation thereto" and make a transcript. (Pen. Code Sec. 1539(a)(i)-(iii)).

During a motion for return of property hearing, on motion by either party, the judge must order witnesses who have not testified to leave the courtroom until they are called, and to avoid conversing with each other. The court may also order them to be kept separated until they have testified, if feasible. (Pen. Code Sec. 1538.5(c)(2)(A)-(C)). The court may hold a hearing on the record to determine whether any person sought to be excluded is in fact excludable under the rule. (Pen. Code Sec. 1538.5(c)(2)(D)). Either party may challenge the exclusion of any person under this rule. (Pen. Code Sec. 1538.5(c)(3)).

The rule on excluding witnesses does not apply to the investigating officer or the defense investigator, nor the officers having custody of persons brought before the court. (Pen. Code Sec. 1538.5(c)(4)).

c. Live testimony is required

In suppression motions, the Government cannot prove its case by affidavit; live testimony is required.

> [T]he language of sections 1538.5 and 1539, as well as the uniform practice over the more than 40 years following the enactment of section 1538.5, make it clear that the suppression hearings provided for in section 1538.5 were intended, and have been understood, to involve the testimony of investigating officers and other pertinent witnesses whose credibility is to be determined by the magistrate or judge presiding at the hearing.

(*People v. Johnson* (2006) 38 Cal.4th 717, 888).

Since Pen. Code Sec. 1538.5 govern both suppression motions and motions for return of property, this principle should apply to motions for return of property as well.

6. Burden of proof on a motion for return of property

In Health and Safety Code forfeiture cases (drug cases) a person other than the criminal defendant who moves for return of property under Health & Saf. Code Sec. 11488.4 must "show standing by proving an interest in the property not assigned subsequent to the seizure or filing of the forfeiture petition." (Health & Saf. Code Sec. 11488.4(g)). The defendant in an underlying criminal action may move for return of property on the grounds that there is no probable cause to believe the property is forfeitable. (Health & Saf. Code Sec. 11488.4(h)(1)).

In return of property cases under the Penal Code, the burdens of proof are apparently the same as in suppression motions, since Pen. Code Sec. 1538.5 contains the procedures for both suppression motions and motions for return of property.

If after the hearing the court finds that the property taken was not that described in the warrant or that there was no probable cause to support the grounds on which the warrant was issued, the court must order the property returned to the person from whom it was taken. (Pen. Code Sec. 1540).

> Sections 1539 and 1540 of the Penal Code provide that, where the grounds for issuance of the warrant are controverted, a hearing shall be held and that, if it is found that there is no probable cause for believing the grounds on which the warrant was issued, the magistrate must restore the property to the person from whom it was taken.

(*People v. Keener* (1961) 55 Cal.3d 714, 719).

7. Appellate review

If the motion for return of property is granted the government may petition for a writ of mandate within 15 days of the ruling. (Health & Saf. Code Sec. 11488.4(h)(2)).

B. Release of seized business records

Where business records are seized in a drug case, the seizing agency must give the claimant copies of them upon request. (Health & Saf. Code Sec. 11470.4(f)).

Pen. Code Sec. 1536.5 contains a procedure for obtaining copies of business records that were seized pursuant to a search warrant. The records' owner must file a written demand and a declaration under penalty of perjury showing "that denial of access to the records in question will either unduly interfere with the entity's ability to conduct its regular course of business or obstruct the entity from fulfilling an affirmative obligation that it has under the law." (Pen. Code Sec. 1536.5(a)).

If the owner files such a demand the seizing agency has 10 days to object by filing a motion requesting an order denying release of the copies of the records, but that period of time may be extended upon request. (Pen. Code Sec. 1536.5(d)). If the agency doesn't discover the risk of harm from releasing the documents until later, it must object as soon as reasonably possible after discovering the risk. *Id.*

If the agency does not file an objection under Pen. Code Sec. 1536.5(d), copies of the records must be released if the owner's declaration makes a prima facie showing that he/she/it "would be impaired or impeded by the ongoing loss of records." (Pen. Code Sec. 1536.5(a)). Within 10 court days of the demand – if the agency has not filed a motion requesting an order denying release – it must make copies of the records available or make the originals available and allow the owner to make copies. (Pen. Code Sec. 1536.5(b)(1)-(2)). If the records are too voluminous to review or copy in the 10-day period the agency may move for additional time, but the motion must be filed within 10 court days of the original demand and the agency must show "that reviewing or producing copies of the records within the 10 court day time period, would create a hardship on the agency." (Pen. Code Sec. 1536.5(b)(6)).

If the records' owner's demand establishes a prima facie case, the agency may not refuse to release them unless the court determines by a preponderance of the evidence that: denying access to the records "will not unduly interfere with the entity's ability to conduct its regular course of business or obstruct the entity from fulfilling an affirmative obligation that it has under the law," (Pen. Code Sec. 1536.5(c)(1)); or "that possession of the business records by the entity will pose a significant risk of ongoing criminal activity, or that the business records are contraband, evidence of criminal conduct by the entity from which the records were seized, or depict a person under the age of 18 years personally engaging in or simulating sexual conduct." (Pen. Code Sec. 1536.5(c)(2)).

If the agency files a motion requesting the court deny the release, a hearing must be set within two court days of the filing, except on agreement of the parties. (Pen. Code Sec. 1536.5(e)). The motion is filed in the courthouse where the search warrant was issued. (Pen. Code Sec. 1536.5h)). The agency may request that the hearing be held ex parte and in camera (in a closed hearing with only the prosecution side present) by alleging in its pleadings that the requesting party is a target of the investigation, or likely to become a target. If they do not allege that in their pleadings, the hearing will not be held in camera unless they make a factual showing in their pleadings that "a hearing in open court would impede or interrupt an ongoing criminal investigation." (Pen. Code Sec. 1536.5(f)(1)).

At the hearing, the agency must present evidence under oath that releasing the records back to their owner "would pose a significant risk of ongoing criminal activity, impede or interrupt an ongoing criminal investigation, or both." (Pen. Code Sec. 1536.5(f)(2)). Any transcript of the hearing is filed under seal. (Pen. Code Sec. 1536.5(f)(3)). After the hearing the court must issue its order in open court after notice to the demanding party. (Pen. Code Sec. 1536.5(f)(4)).

The party seeking release of copies of its own business records must pay the reasonable cost of copying them. (Pen. Code Sec. 1536.5(g)). If there is a dispute over the reasonableness of the costs, the party can file a motion asking the court to resolve it. *Id.*

C. Setting aside defaults

1. Defaults and default judgments

At the beginning of the case, if a claimant fails to file a claim and/or answer, he/she is in default and may permanently lose the right to contest the forfeiture.

In administrative forfeiture cases (drug forfeiture cases involving cash or negotiable instruments totaling $25,000 or more and vehicle code forfeitures) a claimant who fails to file a claim within 30 days after service of the notice of administrative forfeiture is in default. Even if the claimant files a claim, when the government files a petition for forfeiture, the claimant defaults if he/she does not file an answer within 30 days of service of the petition for forfeiture.

In all other forfeiture cases, the case is commenced with the government filing a petition for forfeiture and serving it on persons believed to own interests. A claimant who is served with a petition for forfeiture must file both a claim and an answer within 30 days of service of the petition for forfeiture or they are in default.

If the claimant defaults, at the prosecutor's request the clerk enters an entry of default, and serves the notice of default on all persons who had been served and defaulted. If they do not respond within the deadlines, the prosecutor can move for a default judgment.

Under Code Civ. Proc. Sec. 585,

> the entry of a default terminates a defendant's rights to take any further affirmative steps in the litigation until either the default is set aside or a default judgment is entered. A defendant against whom a default has been entered is out of court and is not entitled to take any further steps in the cause affecting plaintiff's right of action.

(*People v. One 1986 Toyota Pickup* (1995) 31 Cal.App.4th 254, 259, citing *Devlin v. Kearny Mesa AMC/Jeep/Renault, Inc.* (1984) 155 Cal. App.3d 381, 385-386).

In *People v. One 1986 Toyota Pickup* (1995) 31 Cal.App.4th 254, after the claimant defaulted, the prosecutor immediately moved for a default judgment. The claimant, who did not speak English, appeared at the hearing on the motion for default judgment and the court did not allow him to speak nor offer a translator. The court then entered default judgment against the claimant.

On appeal the court reversed. Noting that the forfeiture statute does not contain procedures for default proceedings, the appellate court turned to the Code of Civil Procedure, which is incorporated by reference in Health & Saf. Code Sec. 11488.4(i). Under Code Civ. Proc. Sec. 585(a), the government must obtain an entry of default by the clerk before it can file a motion for default judgment. Since the prosecutor had not obtained an entry of default from the clerk, the appellate court held the claimant's right to be heard was not cut off, and that the lower court's failure to let him appear was an abuse of discretion. It remanded the case to superior court and gave the claimant 30 days to file an answer. (*People v. One 1986 Toyota Pickup*, supra, 31 Cal.App.4th at 259).

2. Deadline for moving to vacate default

Ordinarily the claimant would have 6 months after the entry of default to apply for relief from the default under Code Civ. Proc. Sec. 473(b). However, because forfeiture judgments affect ownership of real or personal property, procedures require the clerk to send the defaulting party and his/her attorney a written notice informing them that the case is in default, and that they have only 90 days after service of the notice to file a Code Civ. Proc. Sec. 473(b) motion to vacate the default. If the defaulting party or his/her attorney receives a 90-day notice, then they have only 90 days to file the motion to vacate.

Parties against whom a default or default judgment are entered but who are not served with the written notice of default have the full 6 months to file a motion to vacate. (Code Civ. Proc. Sec. 473(b)). "No affidavit or declaration of merits shall be required of the moving party." (Code Civ. Proc. Sec. 473(b)).

If more than six months have passed after an entry of default, statutory relief is unavailable but a trial court may still vacate a default on equitable grounds. (*Rappleyea v. Campbell* (1994) 8 Cal.4th 975, 981). Equitable grounds include extrinsic mistake – that is, a mistake which led a court to do what it never intended, such as a clerk's mistakenly quoting the filing fee for a single defendant when multiple defendants were filing answers. (*Id.* at 983).

In ruling on whether to vacate a default on equitable grounds the court considers whether the party had a valid excuse for the failure that resulted in a default, whether his/her defense had merit, and whether they diligently tried to set aside the default once it was discovered. (*Id.* at 983).

A verified answer normally is enough to show merit as long as the answer responds to all of the allegations in the complaint or forfeiture petition. (*Id.* at 983).

Claimants defending themselves in pro per (without a lawyer) should not expect special treatment from the courts. As the California Supreme Court said in *Rappleyea,*

> mere self-representation is not a ground for exceptionally lenient treatment. Except when a particular rule provides otherwise, the rules of civil procedure must apply equally to parties represented by counsel and those who forgo attorney representation.... Although in reaching our decision we have incidentally considered whether parties in defendants' position would reasonably have relied on advice from the clerk's office and whether they would have understood the meaning of a default, our focus is on the clerk's and plaintiff's incorrect advice rather than on defendants' ill-advised self-representation.

(*Rappleyea v. Campbell* (1994) 8 Cal.4th 975, 985-986).

> "[W]hen relief under section 473 is available, there is a strong public policy in favor of granting relief and allowing the requesting party his or her day in court. Beyond this period there is a strong public policy in favor of the finality of judgments and only in exceptional circumstances should relief be granted."

(*Rappleyea v. Campbell* (1994) 8 Cal.4th 975, 982, quoting *In re Marriage of Stevenot,* 154 Cal.App.3d 1051, 1071).

3. Grounds for vacating defaults

a. Mistake, inadvertence, surprise, excusable neglect

If the motion to vacate is made within 6 months, and is accompanied by an attorney's sworn affidavit "attesting to his or her mistake, inadvertence, surprise, or neglect" the court shall "vacate any (1) resulting default entered by the clerk against his or her client, and which will result in entry of a default judgment, or (2) resulting default judgment or dismissal entered against his or her client, unless the court finds that the default or dismissal was not in fact caused by the attorney's mistake, inadvertence, surprise, or neglect." (Code Civ. Proc. Sec. 473(b)).

When the court granting such a motion finds the attorney to be at fault, the court shall order reasonable attorney's fees and costs to opposing parties. (*Id*).

Whenever a court grants relief from any default or dismissal, the court may impose a penalty of up to $1000 on an offending attorney or party, or direct an offending attorney to pay it to the State Bar client security fund. The grant of relief from the default shall not be made conditional on the attorney paying the penalty. (Code Civ. Proc. Sec. 473(c)(1)).

b. Where the lawyer is suspended

If a lawyer is being disciplined by the state bar and a court has assumed jurisdiction over his/her law practice, and a default judgment has been entered against a party who was represented by the lawyer, the defaulting party has 6 months after the court takes jurisdiction over the party's lawyer's law practice to move to vacate the default, or 90 days after receipt of a written notice advising the party they have 90 days to move to vacate. (Code Civ. Proc. Sec. 473.1). "No affidavit or declaration of merits shall be required of the moving party." (Id.)

c. Void default judgments

> "A default judgment is void if the trial court lacked jurisdiction over the parties or the subject matter of the complaint or if the complaint failed to 'apprise[] the defendant of the nature of the plaintiff's demand,' or if the court granted relief which it had no power to grant...."

> (*Falahati v. Kondo*, supra, 127 Cal.App.4th [823], 830, fns. omitted.) A judgment which is void on its face may be set aside at any time after its entry. (*Nagel v. P & M Distributors, Inc.* (1969) 273 Cal.App.2d 176, 179 (Nagel).) "'A judgment absolutely void upon its face may be attacked anywhere, directly or collaterally, whenever it presents itself, either by parties or strangers. It is simply a nullity, and can be neither the basis nor evidence of any right whatsoever....'" (*Id.* at p. 180.)

(*People v. $224,060.89* (Cal. Ct. App. Apr. 4, 2008) No. A115272, 2008 WL 903881 (unpublished)).

d. When notice is received too late to file a claim

When service of a summons has not resulted in the property owner getting actual notice in time to file a claim and answer and a default or default judgment is entered, the party may move to set aside the default. The motion must be filed within a reasonable time not to exceed the earlier of 2 years after entry of default, or 180 days after service on him/her of written notice that default or default judgment has been entered. (Code Civ. Proc. Sec. 473.5(a)).

The motion must be accompanied by an affidavit showing the lack of notice was not caused by avoidance of service or inexcusable neglect. A copy of the proposed pleading (claim and/or answer) must accompany the motion. (Code Civ. Proc. Sec. 473.5(b)). If the court finds the party has shown a lack of notice that was not caused by avoidance of service or inexcusable neglect the court may set aside the default or default judgment. (Code Civ. Proc. Sec. 473.5(c)).

e. Void for lack of constitutionally adequate notice

The court may set aside any void judgment under Code Civ. Proc. Sec. 473(d). A forfeiture judgment obtained without compliance with the statutory and constitutional notice requirements is void. (*United States v. Giraldo* (1st Cir. 1995) 45 F.3d 509, 512). Void judgments are a "nullity." (*United States v. One Toshiba Television* (3rd Cir. 2000) 213 F.3d 147, 157) (holding the court has no discretion to deny a motion to vacate a void judgment, even if the motion is filed after the 1 year statute of limitations on Fed. Rule 60(b) motions. (*Id.* at 157-58)).

Due Process requires notice "reasonably calculated, under all the circumstances" to apprise interested parties of the pendency of a forfeiture action. (*Mullane v. Central Hanover Bank & Trust Co.* (1950) 339 U.S. 306, 313-14). "The means employed must be such as one desirous of actually informing the absentee might reasonably adopt to accomplish it." (*Id*).

"[A]ssessing the adequacy of a particular form of notice requires balancing the 'interest of the State' against 'the individual interest sought to be protected by the [Due Process clause].'" (*Jones v. Flowers* (2006) 547 US 220, 229, quoting *Mullane v. Central Hanover Bank & Trust* (1950) 339 U.S. 306, 314). When the stakes are high for the property owner, the government has a duty to take more extensive efforts to locate him and give notice. See *Jones,* supra, at 230 ("when, as here, the subject matter of the letter concerns such an important and irreversible prospect as the loss of a house" further efforts at giving notice are required when the government learns its initial attempt at giving notice was unsuccessful.)

Jones made it clear that it is not enough for the government to merely demonstrate that its "normal procedures" used in giving notice comply with Due Process. The question is whether the efforts made in the particular case were sufficient. The government must also "consider unique information about an intended recipient regardless of whether a statutory scheme is reasonably calculated to provide notice in the ordinary case." (*Jones,* supra at 230).

"[N]otice of forfeiture proceedings sent to a vehicle owner's home address [is] inadequate when the State knew that the property owner was in prison." (*Jones,* supra at 230, citing *Robinson v. Hanrahan* (1972) 409 U. S. 38, 40). Notice by mailing, posting, and publication is inadequate when the government knew the property owner was incompetent and lacking a guardian. (*Covey v. Town of Somers* (1956) 351 U. S. 141, 146-147).

The government cannot simply ignore information about the property owner that it has reasonably at hand

> any more than it could ignore the information that the owner in *Robinson [v. Hanrahan* (1972) 408 U.S. 38] was in jail, or that the owner in *Covey [v. Town of Summers* (1956) 351 U.S. 141 (1956)] was incompetent.

(*Jones v. Flowers,* supra, 547 U.S. at 237).

The government is not required to check "all possible sources" to locate a potential claimant, but when the agency had several obvious sources at hand, yet failed to pursue them, its minimal effort to locate the property owner fails to provide due process. (*Foehl v. United States* (3rd Cir. 2001) 238 F.3d 474, 480).

> [I]f the United States has some additional piece of information that a reasonable person would use to locate the claimant, it is obliged under *Mullane* to try again, unless it would be burdensome to do so.

Small v. United States (D.C. Cir. 1998) 136 F.3d 1334, 1338.

> For purposes of determining whether the government has made reasonable efforts to notify a claimant, we note that the government is not only chargeable with information it has within its possession but also with information it could have discovered by making reasonable efforts.

(*United States v. Rodgers* (10th Cir. 1997) 108 F.3d 1247, 1251.)

> [I]t was unacceptable for the DEA to rely upon notice by publication while failing to use the information it possessed from the beginning of the forfeiture process to notify plaintiff.

(*Aero-Medical, Inc. v. United States* (10th Cir. 1996) 23 F.3d 328, 331.)

> When such an investigating agency wishes to secure such a prisoner's cooperation in testifying against some important wrongdoer, it has no difficulty delivering the message in a manner that insures receipt.

(*Weng v. United States* (2nd Cir. 1998) 137 F.3d 709, 715).

The government sometimes argues that the claimant's knowledge that the property was seized precludes constitutional challenges based on lack of notice. The First Circuit rejected that argument:

> We reject this proposition. Assuming, arguendo, that the government can show actual notice of the vehicles' seizure on Gonzalez's part at the relevant time, the Second Circuit apparently has retreated from its earlier precedent and intimated that actual knowledge of forfeiture is required to excuse a due process shortfall. See *Ikelionwu v. United States*, 150 F.3d 233, 238 (2nd Cir. 1998). Wholly apart from the Second Circuit's view, we ourselves believe that the actual knowledge required to defeat a notice-based due process challenge is advance notice-in-fact of forfeiture proceedings, as opposed to notice-in-fact of seizure. See *Whiting [v. United States*, 231 F.3d 70, 74 (1st Cir. 2000)] (so stating, albeit in dictum).

(*United States v. Gonzalez-Gonzalez* (1st Cir. 2001) 257 F.3d 31, 380.

> Although, as the district court found, plaintiff may have known that the airplane had been seized, this would not

> necessarily place it on notice that forfeiture was imminent, or advise it of the statutory remedies available.

(*Aeromedical Inc. v. United States* (10th Cir. 1994) 23 F.3d 328, 331).

The government cannot serve process on one claimant and rely on him/her to give notice to the other claimants. (*United States v. Gonzalez-Gonzalez* (1st Cir. 2001) 257 F.3d 31.) Even though the claimant was a fugitive, the First Circuit held, "if the government knew how to notify [him] directly and did not utilize that information," notice to the car's custodians "might well fall short of the constitutional minimum." (*Id.* at 37-38).

In *Jones v. Flowers*, supra, the government argued that its failure to take additional steps to afford notice were excused because "Jones was obliged to ensure that those in whose hands he left his property would alert him if it was in jeopardy." (*Jones v. Flowers,* supra, 547 U.S. at 232). The Supreme Court rejected that argument. "None of these contentions relieves the State of its constitutional obligation to provide adequate notice." (*Id.*) "A party's ability to take steps to safeguard its own interests does not relieve the State of its constitutional obligation." (*Id.,* quoting *Mennonite Bd. of Missions v. Adams* (1983) 462 U. S. 791, 799). "Even fugitives may be entitled to efforts at personal notice." (*Gonzalez-Gonzalez,* supra, 257 F.3d at 36).

> A fundamental requirement of due process is "the opportunity to be heard." *Grannis v. Ordean,* 234 U.S. 385, 394 (1914). It is an opportunity which must be granted at a meaningful time and in a meaningful manner. The trial court could have fully accorded this right to the petitioner only by granting his motion to set aside the decree and consider the case anew. Only that would have wiped the slate clean. Only that would have restored the petitioner to the position he would have occupied had due process

> of law been accorded to him in the first place. His motion should have been granted.

(*Armstrong v. Manzo* (1965) 380 U.S. 545, 552).

f. Void administrative forfeiture

A recent case established that an administrative forfeiture is void if the determination of whether to institute administrative forfeiture was made by police officers rather than prosecutors.

Health & Saf. Code Sec. 11488.4(j) requires "the Attorney General or the district attorney of the county in which property is subject to forfeiture" to make the determination of whether non-judicial administrative forfeiture should be instituted.

Any such procedures initiated by police officers acting on their own are not valid. And because "there was no proper or valid forfeiture proceeding to which [the plaintiff] could make a claim," claimants who defaulted could set aside the non-judicial declaration of forfeiture by filing a civil suit. (*Ramirez v. Tulare County Dist. Attorney's Office* (2017) 9 Cal.App. 5th 911).

15. Federal Adoption

Federal adoption is a statutory process created by federal law that authorizes state and local police to seize property and turn it over to federal law enforcement agencies for forfeiture under federal law. (19 U.S.C. Sec. 1616, 21 U.S.C. Sec. 881(e)(1)(A)).

Local law enforcement agencies are then rewarded with a portion of the federal forfeiture proceeds under the "equitable sharing" program, which authorizes the Justice Department to dole out a portion of the forfeiture proceeds to the local agencies that assisted in the case, proportionate to their contributions to the case. The Department may share up to 80% of the proceeds of any federal forfeiture case with agencies that participated in the federal adoption of the seizure and/or the federal forfeiture case.

Federal law is in many ways easier for the government to win, and local police agencies often get a larger portion of the proceeds under federal adoption than under state law.

The federal forfeiture statutes do not prohibit state and local police from seizing property for federal adoption under a federal forfeiture statute when forfeiture would not be authorized under federal law – such as when there is no state forfeiture statute triggered by that offense, or when state law presents a defense that does not exist under federal law. This presents the potential for abuse. For example, in states that have legalized medical marijuana and/or recreational marijuana, police may try to get around this by using federal forfeiture statutes, which do not exempt medical marijuana.

Because of public outcry over the unfairness of this law, state and federal legislators have repeatedly tried to enact statutory limitations on the practice, but only recently have they succeeded in plugging the loopholes.

A. Restrictions on federal adoption

1. Restrictions imposed by California's SB 443

The amendment of California drug forfeiture statutes by SB 443, effective January 1, 2018, included provisions limiting federal adoption. Under Health & Saf. Code Sec. 11471.2,

> [s]tate or local law enforcement authorities shall not refer or otherwise transfer property seized under state law authorizing the seizure of property to a federal agency seeking the adoption of the seized property by the federal agency for proceeding with federal forfeiture under the federal Controlled Substances Act.

(Health & Saf. Code Sec. 11471.2(a)). This section does not stop the federal government from seizing property under federal law and then sharing it with state or local agencies who work in joint federal investigations or federal task forces, but it should substantially decrease the number of cases initiated by state and local police and handed over to federal agencies for forfeiture under federal law.

To keep the police from using federal adoption to get around SB 443's conviction requirements, Health & Saf. Code Sec. 11471.2(b) now prohibits state and local agencies from receiving an equitable share of federally forfeited property unless a defendant is convicted in an underlying or related criminal case for which Health & Saf. Code Sec. 11470 or 11488 authorize forfeiture, or an offense under the federal CSA which includes all the elements of an offense under Health & Saf. Code Sec. 11470 or 11488. If the subject property is cash or negotiable instruments totaling more than $40,000, there is no conviction requirement as a prerequisite to local police receiving an equitable share.

If the defendant willfully fails to appear in the related criminal case, flees to evade prosecution or dies, there is no conviction requirement as a prerequisite to equitable sharing. (Health & Saf. Code Sec. 11471.2(c)).

2. Restrictions imposed by federal laws

After failing to pass permanent federal statutes to limit federal adoptions of state seizures, sponsors of the legislation successfully added riders to the annual federal budget bill. Those riders expire after a year (or a little longer if the budget bill is temporarily extended) but the sponsors can always seek the same rider in the next budget bill.

This temporary process has been used on two fronts: to prevent federal law from being used to defeat state law on medical marijuana in those states that have legalized it, and to limit federal adoption.

From the time state medical marijuana laws were passed, law enforcement agencies in those states used federal adoption to get around the medical marijuana defense, and to forfeit property for offenses that were legal under state law.

Beginning in December 2014, the Rohrabacher-Farr amendment to the federal omnibus spending bill prohibited the Justice Department from using any of its appropriated funds to prevent states from implementing their state laws that legalized medical marijuana. At first the Justice Department interpreted that statute as merely prohibiting prosecution of state officials. Several rulings in federal courts rejected the Justice Department's interpretation. The Ninth Circuit upheld those rulings in *United States v. McIntosh* (2015) 833 F.3d 1163, holding that the Rohrabacher-Farr amendment prohibited the prosecution of persons who were acting in compliance with the state medical marijuana law.

The *McIntosh* decision will continue to apply as long as Congress continues adding the Rohrabacher-Farr amendment to the federal budget bill, or passes a permanent bill that does the same thing.

A budget rider was also used to limit federal adoption in forfeiture cases not involving medical marijuana.

The 2015 omnibus spending bill took $1.2 billion out of the Justice Department's budget that had been used to fund equitable sharing. The Justice Department had no choice but to suspend equitable sharing payments temporarily, but a DOJ memo issued in December 2015 promised the payments would resume if the budget picture improved.

The International Association of Chiefs of Police immediately issued a press release objecting to the cut-off, complaining that "neither the IACP, nor any of our law enforcement partners, were consulted regarding this announcement." They said they would work with DOJ and Congress to address this situation. (As if the IACP has a say in legislative matters! But maybe they do. The law enforcement lobby is very powerful.)

It didn't take long for the Justice Department to relent. A memo dated March 28, 2016, from the chief of the Asset Forfeiture and Money Laundering Section announced:

> in the months since we had to make that difficult decision, we explored alternative options, while also keeping a close eye on incoming receipts. And now, we are finally at a point where it is no longer necessary to continue the deferral.

In other words, the Justice Department increased their prosecution of federal forfeiture cases and thereby increased the "incoming receipts" of forfeiture revenue, and used it to self-fund the Equitable Sharing program. That way they did not have to use money appropriated to the Justice Department in the budget bill.

That spending bill rider expired and Congress apparently did not bother adding another rider to later budget bills, probably reasoning that the Justice Department would just get around it by self-funding.

3. Restrictions imposed by Justice Department policy

In July 2017, current U.S. Attorney General Jeff Sessions announced a new forfeiture policy order regarding federal adoptions, Order No. 3946-2017. That policy order repealed Obama era Attorney General Eric Holder's policy orders limiting federal adoption, but Holder's order had a loophole: the policy did not apply to state and local task forces that had a federal agent on their force. Holder's policy order had little effect, so Sessions' repeal also had little effect.

However, Sessions' policy order was accompanied by Policy Directive 17-1: "Policy Guidance on the Attorney General's Order on Federal Adoption and Forfeiture of Property Seized by State and Local Law Enforcement Agencies." If the Justice Department follows this policy, Policy Directive 17-1 stands to clean up the worst abuses of the federal adoption program.

First the Policy Directive requires the legal counsel for the federal agency, before adopting the seized property, to "review all seizures for compliance with law, especially seizures made pursuant to an exception to the Fourth Amendment's warrant requirement." Policy Directive 17-1 p. 1-2.

To make sure the federal agency has the information needed to make an informed decision, Policy Directive 17-1 tells agencies to revise the forms state and local agencies have to fill out to request federal adoption, to require the seizing agency to provide enough information to determine if there was probable cause for the seizure, and to state whether a turnover order was obtained. Only a few states require turnover orders.

The policy directive imposed detailed screening requirements for seizures involving cash totaling $10,000 or less. It allows federal adoption of those small cash seizures only if: (1) the seizure was pursuant to a state warrant; (2) it was seized incident to an arrest for a forfeiture triggering offense; (3) it was seized at the same time as contraband was seized "relevant to the forfeiture;" or (4) the person from whom it was seized admitted it was crime proceeds or intended for use to commit a crime. If those small seizures do not fit into one of the above categories, it cannot be adopted unless the agency gets the approval of the U.S. Attorney's Office.

The policy directive advises officials to "proceed with caution" when deciding whether to waive the Justice Department's net equity thresholds for real estate, and in seizing real estate owned by innocent people.

The new policy also requires the government to commence administrative forfeiture within 45 days instead of the 90 days permitted by statute, but, since this is "just a policy," forfeiture victims probably can't force the Justice Department to abide by it, and there are probably no remedies if they miss the deadline.

B. Turnover orders

When state or local police seize property pursuant to a state search warrant and want the federal government to adopt the seizure, they may have to apply for a turnover order from the court that issued the search warrant before transferring the money to the federal government.

In *People v. $25,000* (2005) 131 Cal.App.4th 127, Humboldt County police seized $25,000 during execution of a search warrant. Humboldt DA's office issued an administrative forfeiture notice giving the claimants 30 days to file a claim. Fields filed a claim in Superior Court. A few days later the Humboldt DA referred the case for federal adoption, and advised the DEA that "[n]o turn-over order is required." The Humboldt County Superior Court did not approve the transfer.

The claimant was not told of the federal adoption. A year after the money was seized, his attorney contacted the Humboldt DA requesting return of the money and stating that the statute of limitations had run for initiating a state forfeiture action.

In the meantime the federal government filed a forfeiture complaint, without giving notice to the claimant, and when the complaint went unanswered the court declared it forfeited by default. The claimant found out about the alleged default and successfully moved to vacate the default for defective notice. The 5-year federal statute of limitations hadn't run so the U.S. Attorney's Office filed another forfeiture complaint and served it on the claimant.

The U.S. District Court judge granted the claimant's motion to dismiss that complaint, holding that Humboldt County Superior Court acquired in rem jurisdiction when Fields filed the state claim, and that Humboldt County continued to have exclusive jurisdiction unless or until a turnover order was issued by Superior Court.

The Humboldt D.A. filed a request for release of the property and served it on the claimant's attorney by mail. Two days later, without waiting for a response from the claimant, the court issued an order releasing the property to the DEA.

> If the superior court's turnover order went unchallenged and became a final order, there would be force to the Attorney General's argument that state court jurisdiction has terminated. However, Fields filed a motion to vacate the turnover order and then appealed the court's denial of that motion. We believe that the state courts, specifically this court, retain constructive in rem jurisdiction over the res until review of the validity of the physical disposition of the res is complete. At least one

California court has held, in a case not addressed by the parties in their briefing, that once in rem jurisdiction is acquired, the subsequent disbursement of the res pursuant to court order does not deprive the appellate court of jurisdiction to hear the claimant's appeal challenging the validity of the disbursement order. (*People v. $ 8,921 United States Currency* (1994) 28 Cal.App.4th 1226, 1232-1233 [34 Cal. Rptr. 2d 210].) ...

However, we agree with the Humboldt County District Attorney that the turnover order is valid. "When federal authorities seek to gain control over a res already in the control of a state court, the proper procedure is to seek [a] turnover order from that court." (*In re Seizure of Approx. 28 Grams of Marijuana, supra,* 278 F. Supp. 2d at p. 1107.) Fields claims that the owner of the res is entitled to notice and a hearing before issuance of a turnover order, but fails to provide relevant support for that assertion. A turnover order is not a forfeiture; it does not divest ownership of the property but simply transfers the property to the federal government for a forfeiture proceeding. Upon initiation of the federal forfeiture proceeding, the property owner is provided with notice and a hearing compliant with due process. Accordingly, it has been held that "[t]he mere transfer of jurisdiction as accomplished by [a] turnover order therefore has no effect on the actual ownership of the property" and does not require "preseizure notice." (*Hawkins v. Henderson County* (E.D.Tex. 1998) 22 F. Supp. 2d 573, 579; *accord Ivester v. Lee* (E.D. Mo. 1998) 991 F. Supp. 1113, 1120 ["no preseizure notice or hearing is required before a federal agency may seize personal property subject to forfeiture for violation of federal drug laws"].)

It must also be emphasized that no state forfeiture proceeding was ever initiated. Fields was a claimant, not a defendant, in superior court. Even if we accept Fields's proposition that a property claimant is entitled to a hearing before property is transferred to the federal government for a forfeiture proceeding, Fields had a hearing. While the superior court issued its November 2003 turnover order ex parte, the order was later reconsidered and affirmed only after Fields was afforded the opportunity for briefing and a hearing. It is the later order, which followed a full hearing, that is the subject of this appeal. One is not prejudiced by issuance of an ex parte order where a hearing is subsequently provided before execution of the order. (*Israni v. Superior Court* (2001) 88 Cal.App.4th 621, 633-634 [106 Cal. Rptr. 2d 48].)

Finally, we reach the crux of the matter: Did the superior court have the power to issue a turnover order in November 2003, after the statute of limitations for state forfeiture proceedings expired? The Humboldt County District Attorney now concedes that it "perhaps mistakenly" characterized the turnover order as a retroactive *nunc pro tunc* (literally, now for then) order that would antedate expiration of the statute of limitations. As Fields correctly points out, "[t]he function of a *nunc pro tunc* order is merely to correct the record of the judgment and not to alter the judgment actually rendered – not to make an order now for then, but to enter now for then an order previously made." (*Hamilton v. Laine* (1997) 57 Cal.App.4th 885, 890 [67 Cal. Rptr. 2d 407].) The November 2003 turnover order was the first court order directing transfer of the subject currency. The turnover order was not the correction of a clerical error in a previous court order, and thus may not be given retroactive effect.

> However, we disagree with Fields's claim that the superior court was precluded from issuing a turnover order in November 2003, and had no power other than to "dismiss the case" and return the currency to him. It is true that the expiration of the statute of limitations precludes the state from filing a petition for forfeiture, as the Humboldt County District Attorney rightly concedes. (Health & Saf. Code, § 11488.4, subd. (a).) But expiration of the statute of limitations did not terminate the superior court's jurisdiction over the subject property. It has been established on this appeal that the superior court acquired jurisdiction by virtue of both the search warrant it issued, as well as the claim filed by Fields. The property seized pursuant to the court-issued search warrant remained under the court's control until it issued a dispositional order, as it did here in ordering the property transferred to other governmental authorities. (Pen. Code, § 1536.) The turnover order was a valid exercise of the superior court's continuing in rem jurisdiction over the property."

(*People v. $25,000* (2005) 131 Cal.App.4th 127, 133-135).

About the Author

Brenda Grantland is a lawyer located in Mill Valley, California. She started her legal practice in the District of Columbia in 1982 and Maryland (1985). In 1993, she passed the California bar and moved her practice to California. She defended her first forfeiture case in 1983. Forfeiture defense has made up the bulk of her practice ever since. She handles and/or consults on federal forfeiture cases nationwide but also handles state forfeiture cases in California.

Brenda got her law degree from George Washington University National Law Center, going to law school at night while working full time at the D.C. Public Defender Service as a law clerk/librarian. Before law school she worked at Auto Code/Auto Comp Inc., Bethesda, Maryland, doing writing and editing for Auto Code's official publication of the D.C. Code. Later she was assigned to Auto Comp's high tech team which was working on a government contract to develop a "computer information retrieval system" (database) to do legal research for the Food and Drug Administration. It was like an early version of Lexis or Westlaw, both of which were under development at the time. Compiling and editing the legal digests on food and drug law exposed her to the concepts of civil forfeiture law. It also inspired her to apply for law school.

Her exposure to forfeiture law during her work on the FDA project segued into her experience at the Public Defender Service, where one of her writing projects was a guide for agency lawyers on return of seized property.

After passing the D.C. bar, she left the Public Defender Service and started her solo practice as a court appointed criminal defense lawyer. In her first year in practice she defended her first forfeiture case and won the clients' money back. That case lead to forfeiture referrals from other lawyers and she was able to transition from criminal cases to defending forfeiture cases primarily.

In her tenth year as a sole practitioner in D.C., she made plans to move her practice to California. In her last year in D.C. she became a founding member of Forfeiture Endangers American Rights, a nonprofit that advocated for forfeiture reform and educated the public on the dangers of asset forfeiture. In November 1992, just weeks before moving to California, she had the honor of testifying before Congress, during the House Government Operations Committee hearings into the abuses of civil forfeiture laws. Rep. John Conyers, who chaired that committee, introduced a forfeiture reform bill based on FEAR's position paper, which Brenda wrote. Rep. Conyers remained a champion of forfeiture reform until his retirement in 2017. Brenda worked with the aides for Conyers, and later with Rep. Henry Hyde, who introduced a similar bill. After eight years of consultation and lobbying for forfeiture reform, that bill passed in 2000.

Other publications:

YOUR HOUSE IS UNDER ARREST, 2nd edition, 246-page ebook by Brenda Grantland (published January 2017). This is a new and expanded edition of Brenda Grantland's first book, published in paperback in 1993. It explains the risks forfeiture poses to ordinary law abiding citizens.

FEAR'S FORFEITURE 101 DVD, by Brenda Grantland, Esq. and Judy Osburn, with Joseph Cadle, published by Forfeiture Endangers American Rights Foundation (2009). This is a 2-hour DVD intense crash course in forfeiture law, written for forfeiture lawyers and victims forced to represent themselves in forfeiture cases. http://brendagrantland.com/product/forfeiture-101-dvd/

ASSET FORFEITURE: WHAT TO DO WHEN POLICE SEIZE YOUR PROPERTY (2nd edition, 2016) small ebook (121 pages), written for forfeiture victims to answer the Frequently Asked Questions all forfeiture victims have. It also contains a collection of federal forfeiture statutes and rules which lay out the procedures and pleadings requirements.

All of the above publications and more are available for purchase on BrendaGrantland.com http://brendagrantland.com/.

FEAR'S ASSET FORFEITURE DEFENSE MANUAL, by Brenda Grantland, Esq. and Judy Osburn, with Susan Raffanti, Esq., published by Forfeiture Endangers American Rights Foundation (2002). This 500 page manual covering federal forfeiture law is now out of print and out of stock, the last volume having sold in September 2017.

FORFEITURE AND DOUBLE JEOPARDY, by Brenda Grantland, Esq., Jeffrey Steinborn, Esq., and Reba Weiss, Esq., published by Forfeiture Endangers American Rights Foundation (1994, 1995) (103-page paperback) out of print and out of stock. Note: the Supreme Court invalidated this entire issue in 1996 with its decision in *United States v. Ursery*, 518 U.S. 267, holding double jeopardy did not apply to civil forfeiture.

###

Index

www.ingramcontent.com/pod-product-compliance
Lightning Source LLC
LaVergne TN
LVHW091523200926
848483LV00002B/283
* 9 7 8 0 9 8 4 7 8 5 9 3 3 *